PRAISE FOR JEROME CORSI'S ATOMIC IRAN

"Jerry Corsi has 'connected the dots'—offering readers accustomed from *Unfit for Command* to his incisive analysis and vivid commentary, an understanding of the grave danger posed to America, Israel, and other freedom-loving nations by the 'mad mullahs' of Iran, with their nuclear ambitions and global support for terror."

> —*Frank J. Gaffney Jr.*
> *President*
> *Center for Security Policy*

"If a society has no religious freedom, it lacks freedom of speech, press, and assembly and is by definition therefore tyrannical. In *Atomic Iran* Jerry Corsi has exposed how this core deficit of religious freedom in Iran has led to a tyranny with a nuclear capacity it is willing to use to spread its intolerant brand of enforced religious beliefs. [Corsi] gives vivid details of the nuclear disaster that could result inside the borders of the United States."

> —*William J. Murray*
> *Chairman*
> *Religious Freedom Coalition*
> *Washington, DC*

"Jerry Corsi has pieced together the powerful Iranian mullah network of influence. Corrupt dealings and cashed checks by American leadership, including Kerry-Edwards, the Clintons, Kennedy, Biden, and Soros, have put our national security in peril.

"Corsi understands Iran's Islamic theocracy and the mullahs' powerful motive in Iran's quest for nuclear weapons, and he spells out the cost if we fail to carry out the Bush National Security Strategy."

> —*Steve King*
> *Congressman (R-IA)*

"I'm a former U.S. Marine and don't scare easily, but after reading *Atomic Iran,* I'm scared. I'm scared for my country, scared for the Middle East, and scared for Europe. Nuclear conflict is going to happen unless the United States helps bring about regime change in Iran. The mad mullahs are unfit to rule."

—James L. Martin
President, The 60 Plus Association

"For too long the mainstream media have failed to inform the public on Iran. While the people of Iran are largely pro-American, their regime is now the greatest threat to U.S. national security. Dr. Corsi provides a critical service to us all by exposing the true nature of the regime, its mission, and, even more shockingly, their American political allies at the highest levels of the U.S. government."

—Gary Metz
RegimeChangeIran.com

ATOMIC IRAN

ATOMIC IRAN

How the Terrorist Regime Bought the Bomb and American Politicians

Jerome R. Corsi, Ph.D.

INTRODUCTION BY CRAIG R. SMITH, CEO SWISS AMERICA

WND BOOKS

AN IMPRINT OF CUMBERLAND HOUSE PUBLISHING, INC.
NASHVILLE, TENNESSEE

ATOMIC IRAN
A WND BOOK
PUBLISHED BY CUMBERLAND HOUSE PUBLISHING
431 Harding Industrial Drive
Nashville, Tennessee 37211

Cover design by James Duncan Design, Nashville, Tennessee

Library of Congress Cataloging-in-Publication Data

Corsi, Jerome R.
   Atomic Iran : how the terrorist regime bought the bomb and American politicians / Jerome R. Corsi.
        p.   cm.
   Includes bibliographical references and index.
   ISBN 1-58182-458-0 (hardcover : alk. paper)
   1. Nuclear weapons—Iran. 2. Iran—Military policy. 3. Nuclear arms control—Iran.
   4. United States—Foreign relations—Iran. 5. Iran—Foreign relations—United States.
   I. Title.
   UA853.I7C635 2005
   355.02'17'0955—dc22

                                                                                    2005001596

Printed in Canada
1 2 3 4 5 6 7 8 9 10—08 07 06 05

To two people who have passed on to a better life:

Louis E. Corsi,

my father, with profound appreciation for allowing me
to see politics through his eyes and for sharing
with me his enthusiasm for effective change.

and

Melania M. Menzani,

with continuing gratitude for sharing with me her daughter,
Monica, my wife, the greatest treasure of both our lives.

Contents

Foreword

The truth is stranger than fiction.

—Mark Twain

NUCLEAR PROLIFERATION is the most serious international security threat the world faces today.

When the cold war ended and the Soviet Union imploded, many Americans thought the risk of nuclear war had been greatly reduced. But today, because of terrorism, the threat of a nuclear attack on a major city—in the United States or somewhere else in the world—may be higher than ever.

This threat is only increased as terror-sponsoring states achieve nuclear capability. Iran, arguably the leading terror-sponsoring state in the world, is about to join that club.

In *Atomic Iran*, Jerome R. Corsi brings this issue home, starkly raising the question: Can the free world tolerate the growing threat that a major city could be blown off the face of the earth by a softball-sized lump of uranium-235 "yellowcake" that could easily be smuggled across borders in a briefcase by a terrorist under orders from Osama bin Laden or a mad Iranian mullah?

Corsi's impeccable research, similar to that which undergirded the runaway *New York Times* best seller *Unfit for Command*, explains exactly how close Iran is to achieving this nuclear capability. You are about to discover the shocking truth, which has until now been largely overlooked by the U.S. mass media—even after the glaring agreement on this crucial issue by both candidates during the 2004 presidential debates.

Hold on tight as you travel with Corsi on a nuclear fact-finding mission that reads more like a best-selling suspense novel than the journalistic exposé it is. This book documents the cold, harsh truth about this urgent issue with style. It is simultaneously easy to understand for the layman yet meticulously documented for the skeptic or naysayer.

Americans are typically short-term thinkers. We're so busy working to produce and enjoy the "good life" that it's easy to miss our growing vulnerability to another major terrorist attack. Tom Ridge, former secretary of the Department of Homeland Security, observed: "Homeland Security has to be right 100 percent of the time, but the terrorists only have to be right *once!*"

My hope is that this book will serve as a wake-up call, not only to Americans who have grown complacent about their security since the end of the cold war and even since September 11, 2001, but to our policy makers as well.

As a businessman—and as an American—I urge you to take Corsi's admonitions seriously and to use them to make wise decisions about preparing for your future and the future of your country.

I shudder to think about the potential consequences if the message of this book is not heeded by our leaders and elected officials at all levels—especially by our president, vice president, senators, and representatives.

After reading this book, I felt compelled to share it with my family, friends, and associates. I hope you will do the same.

Craig R. Smith
CEO, Swiss America

Preface

WHILE I was working on *Unfit for Command*,[1] my coauthor, John O'Neill, telephoned me regarding an Iranian named Aryo Pirouznia. As John explained the situation, Aryo was a pro-democracy Iranian who lived in Texas. Hassan Nemazee, a New York investor who was one of John Kerry's top fund-raisers in the 2004 presidential campaign, had filed a libel suit against Aryo, charging Aryo with defamation. Evidently Aryo had accused Nemazee of being an agent of the mullahs who control the terror-supporting theocracy in Iran.

John O'Neill, a Swift Boat veteran himself, clearly needed to remain focused on his efforts with the Swift Boat Veterans for the Truth. Still, John suggested that I might want to follow up with Aryo to learn more about the situation. I gave Aryo a phone call and began the discussion that led to the writing of this book.

Iran has interested me since the 1979 student revolution that brought Ayatollah Ruhollah Khomeini to power. In 1981 I published an academic paper containing an early computer model designed to predict the outcome of terrorist events in an international journal on conflict resolution.[2] I had delivered an earlier version of the paper at an international conference on terrorism and political violence at the National Academy of Sciences in Washington DC.

As a result of that work, security officials for the Agency for International Aid (AID) recruited me to participate in a task force being assembled to assist State Department embassy personnel in hostage survival strategies. For this I received a top-secret security clearance from the U.S. Government. For almost two years I participated in this anti-terrorism effort. The 1979 Iranian hostage crisis was clearly the driving motive for this AID-led anti-terrorism effort during the early years of the Reagan administration. With Aryo Pirouznia's phone call in 2004 I was drawn back to the work I had done on Iran and Islamic terrorism.

I firmly believe that Islam is a genuine and important religion. With more than one billion believers throughout the world, Islam rightly qualifies as one of the world's greatest and most successful religions ever. The hijacking of Islam by radical terrorists is what I consider despicable. The evil done by these radical terrorists proclaiming Islam has nothing to do with true Islam. In this book I am determined to add my voice to those calling out for the responsible principles of Islam to be proclaimed with rightful pride. True Islam can and should stand alongside the other major and legitimate religions of the world.

Iran has a proud three-thousand-year history of accomplishment and culture. The people of Iran are educated and capable. The Iranian community within the United States now reaches nearly one million people who continue to maintain strong bonds of contact and commitment to their seventy million brothers and sisters in Iran.

I agree with President George W. Bush that freedom is within the heart of every living human being. The world will not be safe until freedom and democracy are brought to those Middle Eastern countries now in the grip of radical Islamic terrorists. As the speaking out of the Swift Boat veterans led to a movement, hopefully this book will support what is developing as a movement of individuals and groups within America and around the world who want to see freedom in Iran.

If we are to preserve freedom in America, we must also be committed to supporting the cause of freedom in Iran. The goal of this book is to bring down the mad mullahs currently ruling Iran.

ACKNOWLEDGMENTS

MANY PEOPLE contributed to this book. I am particularly appreciative of Joseph Farah who had the initial vision and enthusiasm to see the value of this project. At every step of the way, Joseph was there to provide encouragement. By offering me a weekly Friday commentary column on WorldNetDaily.com, Joseph provided a forum where I could first test many of the ideas that now appear in these pages. Aryo Pirouznia was the first to suggest to me the importance of the topic. Aryo, together with his attorney, Bob Jenevein, played a key role for my understanding of the politics behind the scenes in the Iranian freedom movement. Bahman Batmanghelidj offered enormous wisdom in explaining the background and history that remain the context of this story. His friendship is greatly treasured. Also important was Bijan Sepasy whose executive skills have helped me enormously to organize this project into the beginnings of a movement. Jim Martin's always helpful insights were invaluable in guiding my thinking through the intricacies of Washington politics, as together we contemplated how this book would fit into our ongoing national policy debate. Ed Lubin shared a breakthrough perception with me that positively influenced the work at an important point in the project. Chris Bauerle's considerable editorial skills provided expert guidance from the first draft outline through the final manuscript editing. His suggestions were consistently on target and always delivered with great grace and thoughtfulness. The production of the book took a team effort. Without the confidence and support of the publisher, Ron Pitkin, none of this would be possible. I am also grateful for the efforts of my editor, Ed Curtis, and Stacie Bauerle, the publicity manager, who have worked diligently to lay a solid foundation from which the message can be launched. Finally, I want to thank my family, especially my wife, Monica, and my daughter, Alexis, for their patience, understanding, and love as I struggled through the countless hours needed to deal with this difficult subject.

Many personal friends provided more assistance than they realize with their heartfelt prayers and their steady belief in the success of the work. We are all deeply indebted to Bernard Lewis for the countless scholarly contributions he has made to illuminate our understanding of the richness and complexities that are the Middle East.

Introduction

No serious person can believe that the negotiations are going to block, or even seriously delay, the Iranian race to acquire atomic bombs.

—Michael Ledeen, Resident Scholar in the Freedom Chair
at the American Enterprise Institute[1]

1979: The American Embassy in Tehran

A NEW world war may well have begun on January 31, 1979, the day Ayatollah Khomeini left Paris on a flight to Tehran.

One impression was that the ayatollah was a harmless old man at worst or a religious figure of some importance at best. He was striking, tall, and somber with his long gray robes and a ponderous face framed by a black head scarf and a long white flowing beard.

Yet looking closer, the ayatollah could appear threatening. His penetrating dark eyes were ominous. He held an almost hypnotic command over the throngs of Iranians who mobbed fanatically before him in the streets. The image was certainly haunting as the ayatollah stood there with his right hand extended palm down, moving in a slow waving motion that seemed to orchestrate the movement in the crowd itself.

Then on November 4, 1979, hundreds of militant Islamic students surged over the walls of the American Embassy in Tehran, spearheading a radical revolution that was about to start. The television images that flooded from Tehran were humiliating as fifty-two embassy workers were held captive, paraded with their eyes covered and their hands tied submissively behind their backs through angry Iranian mobs. For 444 days, each painful day followed by another painful day, the seemingly endless sequence reminded the American public that President Jimmy Carter was helpless to force a diplomatic solution to this tragedy.

On April 24, 1980, a top-secret team of Army Special Forces and CIA operatives failed in a rescue attempt. A helicopter crashed into a C-130 transport plane filled with gas, and the mission turned into a disaster. The public watched more humiliating images, this time of burned-out U.S. helicopters lying on a barren stretch of desert. Eight brave American soldiers were killed. Carter, a good man with a religious heart, now appeared even more helpless as he explained the poorly conceived mission to the American people.

Our military was disgraced. Was it Vietnam all over again? The images of the fall of Saigon were only five years old, chaotic scenes of desperate Vietnamese scrambling on ladders to rooftops, fighting one another to be one of the lucky few to get aboard the final helicopters before the Communists took over.

The turning point to the Iranian hostage drama was Ronald Reagan's defeat of Jimmy Carter in the 1980 presidential election. The very day Reagan was inaugurated, January 20, 1981, the hostages were released by the ayatollah. He had kept them captive throughout the presidential campaign as if to demonstrate to the world his supreme power to defeat an American president, denying Carter reelection.

When Ronald Reagan stood to give his inaugural address, the clouds seemed to break as the sun shone down upon him—a magical moment worthy of a Hollywood film. Here Reagan stood, a Westerner come to Washington, and even the ayatollah seemed to realize that a new, tougher sheriff had come to town. The television images shifted to the positive. The hostages were finally coming home, and the 444-day ordeal was over. The nation watched as the freed hostages were flown to freedom and greeted joyously on an Algerian tarmac, having been released some twenty minutes after Reagan began his inaugural address.

In the American imagination the ayatollah and the radical Islamic revolutionaries he led were firmly branded as enemies, dangerous adversaries from a distant land and a forbidding culture. President Reagan moved on to continue his legacy of freedom fighting. His administration, which began with the freeing of the hostages, also brought down the Berlin Wall, something most Americans had never imagined would happen in their lifetime.

A generation before, Neville Chamberlain, despite his passion to avoid war, had failed to stop Adolf Hitler with appeasement. The Iranian hostage crisis raised the question once again. Would the calm determination of men of peace be sufficient to carry the day against radical Islamic terrorists, our enemies of today? Reagan had not fired a shot, but his firm resolve communicated where Carter's preference for diplomacy and ineptitude with the military had failed to achieve results.

September 30, 2004: First Presidential Debate

THE FIRST presidential debate in the 2004 election was held at the University of Miami in Coral Gables, Florida. Toward the end of the debate, moderator Jim Lehrer asked President George W. Bush and Senator John Kerry whether they believed that diplomacy and sanctions could resolve the nuclear problems with North Korea and Iran. In a little noticed response to that question, Kerry answered with regard to Iran: "I think the United States should have offered the opportunity to provide the nuclear fuel, test them, see whether or not they were actually looking for it for peaceful purposes."[2] This was basically the substance of the EU-3 (the European Union states of France, Germany, and the Great Britain) proposal, the same failed policy that had been tried with North Korea.

Rather than set off a firestorm of criticism, Kerry's response went virtually unchallenged. To provide nuclear fuel to the mullahs in charge of Iran's radical theocracy somehow seemed reasonable to Kerry and the mainstream media covering the debate.

President Bush's answer to the question, however, placed much more emphasis on the need for the mullahs to abandon their desire for nuclear weapons. "We worked very closely with the foreign ministers of France, Germany, and Great Britain, who have been the folks delivering the message to the mullahs that if you expect to be part of the world of nations, get rid of your nuclear programs."[3]

Why be concerned that the mullahs might not keep their promise to use the nuclear material that John Kerry or the EU-3 would give them only for peaceful purposes? Iran is clearly a rogue regime, one known for its support of terrorism. In his 2002 State of the Union address President Bush marked Iran as one of three countries comprising the "Axis of Evil."[4] Even the 9/11 Commission Report on pages 240–41 had documented the assistance the nineteen al-Qaeda terrorists-hijackers who attacked the World Trade Center and Pentagon had received from Iran.[5] The preceding two pages of the report published headshot photographs of the terrorists grouped according to the aircraft they had hijacked.

In sharp contrast to this, the *Tehran Times* on February 8, 2004, published an e-mail memo that was received by the Iranian government's Mehr News Agency (a noted mouthpiece for the mullahs) from John Kerry's campaign that indicated the Democratic candidate, if he were elected, could be expected to be much more favorable to the mullahs than President Bush would be. The e-mail held out to the mullahs a heartwarming message: "It is in the urgent interests of the people of the United States to restore our country's credibility in the eyes of the world. America needs the kind of leadership that will repair alliances with countries on every continent that have been so damaged in the past few years, as well as build new friendships and overcome tensions with others."[6] The news agency highlighted the importance of the e-mail by publishing it under the headline, KERRY SAYS HE WILL REPAIR DAMAGE IF HE WINS ELECTION.

Kerry's campaign initially disputed the authenticity of the e-mail, but finally Kerry's top foreign policy aide, Randy Beers, admitted: "I have no idea how they got hold of that letter, which was prepared for Democrats Abroad. I scratched my head when I saw that. The only way they could have gotten it was if someone in Iran was with Democrats Abroad."[7]

Why was Kerry willing to look past the State Department's listing of the Iranian theocracy at the top of the roll of rogue regimes supporting international terrorism?

Some of the answer comes later in this book when we examine the list of Kerry's top campaign contributors. We will see a pattern that involves the senator's wanting to work with the mullahs, overlooking their nature to support terror, and accepting political contributions from the strong pro-mullah lobby within the United States. The list of politicians who have accepted such contributions includes many high-profile Democrats, including Bill and Hillary Clinton, Ted Kennedy, and Joseph Biden in addition to John Kerry.

The Carter example from more than twenty-five years ago—relying on diplomacy to achieve goals with Iran—appears to be the continuing modus operandi of the liberal-oriented foreign policy wing of the Democratic Party.

October 31, 2004: The Majlis, the Iranian Parliament

IRAN'S TOP nuclear negotiators were engaged in a final round of negotiations with the EU-3 toward bringing Iran's nuclear program under the control of the International Atomic Energy Agency (IAEA). The EU-3 sought Iran's agreement to end all programs designed to enrich uranium to weapons grade. In return, the IAEA was prepared to give Iran nuclear fuel for peaceful purposes and to implement inspection procedures to make sure that Iran would follow all agreed-upon restrictions. The world was watching this negotiation carefully to discern Iran's true purposes.

As the negotiations entered the final phase, the EU-3 wanted to avoid the necessity of taking Iran's refusal to comply to the United Nations Security Council, where more sanctions could be placed upon Iran.

On Sunday, October 31, 2004, virtually on the eve of the U.S. presidential election, the Majlis, Iran's Parliament, met in Tehran. The 247 lawmakers present of the 290 total considered an inflammatory resolution. The bill before the Majlis would require the government to enrich uranium. The session was carried live on national radio. As the assembly voted unanimously to enrich uranium, the members of parliament took up an eerie chant: "Death to America! . . . Death to Israel!"

With the vote and the incendiary rhetoric, Iran sent a message to the world. The mullahs, to fool the EU-3 for tactical reasons, might agree to suspend uranium enrichment temporarily, but two possibilities were being taken off the table. Iran would not agree to suspend uranium enrichment permanently. Nor would the country's leaders ever abandon the determined goal of developing nuclear weapons.

Earlier in October a report circulating in the international intelligence news community quoted Iranian leader Ayatollah Ali Khamenei as urging Iran to have nuclear weapons available almost immediately. "We must have two bombs ready to go in January [2005] or you are not Muslims," Khamenei instructed his senior military and government leaders working on his nuclear weapons program.[8]

The moment Iran has deliverable nuclear weapons, the entire political and military equation will change in the Middle East. Israel, which has lived since the Holocaust under the pledge "Never Again," will reasonably fear for its survival once Iran can unleash a nuclear weapon on Tel Aviv with nearly unimaginable consequences. The vote of the mullah-controlled Majlis communicated their true intentions to anyone who knew how to listen.

HOW LONG do we have before Iran plays out the game, deceiving anyone who will listen to them in the meantime, with the final result that they have deliverable nuclear weapons? Is a war inevitable? Will Israel simply strike, not waiting for anyone's permission, not caring how complicated it will be to take out a nuclear weapons capability that Iran may have hidden among hundreds of sites, some embedded in population centers? Are there any alternatives to war? How can we stimulate a democracy movement we know is building momentum within Iran?

The Iranian mullahs are a terror-supporting rogue regime that has exported terrorism abroad and suppressed dissent within, all with ruthless calculation and religious determination. Ironically, the theocracy in Iran presents to the world a clear and present danger of nuclear war. The mullahs are mad religious zealots who will soon have access to nuclear weapons. The prospect for the world is chilling. When one considers the ease with which drugs are smuggled into the United States each year, how hard would it be for Iranian terrorists to slip a softball-size lump of uranium-235 across our borders? Even a small nuclear explosion in a major American city would be as horrible for us to contemplate as the loss of Tel Aviv is to Israel.

These are the questions I hope to answer in this book. How has Iran acquired the capability to build atomic bombs? And what steps have the mullahs taken to buy the support of American politicians?

The world does not have long to calculate a winning strategy in dealing with atomic Iran. The war against terrorism in which we are now engaged will leap to a frightening new level of intensity should we be foolish enough to leave Iran alone with deliverable nuclear weapons.

Abbreviations

AEOI	Atomic Energy Organization of Iran
AIC	American Iranian Council
AID	Agency for International Aid
AIG	American International Group
AIPAC	American Israel Public Affairs Committee
CAIR	Council on American-Islamic Relations
CalPERS	California Public Employees' Retirement System
CPD	Committee on the Present Danger
CSIS	Center for Strategic and International Studies
DNC	Democratic National Committee
EIA	Energy Information Agency
EU-3	European Union states of France, Germany, and Great Britain
FCA	First Capital Advisors
FIDH	International Federation of Human Rights Leagues
FISA	Foreign Intelligence Surveillance Act
G8	Group of Eight: coalition of the world's eight leading industrialized nations (Canada, France, Germany, Italy, Japan, Russia, United Kingdom, United States) plus the European Union
HEU	highly enriched uranium
HLF	Holy Land Foundation
IAEA	International Atomic Energy Agency
IDF	Israeli Defense Force
IMAM	Iranian Muslim Association of North America
INC	Iraqi National Congress
IND	improvised nuclear device
IRGC	[Iranian] Revolutionary Guards Corps
JDAM	joint direct action munition

MAD	mutual assured destruction
MEK	People's Mujahedin of Iran, Mujahedeen Khalq; political front of which is NCRI
MEMRI	Middle East Media Research Institute
MOIS	Iranian Intelligence Ministry
NATO	North Atlantic Treaty Organization
NCLC	National Caucus of Labor Committees
NCRI	National Council for Resistance for Iran; political front for MEK
NESA	Near East and South Asia Bureau
NPT	Nuclear Nonproliferation Treaty
NSL	national security letter
RED	radiation explosive device
Rosatom	Russia's Atomic Energy Agency
SAVAK	Iranian Secret Police (under the Shah)
SIDE	Secretariat of State Intelligence (Argentina)
SMCCDI	Student Movement Coordination Committee for Democracy in Iran
UASR	United Association for Studies and Research
UNRWA	U.N. Relief and Works Agency
USAID	U.S. Agency for International Development
VVAW	Vietnam Veterans Against the War
WMD	weapons of mass destruction
WTC	World Trade Center
WTO	World Trade Organization

ATOMIC
IRAN

1

Iran's Quest for Nuclear Weapons

The prospect of a nuclear Iran is particularly frightening, not simply because of the threat that Iran itself poses to the United States and our friends in the Middle East, but also because the regime could supply terrorist groups with nuclear weapons.

Bill Gertz, *Washington Times* investigative reporter[1]

IRAN HAS PURSUED NUCLEAR weapons as if they were the weapons of mass destruction of choice. No other WMD, neither chemical nor biological, can be delivered as elegantly, as destructively, or as reliably from great distances. The image of a missile arching into the sky, aimed to deliver hundreds of thousands of deaths in the brilliant flash of an instant has been impossible for the mad mullahs to resist.

In November 2004, just after the U.S. presidential election, the CIA released the year's 721 Report. The report is so named because it is submitted to Congress in accordance with Section 721 of the 1997 Intelligence Authorization Act. The unclassified report is required to detail the acquisition of nuclear weapons technology by foreign countries during the preceding six months. The 2004 report presented a frightening picture of Iran.

The CIA report left no doubt that Iran was secretly pursuing the development of nuclear weapons:

The United States remains convinced that Tehran has been pursuing a clandestine nuclear weapons program, in contradiction to its obligations as a

25

party to the Nuclear Nonproliferation Treaty (NPT). During 2003, Iran continued to pursue an indigenous nuclear fuel cycle ostensibly for civilian purposes but with clear weapons potential. International scrutiny and International Atomic Energy Agency (IAEA) inspections and safeguards will most likely prevent Tehran from using facilities declared to the IAEA directly for its weapons programs as long as Tehran remains a party to the NPT. However, Iran could use the same technology at other, covert locations for military applications.[2]

The CIA clearly said that Iran has been lying to the world. The mullahs have pursued nuclear weapons clandestinely with a clear intent to ignore their NPT obligations and deceive the IAEA. Iran continues to display the characteristics of a rogue regime actively pursuing nuclear weapons, willing to both defy and deceive attempts at international control. Clearly stated, Iran has been playing the world for a fool.

The Bush Administration Gets Serious

IN THE 1940s, when the United States decided to develop the atomic bomb, we established the hugely expensive Manhattan Project, which was hidden away in then remote Los Alamos, New Mexico, and peopled with top international physicists. The project was difficult and unsure of success. Today a gifted high school student with access to the Internet can determine in a few hours all the theoretical physics needed to create an atomic bomb.

The barriers to developing a nuclear weapon today are not intellectual; the barriers instead are the physical requirements needed to make a deliverable weapon that will function reliably. To get to this point a nation must have weapons-grade nuclear fuel, the technology to miniaturize a bomb to fit into the confines of a missile warhead, and a missile capable of covering the distance to its target. These physical requirements take time and money, even for a rogue regime such as Iran.

Iran's nuclear program began during the Clinton administration and has continued to the point where Iran might have a deliverable nuclear weapon at any day. The evidence for this conclusion is overwhelming.

In the days preceding the release of the CIA's 2004 721 Report, the Bush administration gave off clear signals suggesting Iran was very close to having a deliverable nuclear bomb. En route to Santiago, Chile, to attend an economic summit with Pacific Rim leaders, Secretary of State Colin Powell gave an impromptu news conference to reporters traveling with him. "I have seen some information that would suggest that they [the Iranians] have been actively working on delivery systems. . . . You don't have a weapon until you put it in something that can deliver a weapon," Powell said. "I'm not talking about uranium or fissile material, or the warhead; I'm talking about what one does with a warhead."[3]

He added: "There is no doubt in my mind—and it's fairly straightforward from what we've been saying for years—that they have been interested in a nuclear weapon that has utility, meaning that there is something they would be able to deliver, not just something that sits there."[4] The ringing alarm bell here was Powell's disclosure that Iran had made significant advances toward developing a nuclear device small enough that it could be delivered by the missiles in its arsenal.

Almost immediately the liberal press questioned the fact that Powell's source for this information was a "walk-in" source that had brought to U.S. intelligence officials some one thousand unverified pages purporting to be technical documents and drawings of Iranian nuclear warhead design modifications that would allow ballistic missiles to deliver an atomic strike.[5] The *New York Times* engaged the political battle by sounding themes suggesting the administration was simply replaying another unfounded WMD scare. Reporter Steven Weisman noted that Powell's comments seemed "an eerie repetition of the prelude to the Iraq war, hawks in the administration and Congress are trumpeting ominous disclosures about Iran's nuclear capabilities to make the case that Iran is a threat that must be confronted, either by economic sanctions, military action, or 'regime change.'"[6]

The underlying message in the *New York Times* article was political. The newspaper echoed the argument made repeatedly by Democrats in the 2004 presidential campaign, namely, that President Bush had launched an unjustified preemptive war on Iraq based on false intelligence reports of WMDs and an imminent threat to U.S. national security in the person of Saddam Hussein. The *Times* suggested that the Bush administration was merely repeating the same unfounded prewar themes with the mullahs with the intent to launch another war without justification.

Secretary Powell's comments were made as France, Germany, and Great Britain, the Economic Union 3 (EU-3), were working desperately to hammer out yet another agreement with Iran to stop enriching uranium. The EU-3 and their supporters in the liberal U.S. mainstream media clearly favored more of the same: a continued diplomatic dance with Iran, even though that dance had not prevented Iran from pursuing nuclear weapons.

Quickly, State Department officials countered the suggestion by the *Washington Post* that Powell's statements were based on a source the *Post* had identified. Spokesperson Tom Casey insisted that the State Department had reliable information that the Iranians were developing workable delivery systems as part of their clandestine nuclear weapons program. "Powell said what he said and he stands by it," was Casey's assertion.[7]

The liberal mainstream media attacked the source of Powell's statement for an important reason. Powell was an active supporter of the diplomacy road with Iran. If he was becoming more hawkish on the question of Iranian nuclear weapons, then a clear signal was being given to the world that U.S. intelligence had reason to believe a deliverable Iranian nuclear bomb was closer to reality than anyone had previously thought.

The firestorm caused by Powell's comments had serious political implications. The moment Iran is able to put the two components together—nuclear warheads and ballistic missiles—then the rogue regime has become a deadly serious threat; if that moment is close, the threat is imminent.

President Bush in Santiago, Chile, for the Pacific Rim meeting made comments that strongly suggested that Secretary Powell's comments were calculated, part of a determined effort by the administration to send a warning to Iran and the EU-3. Echoing President Reagan's famous admonition to "trust but verify" when it came to evaluating Soviet Union arms control agreements, President Bush spoke in equally firm terms: "I think the definition of truth is the willingness of the Iranian regime to allow for verification. You know, they have said some things in the past, and it's very important for them to verify and earn the trust of those of us who are worried about them developing a nuclear weapon."[8]

The EU-3 and the IAEA Continue the Charade

BUSH'S AND Powell's comments coincided with meetings being held in Vienna by Mohamed ElBaradei (the director general of the IAEA), the EU-3, and the Iranians. The United States had not objected to the EU-3 and the IAEA taking the lead in trying to work out yet another agreement in a seemingly endless stream of meaningless agreements with Iran. Yet this time the United States would not accept just any agreement; the Iranians had broken too many prior accords.

The Bush administration asserted its right to take Iran to the U.N. Security Council unless the IAEA agreement provided more than cursory verification schemes. The Iranians had proven adept at circumventing all previous inspection schemes contained in prior broken agreements. What was different now? That was the challenge put forth by the president.

On November 17, 2004, the National Council for Resistance for Iran (NCRI), an Iranian opposition group, held press conferences in Paris and Vienna to reveal that Iran was continuing to enrich nuclear fuel at a secret site in Tehran. The NCRI functions as the political front for the People's Mujahedeen, itself a questionable group designated as a terrorist group by the U.S. government and banned from the United States. Still, the NCRI's information had proven useful before. In 2002 the NCRI revealed the existence of two clandestine Iranian nuclear facilities, including a uranium enrichment plant in the town of Natanz. The disclosures by the NCRI this time were being taken seriously as well. Paul Leventhal of the Nuclear Control Institute in Washington DC, noted that NCRI information "has been accurate in the past. Everything that came out initially about the Iranian clandestine information was from this organization."[9]

Only the day before, November 16, 2004, the liberal mainstream media in the United States were printing glowing stories about a new IAEA deal in which Iran had agreed to stop enriching uranium on November 22, 2004. To make everyone stop worrying, Dafna Linzer wrote in the *Washington Post*: "In its most positive assessment of Iran in two years, the International Atomic Energy Agency reported yesterday that it found no evidence that the nation had a nuclear weapons program and that Tehran's recent cooperation with the agency has been very good."[10] Linzer went on to cite a thirty-two-page IAEA report released the day before in which Mohamed ElBaradei noted that "all the declared nuclear material in Iran has been accounted for, and therefore such material is not diverted to prohibited activities [such as weapons programs]."[11] Still, Linzer noted, ElBaradei could not rule out the possibility that Iran might be conducting clandestine nuclear weapons activities, a loophole that allowed more than enough room for the doubt raised by the NCRI.

Nor was Israel convinced by the spin being put on events by the *New York Times* and the *Washington Post*. An article published in the *Jerusalem Post* on November 21 clearly indicated that Israel had reason to believe that Iran was running a secret nuclear weapons program parallel to the one Iran had agreed—with the EU-3—to suspend temporarily. "The Iranians have a 'declared' secret program which they have agreed to temporarily suspend," said one senior Israeli officer. "But they also have a 'secret' secret program. The agreement with the Europeans is not touching this program. Furthermore, it is our understanding that the suspension is only temporary and partial."

The military source went on to characterize the "negotiations" with the IAEA and the EU-3 as a "Persian bazaar" that could be expected to have little or no impact on continuing clandestine efforts by Iran to enrich uranium to weapons grade.

Just when the EU-3 and the IAEA believed they had a firm agreement with Iran to stop enriching uranium, the Iranians backtracked and opened another loophole. Iran unexpectedly announced on November 24—two days after the country was supposed to have stopped all uranium enrichment—that the deal had to be amended to permit Iran to operate about twenty-four enrichment centrifuges for "research purposes."[12]

The Bush administration objected that this new agreement included no "trigger provision" that would send Iran to the Security Council for sanctions if it was learned that Iran had broken the agreement. Now Iran wanted to exempt some centrifuges from the agreement. One could speculate that an intelligence source in Tehran had notified the mullahs that U.S. satellites could detect the signature sound of the centrifuges in operation, so something would have to be done to obfuscate the issue once continued enrichment efforts were detected. The Iranian cat-and-mouse game continued.

Still, on November 30 the IAEA accepted all of Iran's assurances and announced that an agreement had been reached with Iran to stop enriching uranium and to abandon its nuclear weapons program. Predictably, the *New York Times* presented the announcement as a defeat for the Bush administration: "In a defeat for the Bush administration, the 35-country ruling board of the International Atomic Energy Agency passed a mildly worded resolution on Monday welcoming Iran's total freeze on a sensitive part of its nuclear program."[13] In more politically loaded language, the article strongly suggested that this agreement would preempt any thought the administration might have about taking Iran to the U.N. Security Council: "The resolution, passed by consensus without a vote, removes the possibility that the group will drag Iran before the Security Council for possible censure or even sanctions."[14]

Buried in the article was the report that Jane Wolcott Sanders, the head of the American delegation to the IAEA, gave a nine-page statement behind closed doors to the board after the resolution had passed. She accused Iran of deceit and suggested that the IAEA board was acting irresponsibly in agreeing to such a softly worded accord that contained little or no verification teeth. Wolcott accused Iran of continuing a clandestine nuclear weapons program, and she held open the possibility that the United States could decide unilaterally to take Iran before the U.N. Security Council despite expected objections from the EU-3, China, and Russia. Examining the resolution closely, the language called only for Iran to suspend enriching uranium as a "voluntary confidence builder," not as a legal obligation.

Not only was the final agreement lukewarm, Mossein Mousavian, the lead Iranian delegate to the IAEA, insisted right after the agreement's announcement that Iran had not agreed to shut down all centrifuges. Some twenty machines would still be used for testing purposes; besides, he added, "There are technical issues I don't know about."[15] Obviously, the hard line within Iran was to resist any appearance that the mullahs had given up their intention to ultimately enrich uranium and develop nuclear weapons. At most, this "agreement" was temporary, subject to improvement only if the EU-3 could come up with further inducements.

Clearly, the gamesmanship continued as Iran invited the IAEA and the EU-3 to come up with more carrots. ElBaradei claimed the agreement was a "step in the right direction," while Hassan Rohani, a cleric who heads Iran's Supreme National Security Council and is also his country's main nuclear negotiator, asserted that enriching uranium was still "Iran's right, and Iran will never give up its right to enrich uranium."[16]

America Signals Resolve

As if to underscore the Bush administration's firmness, in December 2004 U.S. Undersecretary of Defense for Policy Douglas J. Feith gave an interview to the *Jerusalem Post* in which he refused to rule out the possibility of military action against Tehran if the agreements reached with the IAEA the preceding month were violated by Iran. Feith stated that the United States was focusing now on "a process to get the existing international mechanisms—the non-proliferation treaty (and) the International Atomic Energy Agency—to work, to bring the kind of pressure to bear on Iran that would induce the Iranians to follow the path that Libya took in deciding that they were actually better off in abandoning their WMD programs." Feith took exception with the statement of British Foreign Secretary Jack Straw that ruled out military action should diplomacy fail. "I don't think that anyone should be ruling in or out anything while we are conducting diplomacy," Feith added.[17]

Feith, widely disliked by American liberals and the mainstream media in the United States, is widely regarded as a principal architect of U.S. military action in both Afghanistan and Iraq. Feith began his government career in 1981 as an assistant to Richard Pipes at the U.S. National Security Council during the Reagan administration. He played a major role in the fall of the Soviet Union and the end of the cold war, advocating democracy and human rights for those living in the grip of the Soviet bloc, themes delivered by a U.S. president willing to oppose the USSR militarily. The aggressive themes Feith articulated once again were certain to be rejected by the EU-3, the IAEA, and those American liberals who preferred soft diplomacy as the approach of choice in dealing with the terror-supporting mullahs.

But Israel was expressing the same sentiments. At a conference on security and economics in Tel Aviv on December 13, 2004, IDF Chief of Staff Lt. Gen. Moshe Ya'alon indicated that Israel and the West should be prepared for "other options" should Tehran continue its drive toward nuclear weapons. Ya'alon made clear he had in mind military solutions to the problem: "We believe there is a chance of success when talking about the elimination of the Iranian capabilities of weapons of mass destruction, first of all using political and economic resolutions. From my point of view and my recommendation, this has to be used first of all. If not we have to be prepared, and I am talking about the Western community, to use other options in order to eliminate the Iranian capabilities."[18]

In December 2004 the United States took steps to block Iran's application to open membership in the World Trade Organization (WTO). The General Council of the 148-nation trade organization voted by consensus to accept the applications of Iraq and Afghanistan for membership but rejected for the sixteenth time Iran's application. The U.S. action was taken just as the IAEA and Iran's nuclear negotiator, Hassan Rohani, were beginning meetings in Brussels to transform Iran's voluntary agreement in November into a permanent and binding agreement. The Europeans and the IAEA were clearly disappointed with the U.S. action, as entry into the WTO was one of the incentives being offered to Iran.[19]

By the end of 2004 the EU-3 and the IAEA had made clear they had no problems in giving the Iranian rogue regime full access to nuclear fuel for peaceful purposes, and they were willing to trust that the mullahs would not cheat to enrich uranium or develop nuclear weapons. After all, U.S. forces did not find Saddam Hussein's stockpiles of WMDs, so why would anyone believe the mullahs would eventually have nuclear bombs? Thus went the argument from the Left.

So, what was the scorecard at the end of 2004? The Europeans had settled on diplomacy, economic incentives, and reliance on multinational organizations as their approach to containing Iran's desires for nuclear weapons. The United States achieved neither hard language nor reliable verification procedures, while the EU-3 and the IAEA maneuvered to make sure the Iran question never reached the U.N. Security Council.[20] That the United States and Israel both began talking about military options is not unreasonable given the threat they perceive in the mullahs' determination to attain nuclear weapons.

From Iran's point of view, the negotiation process could be seen as buying time. Working from the premise that terrorists do not view the world as others do, the EU-3 and the IAEA could easily be perceived by Iranian hard-liners as weak and easily deceived. The mullahs see the Europeans and the IAEA as ready to give away almost everything, even economic incentives, and probably even security guarantees, in return for little other than a promise to be good. To the terrorist mind-set what could be better than being paid for not causing harm? Never was the protection racket this perfect. Besides, if the mullahs continue to develop nuclear weapons secretly, what would the Europeans or the IAEA do when the deception is uncovered? Probably nothing except demand more negotiations and offer more bribes.

Iran's Extensive Nuclear Weapons Capability

MOST ANALYSTS agree that Iran has diversified its nuclear technology infrastructure over an estimated three hundred different sites, possibly many more. One strategy at play here may be defense oriented: a large number of sites geographically distributed are more difficult to attack. An examination of a few critical sites provides a snapshot of the size and scope of Iran's nuclear endeavor as well as an appreciation of how the technology in place could be adapted to the development of nuclear weapons.

Access to Uranium

SINCE 1988 Iran has opened an estimated ten uranium mines. The explorations at these sites suggest that the uranium resources of Iran might be in the range of twenty thousand to thirty thousand tons throughout the country, more than enough to fuel Iran's civilian nuclear power plants well into the future.[21]

On September 1, 2004, Mohamed ElBaradei, the director general of the IAEA, reported to the organization's board of governors that Iran planned to convert twenty-seven tons of yellowcake uranium into uranium hexafluoride gas, the form in which uranium is fed into centrifuges for enrichment.[22] This quantity would be small enough for a peaceful nuclear program, but it would also be sufficient to make about five crude nuclear weapons. It should be no surprise that the steps Iran has taken to enrich this uranium violated the agreement signed with the EU in October 2003, in which Iran had accepted economic benefits for an agreement to suspend enriching uranium. Iran violated the deal when it started assembling centrifuges for further processing of the hexafluoride gas.

According to a Reuters story printed in the *Tehran Times*, a Western diplomat claimed "ElBaradei and the IAEA have offered to guarantee Iran's fuel supply." According to the source, the Iranians argued that if they gave up their nuclear fuel production capabilities, they would never have a reliable source of fuel for their nuclear reactors. So Iran demanded a guaranteed fuel supply to ensure the country's fuel supply would not be subject "to the political whims of countries such as Russia, which plans to provide fuel for the Russian-built Bushehr reactor and to take back to Russia all the spent fuel." The diplomat noted, "Iran is afraid that the U.S. could put pressure on Russia to halt its fuel supplies to Iran and they would not have fuel for their reactors."[23]

What makes sense is that Iran decided to affirm the Nuclear Nonproliferation Treaty (NPT) and continue negotiations with the IAEA to see if the IAEA would guarantee an abundant supply of nuclear fuel to run its reactors. Nuclear fuel required for peaceful purposes is about half the enrichment grade needed to make weapons. But even without the IAEA-supplied fuel, Iran appears to be well on its way to being nuclear fuel self-sufficient.

The Bushehr Nuclear Reactor

In 1992 Russia agreed to build a nuclear reactor for Iran at Bushehr for a cost of between $800 million and $1 billion. The reactor deal caused great concern in the United States. As reported by GlobalSecurity.org: "US opposition to Russian construction of Bushehr rests on three issues; first that weapons

grade plutonium could be extracted from the reactor allowing the Iranians to construct nuclear weapons. Secondly, the US fears that the Russians and the Iranians are using Bushehr as a cover for the transfer of other sensitive technology that would normally be prohibited. Finally, the US is concerned that knowledge gained by Iranian scientists working at Bushehr could further Iran's nuclear weapons program."[24]

The United States argued that Iran was sitting on top of perhaps one-quarter of the world's known oil reserves, with sufficient natural gas and oil to provide electric power for more than four generations of Iranians. Iran's estimated 26.6 trillion-cubic-meter natural gas reserve is the second largest in the world. By comparison to oil and gas, nuclear power is expensive. To the United States, Iran's arguments were merely subterfuge for obtaining nuclear technology with the objective being the transfer of that technology to weapons purposes.

The Russians finished the Bushehr nuclear reactor in October 2004. "We're done," was the statement of a spokesperson for Russia's Atomic Energy Agency (Rosatom). "All we need to do now is work out an agreement on

sending spent fuel back to Russia." According to Alaeddin Boroujerdi, head of
the Iranian parliament's Foreign Affairs and National Security Commission,
making the reactor operational was imminent: "The (nuclear fuel) agreement
is practically ready. If experts agree on a few remaining commercial matters, it
could be signed in November."

Interestingly, the Russians publicly handed over the reactor to the Iranians without demanding concessions from Iran in accord with the IAEA or
demanding that Iran abandon its nuclear weapons program. And Russia is a
member of the U.N. Security Council, one not likely to be a strong supporter of sanctions against Iran if the United States were to bring Iran before the Security Council.[25] Reports indicate that Iran is considering the
construction of three to five additional nuclear reactors at an estimated cost
of $3.2 billion.[26]

Esfahan (Isfahan) Nuclear Technology Research Center

THE NUCLEAR Technology Research Center is the country's largest nuclear research center, employing an estimated three thousand scientists. One goal is
to train personnel to operate the Bushehr reactor. An agreement with France
in 1975 permitted the center to be piggybacked onto the University of Isfahan, which has more than fifty years of experience as one of Iran's leading
universities. The French have reputedly provided a light-water subcritical reactor at Esfahan, and the Chinese have constructed a plutonium production
reactor at the site. Esfahan is also the site of Iran's largest missile assembly and
production plant, which was built with North Korean assistance.[27]

Natanz (Kashan) Uranium Enrichment Facility

THE NUCLEAR facility at Natanz was clandestine until the National Council of
Resistance for Iran (NCRI) revealed the site in a mid-August 2002 press conference in Washington DC. The site contains two large underground structures designed to house the centrifuges necessary to enrich uranium to
weapons grade. Each of the underground structures is buried twenty-five feet
underground, protected by eight feet of concrete, and surrounded by a protective shield to make the structure resistant to explosions.[28] The underground
enclosures measure approximately thirty-two thousand square meters, enough
to operate between fifty thousand to sixty thousand centrifuges. Here uranium
hexafluoride gas could be processed into a grade sufficient to fuel a reactor,
such as the Bushehr reactor, or into weapons-grade uranium-235. The Insti-

tute for Science and International Security estimates that the Natanz facility could make enough highly enriched uranium to produce three nuclear weapons per year.[29]

Arak Heavy Water Reactor

THE SECRET site at Arak was also revealed by the NCRI at its August 2002 Washington press conference. Here Iran has built a heavy water production plant and reactor. Heavy water is required to moderate the chain reaction needed to produce weapons-grade plutonium. The Atomic Energy Organization of Iran (AEOI) is overseeing the construction of the heavy water plant, operating through a fronting company, the Mesbah Energy Company.[30] Fission bombs requiring plutonium are more sophisticated to design and detonate than bombs using uranium-235, but their explosive magnitude is many times greater. The reactor at Bushehr does not use heavy water.

America Does Not Buy Iran's Lies

THE ARAK facility has raised serious concerns from the U.S. government that Iran's intention is to weaponize its nuclear program. Consider the comment of Richard Boucher, a State Department spokesperson, at the daily press briefing of May 8, 2003:

> Iran's only nuclear power reactor expected to become operational within the next decade is the light-water reactor under construction with Russian help at Bushehr. This raises serious questions about Iran's intentions in constructing an industrial-scale heavy water plant at Arak. Heavy-water moderated reactors are better suited for plutonium production than are light water reactors. We believe Iran's true intent is to develop the capability to produce fissile material for nuclear weapons, using both the plutonium route (supported ultimately by a heavy-water research reactor) and the highly enriched uranium route (supported by a gas centrifuge enrichment plant).[31]

Boucher raised the same concerns about the nuclear facility at Natanz:

> Iran has also confirmed to the IAEA that it is constructing a gas centrifuge uranium facility near the town of Natanz. Although Iran initially delayed the visit, IAEA Director General ElBaradei visited the Natanz site in late February and found what appeared to be a "sophisticated" centrifuge uranium enrichment

program. We are deeply concerned at Iran's efforts to build that facility clandestinely, and believe there is no logical reason for Iran to pursue uranium enrichment other than to support a weapons capability, especially in light of Russia's pledge to provide all the fuel for the lifetime of the Bushehr reactor.[32]

On August 17, 2004, James Bolton, undersecretary of state for arms control and international security, gave an important address to the Hudson Institute in Washington DC in which he put together the various elements of the Iranian nuclear program. His conclusion was firm but frightening. Referring specifically to Iran's uranium enrichment plant in Natanz and the heavy water processing plant at Arak, Bolton said:

> The costly infrastructure to perform all these activities goes well beyond any conceivable peaceful nuclear program. No comparable oil-rich nation has ever engaged, or would be engaged, in this set of activities—or would pursue them for nearly two decades behind a continuing cloud of secrecy and lies to IAEA inspectors and the international community—unless it was dead set on building nuclear weapons.[33]

Reinforcing the conclusion that Iran was weaponizing its nuclear program was its incredible pattern of lying and deception. As Bolton continued:

> Another unmistakable indicator of Iran's intentions is the pattern of repeatedly lying to and providing false reports to the IAEA. For example, Iran denied testing centrifuges with uranium, denied the existence of a laser enrichment program, denied producing enriched uranium, and denied receiving any foreign assistance in its centrifuge program. In each case, Iran confessed the truth only when confronted with irrefutable technical evidence from IAEA inspections. Iran's October 2003 submission to the IAEA, a declaration that was supposed to be the correct, complete, and final story of Iran's nuclear program, omitted any mention of the development and testing of advanced P-2 centrifuges, which IAEA inspectors discovered in early 2004.[34]

Simply put, Iran is determined to develop nuclear weapons, as it has always said to anyone who would listen. The Europeans and the IAEA continue to put on the blinders and believe the Iranians can be trusted, allowing the Iranians to play them for fools. They are intent on carrying out the process of meaningless negotiations whose only point for the mullahs is to buy time while they secretly make atomic bombs.

Iran's Secret Missile Program

THE MAINSTAY of Iran's missile system is the Shahab-3 missile, a single-stage, liquid-fueled missile based on the North Korean "Nodong" missile series. The missile is road mobile with a reliable range of sixteen hundred kilometers—more than enough to hit Tel Aviv. The warhead is capable of carrying chemical, nuclear, or biological payloads. The Shahab-3 was successfully tested on August 11, 2004, and again on September 19. On September 21 a Shahab-3 missile was paraded by Iran, covered with banners proclaiming "We will crush America under our feet" and "Wipe Israel off the map."[35]

Tehran claims that the Shahab-3 can reach targets as far away as 2,000 meters (1,250 miles), which would allow the missile to be deployed farther away from Israel's air force and its Jericho-2 ballistic missiles. On November 9, 2004, Iran announced it was capable of mass-producing the Shahab-3 missile and reserved the right to use the missile in preemptive strikes should its nuclear facilities be threatened with attack.[36] Iran's ballistic missile inventory is among the largest in the Middle East, "thanks to all the missile-related cooperation it has received over the years from Russia, North Korea, China, and others."[37]

On December 3, 2004, the NCIR disclosed not one but two clandestine Iranian missile programs. According to the NCIR press release, Iran's Defense Ministry is pursuing two top-secret missiles: the Ghadr and the Shahab-4. The Ghadr differs from the Shahab series in that the Ghadr has more maneuverability. The Ghadr can evidently be prepared for launch within thirty minutes, whereas the Shahab-3 missile takes several hours of preparation prior to launch. The Ghadr is said to have a range of 2,500–3,000 kilometers. The Shahab-4 is a three-stage missile capable of delivering a warhead with a range of 3,000 kilometers, which would be sufficient to hit targets as far away as Berlin.[38]

The NCRI also revealed that Iran was making progress in manufacturing nuclear warheads. The Shahid Karimi Industrial Group in the Hemmat Complex is directing the nuclear warhead project, according to the NCRI. Adding detail to give the report credibility, the NCRI revealed the name of the project director as well as the project code number.

Investigative reporter Bill Gertz of the *Washington Times* wrote on December 3, 2004, that Bush administration officials added, "Iranians belonging to the Atomic Energy Agency of Iran were conducting research and testing on development of a nuclear warhead for a missile. The information came from reliable intelligence sources and was not provided by an Iranian opposition group."[39]

A. Q. Khan's Nuclear Smuggling Network

ON FEBRUARY 4, 2004, Abdul Qadeer Khan, the father of Pakistan's nuclear weapons program, went on Pakistani television to confess and apologize to the nation for selling Pakistani nuclear secrets to other countries. "It pains me to realize that my lifetime achievement could have been placed in jeopardy," he said with an emotion that looked like regret.[40]

From the available record, Khan sold nuclear technology, including weapons blueprints and uranium enrichment equipment, to a rogue's gallery of target states—North Korea, Syria, Iraq, Iran, Libya—if the country had the multimillions required. Khan visited each country to make available his extensive expertise of trafficking in the world's underground nuclear smuggling network. Instead of being turned over to an international tribunal for justice, Khan was permitted to retire into semiprivate life in Pakistan, evidently secure with the hundreds of millions he had been paid for his services since around 1990.

Typically, the IAEA's ElBaradei appeared at a loss for words after Khan's public apology. He told reporters, "The Khan case raises more questions than it answers." He added, "We need to know who supplied what, when, to whom. Dr. Khan was not acting alone."[41] ElBaradei appeared flat-footed, probably because Khan's confession made clear to the world that IAEA safeguards had been totally ineffective. Not only had the IAEA not stopped Khan's smuggling ring from proliferating nuclear technology to a host of rogue states around the globe, the IAEA did not appear even to know Khan's black market existed.

The CIA's 721 Report released in November 2004 admitted that Iran's nuclear program "received significant assistance" in the past from "the proliferation network headed by Pakistani scientist A. Q. Khan."[42] In a closed-door speech, former CIA Director George J. Tenet called Khan "at least as dangerous as Osama bin Laden" because of his role in spreading nuclear technology to rogue states throughout the world.[43]

What was the importance of Khan's contribution to Iran? According to the NCRI, as far back as sometime between 1994 and 1996 Khan provided Iranian nuclear scientists with the blueprints of a Chinese-designed warhead.[44] Even if the design was outmoded or not precisely the specifications the Iranians needed, the availability of the Chinese nuclear warhead design would have assisted the Iranians in designing their own. Moreover, the NCRI claimed that in 2001 Khan provided the Iranians with a quantity of highly enriched uranium, perhaps not enough to make a bomb, but still a sizable quantity. None of this was good news. What Khan's confession and the subsequent revelations made clear was that the Iranians had access through Khan to key design information and weapons-grade uranium, breakthrough elements Iran would need if it were to build a bomb.

With Khan's revelations and with Libya deciding to hand over to the United States its illicit nuclear weapons program, there was abundant evidence that the Nuclear Proliferation Treaty and the United Nations had been completely ineffective in stopping rogue states from communicating and trafficking in nuclear technology, probably even in nuclear fuel. With both available on the world black market, how could a terror-supporting rogue state like Iran *not* get involved, especially with abundant oil revenue flowing into the hands of the few mullah criminals who dominated power? The setup would have been hard for any criminal mentality to resist.

As yet there has been no thorough international investigation of the countries whose corporations served as the middlemen, the suppliers, in this black market setup. Selling "dual use" technology—nuclear technology that could be used in either peaceful purposes or to produce weapons—would be a hot commodity on a cash-rich smuggling network where sanctions imposed by multinational organizations amounted to little more than inconveniences. The participating countries undoubtedly included the usual suspects. If the United Nations oil-for-food crisis with Iraq served as the model, the same countries most supporting Iran probably were the countries whose internal suppliers profited most from the opportunity to participate in a worldwide nuclear technology black market that served the interests of rogue states.

It should be no surprise that the IAEA did not lead the investigation into Khan's network or the ties from that network back to Iran. In its entire history, the IAEA has never once uncovered a clandestine national nuclear weapons program—a record truly worthy of Peter Sellers and Inspector Clouseau.

The Mad Mullahs Threaten

HITLER REVEALED in *Mein Kampf* that he intended to commit genocide on the Jews of Germany. Many did not take him seriously; the thought was simply too extreme, too mad. Yet he communicated his true intentions, even if only those who knew how to listen to disturbed personalities believed him at the time.

So, too, the mad mullahs who rule Iran have been clearly telling the world that they intend to use their missiles and, when they have them, their nuclear weapons. Iran's President Muhammad Khatami speaks in radical terms. "Haven't the Jews and Christians achieved their progress by means of toughness and repression?" he asks.[45] Take him seriously, for he has a strategy drawn to destroy Jewish and Christian civilization, regardless how fourteenth century the whole discussion seems. "Our missiles are now ready to strike at their civilization, and as soon as the instructions arrive from the Leader 'Ali Khamenei, we will launch our missiles at their cities and installations."

Yes, the talk is mad, but it is also serious. Yes, other representatives of the theocracy will come forward calmly, well-dressed, with impeccable manners, and announce in the forums of international diplomacy that all Iran cares about is national defense and protection from Iran's historical enemies. These more responsible spokespersons will defend Iran's honor and argue that having nuclear technology is a right the theocracy derives from the legitimacy of its twenty-five years in power. Aren't other states permitted by the international community to have nuclear technology, even nuclear weapons?

Yet President Khatami rants on: "The global infidel is a front against Allah and the Muslims, and we must make use of everything we have at hand to strike at this front, by means of our suicide operations or by means of our missiles. There are 29 sensitive sites in the U.S. and the West. We have already spied on these sites and we know how we are going to attack them." Recall that a number of Iranian U.N. diplomats have been deported from the United States for photographing strategic sites without authorization or explanation. Suddenly the inflammatory words become quite serious.

Nor is Israel exempt from this radical Islamic fury. "If Israel dare attack our installations at Bushehr, our losses will be very low, because only one structure will be destroyed, while we have the means of attacking Israel's nuclear facilities and arsenals such that no trace of Israel will remain." Yes, Iran probably has its Shahab missiles pointed at Israel's nuclear facilities. Ponder how a nuclear attack on Tel Aviv and the possibility of nearly eradicating the State of Israel must appeal to the terrorist Iranian mind.

These statements of Khatami are not idle threats or the raging of an insane mind, no more than were Hitler's speeches against the Jews, the British, and the Americans.

Insight into the Terrorist Mind

WHEN I received a top-secret clearance in the early 1980s to participate in the hostage survival program, some psychiatrists and psychologists trained me. As part of my training, I watched countless filmed interviews and participated personally in interviews with hardcore criminals and terrorists. I began the work with Dr. David Hubbard who conducted pioneering research to develop successful techniques to stop skyjacking and deal with skyjacking perpetrators.[46] Over and over again, one key lesson was drummed into me: terrorists do not think like average human beings who have never committed a crime. Put simply: terrorists do not think like you or me.

To a terrorist, a person who pleads for his life when threatened with a gun not only increases the likelihood he will be killed, but he also earns the disdain of the terrorist. Thus the terrorist concludes that his victims are weak and don't deserve to live.

In the realm of foreign policy many analysts today try to map on the Iranian terrorists the same reactions that other nations have experienced after developing nuclear weapons. Highly respected analysts have reasonably argued that countries that develop nuclear weapons end up moderating their foreign policy toughness. Initially, the availability of nuclear weapons induces some bravado, but after a time the reality of deterrence sets in, so goes the argument. Not so with a terrorist regime. The very ability to induce chaos by an atomic strike to the terrorist mind may present an almost overwhelming temptation to use the weapon. That other nations might respond with their own massive conventional or even nuclear retaliations may ironically turn out to be an even greater enticement to the terrorist to use the weapon.

Iranian terrorists have repeatedly demonstrated suicidal tendencies. Simply examine the car-bombing techniques and vest-bomb methodologies invented by Hezbollah, an Iranian created and funded surrogate group. Another example are the human-wave attacks, often led by children, that Iran perfected as a key battle strategy in its nearly ten-year-long war against Iraq in the 1980s. The mullahs sent countless thousands of children to brutal deaths in battle with plastic keys around their necks, to remind the children how soon they were to enter the glory of heaven after their soon-to-be-realized martyrdom. Many of the youths who went into those suicidal battles went unarmed; they expected to be able to pick up from the dead the few weapons that were given to those who led the charge.

Long drawn-out negotiations appeal to terrorists who need more time. How the EU-3 and the IAEA have behaved in their drive to force a diplomatic settlement looks like weakness to the terrorist mind, especially if the terrorists' only goal is to get nuclear weapons and to use them. The possibility that this is the game being played today by the Iranian mullahs must be taken seriously.

North Korea acted like a rogue state and played the Clinton administration for fools. Kim Jong Il signed treaties when convenient but never stopped advancing and developing clandestine nuclear weapons programs. In this regard North Korea and Iran are similar. There is, however, a major difference. Iran is in the Middle East, a region Iran has been actively destabilizing for a quarter of a century. Korea appears to have a somewhat longer time horizon and for now is acting in a relatively stable manner—for the time being. Drastic, dramatic steps taken now, such as sending a nuclear weapon to Tel Aviv, could easily appeal to the mullahs.

One or two nuclear weapons detonated on Israel in a surprise attack could be enough to wipe Israel off the face of the earth. That will be a powerful image, perhaps irresistible, to the Jew-hating mullahs who have sworn to destroy Israel and eliminate the Jewish state for all time.

PART 1

THE AMERICAN POLITICIANS

2

Kerry-Edwards '04 Endorses the Mullahs

DURING THE 2004 PRESIDENTIAL election, Democratic vice presidential candidate John Edwards gave an important interview to the *Washington Post*. The interview came at the end of August and was mostly eclipsed by the Swift Boat controversy that grabbed the headlines at the time. And the press had given most of the foreign policy attention in the campaign to the war in Iraq and was little prepared to handle a new, more complicated story on Iran. Still, the *Post*'s interview with Edwards was important.

Edwards laid out the Kerry campaign position that Iran should be given nuclear fuel for peaceful purposes, explaining that we would only know for sure if Iran was going to build a bomb if we tested the mullahs. Somehow, in the Kerry-Edwards logic, if the mullahs built bombs, the blame would not be so much on the United States for calling them bad guys if they proved themselves to be bad guys. The *Washington Post* reporters wrote: "Edwards said that if Iran failed to take what he called a 'great bargain,' it would essentially confirm that it is building nuclear weapons under the cover of a supposedly peaceful nuclear power initiative."[1]

This is essentially the same failed policy the Clinton administration tried toward North Korea. In 1994, under an "Agreed Framework" treaty, the Clinton administration agreed to provide enough nuclear fuel to North Korea to run two power plants (plus a ton of economic aid) with the stipulation that North Korea would halt its plutonium weapons program.

Somehow, Clinton officials and their supporters even today still claim to be shocked that rogue-state dictator Kim Jong Il deceived them, withdrew from the Nuclear Proliferation Treaty, and proceeded to make nuclear warheads for Nodong missiles. The Clinton administration was never able to get North Korea to agree to abandon its development of ballistic missiles. Evidently the nuclear fuel to run two power plants was all the nuclear fuel the North Koreans needed, so why bother making more meaningless agreements with the Americans?

Now, in the 2004 presidential campaign, Edwards made clear in his August tête-à-tête with the *Washington Post* reporters that the Kerry administration was going to walk the same path with the mad mullahs in Iran. He explained that, if elected, he and John Kerry would ensure that America's historic European allies would join the United States in imposing strong sanctions if Iran rejected this proposal. "If we are engaging with the Iranians in an effort to reach this great bargain and if in fact this is a bluff that they are trying to develop nuclear weapons capability, then we know that our European friends will stand with us," Edwards argued.[2]

The *Washington Post* predictably spun the story positively for Kerry: "Edward's notion of proposing such a bargain with Iran, combined with Kerry's statement in December that he was prepared to explore 'areas of mutual interest' with Iran, suggests that Kerry would take a sharply different approach with Iran than has President Bush," the reporters wrote. To the liberal mind-set, all President Bush's foreign policy initiatives were considered ill advised at best, if not downright stupid. So any change had to be for the good, and reporting the story was something the *Post* could easily have calculated would sway their readers to vote for Kerry (despite the obvious fact that a great number of their readers were already determined to vote Democratic).

The *Post* did not challenge Edwards on this policy nor compare it to the nuclear fuel gambit that had already failed with North Korea. The *Post* acted as if Edwards were articulating a major policy breakthrough that would prove devastating to the failed Middle East foreign policy of George W. Bush.

Undoubtedly the mullahs had gone to school on the North Korean model. Easily Ayatollah Khamenei could have concluded that the West was again trying to appease them, a familiar pattern that Western democracies since Neville Chamberlain's time had followed in their anxiousness to avoid war.

Khamenei and the ruling mullahs of Iran could see what had happened with North Korea. All Kim Jong Il had to do was say that he would give up his nuclear weapons programs, and the West would ship free of charge all the nuclear fuel for peaceful purposes he wanted. Since nuclear fuel in this form was halfway to weapons grade already, enriching it to weapons grade would be easier. Besides, with the nuclear plants open ostensibly for peaceful purposes, North Korea would have a ready excuse for importing all the nuclear technology it wanted, a perfect cover to access whatever additional nuclear expertise and equipment North Korea could find anywhere worldwide. Why not import some additional uranium or plutonium as well? Clearly Pakistani A. Q. Khan read the situation as a clear invitation to visit North Korea, something he did regularly from 1994 on.

North Korea set the path for Iran to follow. There had been no downside for accepting President Clinton's offer of nuclear fuel. And the weak West did nothing when Kim Jong Il proceeded to make nuclear weapons anyway. With nuclear weapons in hand, North Korea would be even harder to attack militarily. All Kim Jong Il had to do was lie. Again, there was no downside. The world is accustomed to dictators who lie. The case was proved in the 1930s with Adolf Hitler, and very little had changed in diplomacy tactics since then.

Yet the Kerry-Edwards team believed they were on to something here. Edwards gave the interview to the *Washington Post* on the eve of a major foreign policy address. As the *Post* article noted: "Edwards will deliver a speech today in Wilmington, N.C., that aides say will seek to sharpen the differences with the Bush administration on a range of foreign policy issues. Seizing on Bush's statement last week that he miscalculated the postwar conditions in Iraq, Edwards will lay out a broad indictment of how he believes the administration has miscalculated on Iraq, overseas alliances, Afghanistan and other issues."[3]

Kerry-Edwards had with Iran exactly what they wanted—a chance to argue the importance of relying on international diplomacy and multinational organizations while attacking President Bush on his failure to form as extensive an international coalition as Bush's father had formed when fighting the first Gulf War. The Kerry campaign was happy to advance its Iran policy in lockstep with the strategy of negotiations the EU-3 and the IAEA had on-going with the mullah's nuclear team in Vienna and Brussels.

So when John Kerry said in the first debate that he wanted to provide nuclear fuel to Iran to test Iran's intentions, he was on theme. Kerry was merely following the approach to terrorists that Democrats had taken since the Carter administration. Dealing with terrorists was a subject of law enforcement; the use of military action represented not the only alternative but an admission that sound policy options had not been formed or followed.

Kerry's campaign Web site explained: "As president, John Kerry will work with every country to toughen export controls, stiffen penalties, and strengthen law enforcement and intelligence sharing so that disasters like the A. Q. Khan network can never happen again. And he will work through the United Nations and international treaties to make trade in the technologies of mass destruction an international crime, like slavery and piracy."

Evidently, the Kerry campaign was not thinking about the Barbary pirates and the homage paid in the Marine Corps hymn to the shores of Tripoli. President Thomas Jefferson was forced to take military action to bring the situation under control. Paying tribute did not work with those pirates any more than Kim Jong Il had been swayed to stay in line by the economic incentives that went along with President Clinton's 1994 "Agreed Framework" agreements.

Once Kim Jong Il or Ayatollah Khamenei has nuclear weapons, how could anyone seriously think that a United Nations resolution of censure would bother them? Economic sanctions issued by a multinational organization such as the United Nations may be a nuisance, but there are plenty of states, including members of the U.N. Security Council, who will be willing to trade under the table with censured rogue states. The oil-for-food scandal at the United Nations under Saddam Hussein's rule in Iraq should prove the point that U.N. sanctions and censures are mere words to dictators who have already stepped beyond the law.

Besides, just among the French, the Germans, the Russians, and the Chinese, to name just a few, there are plenty of international players (read "allies" in "Kerry/Edwards-Speak") who will let personal gain cloud their vision so completely that one begins to wonder if the morality of the sanctions and censures they voted for have any meaning even to them. Dictators rarely seem to lose sight of the old saw, ". . . but words will never hurt me."

By offering the nuclear-fuel-for-peaceful-purposes gambit to Iran, the Kerry-Edwards campaign was obviously calculating that the theme of speaking softly to dictators and carrying a polite stick limited to "law enforcement" was a theme their liberal supporters wanted to hear. This was especially true in point-counterpoint contrast to the way the Kerry campaign was portraying the Bush administration, as a cabal of second-rate warmongers of minor intellect.

The Kerry-Edwards campaign went all the way, advocating not only that Iran be given nuclear fuel for peaceful purposes but also full economic and diplomatic recognition by the United States, plus a entry into the World Trade Organization (WTO).

The *New York Times*, another central player in the liberal mainstream media promoting Kerry's candidacy, reported on a Kerry speech delivered in December to the sympathetic Council of Foreign Relations in New York City. Here, John Kerry attacked President Bush as conducting an "arrogant, inept, and reckless" foreign policy. Kerry went on to suggest that the Bush administration was "intoxicated" with America's military power. He invented a new word, charging that the administration's "triumphalism" as a lone superpower had only made the United States "less safe than we were three years ago."[4] Kerry elaborated, making sure to drive home his newly coined pejorative term: "Triumphalism may make the armchair warriors in the seats of power feel good, but it does not serve America or the world's interests." And: "This is the consequence of a policy that regards legitimacy as largely a product of force, and victory as primarily a triumph of arms."

Kerry and Edwards wanted to "find common ground with Iran" by exploring areas of mutual interest. What exactly did the Democrats have in mind? According to the *New York Times*, Kerry felt he could work with Iran "by fighting the flow of drugs from Afghanistan and by exchanging anti-Iranian terrorists operating out of Iraq for members of al-Qaeda and the Taliban in Iran."[5] Why Iran would ever want to do this, Kerry did not explain. Kerry further claimed that the Bush administration's aggressive military stance in the Middle East only "diminishes Islamic moderates and fuels the fire of the Jihadists." He added: "Instead of demeaning diplomacy, I will restore diplomacy as a tool of the strong."

This was Kerry the Vietnam antiwar activist speaking, not Kerry the war hero saluting and reporting for duty. To make sure no one missed the point, Randy Beers, one of John Kerry's top foreign policy advisers (the same adviser who tried to explain away the Kerry campaign e-mail that was published in the *Tehran Times* as an endorsement of the mullahs) spoke up. Beers volunteered that, if elected, Kerry would name a special envoy to the Middle East peace process. He offered as candidates for the positions the names of Bill Clinton (under whose watch North Korea abandoned the Agreed Framework and resumed developing nuclear weapons), or possibly Jimmy Carter (under whose watch the mess with Iran started in the first place, with the 1979 hostage taking at the American Embassy in Tehran).

To balance out the slate, and to appear nonpartisan at least for the moment, Beers also mentioned President Bush's father and James A. Baker III. Neither of these alternatives was taken very seriously. The Democratic Party's extreme left wing had not yet forgiven Baker for his role in the Florida ballot recount defeat of Al Gore in 2000. Kerry had not voted for the first Gulf War; he was not about to nominate George Herbert Walker Bush to be his new special ambassador to the Middle East, no matter what he said during the campaign.

Politically, the speech must have been music to the ears of the *New York Times*. The article concluded on a upbeat note: "He proposed ideas for reaching out to Muslim nations, in part by charging American diplomats with appealing to 'populations, not just to governments,' and naming a presidential envoy to the Islamic world. 'We must speak,' he said, 'and we must listen.'"

The Kerry-Edwards theme on Iran was hard to distinguish from Chamberlain's approach to Hitler. Hadn't Germany suffered enough at the end of World War I, not to mention anything of the Depression and the hyperinflation that destroyed the German mark? If we could only reach out and understand Hitler, we might see why the return of the Sudetenland was part of Germany's rightful heritage and the return of Danzig something that rightfully belonged to Germany anyway. Hitler was misunderstood; we weren't sympathetic enough. That evidently was the problem, if only we could extend the Kerry-Edwards logic backward.

Are the Mad Iranian Mullahs in Touch with Reality?

KERRY'S APPROACH to the Iranian problem was predicated on the assumption that within Iran was a responsible ruling group that could be trusted to make and keep agreements. Otherwise, the exercise would merely be a charade. This was a fundamental failing in the Kerry-Edwards thinking. The theocracy ruling Iran not only supports terrorism, they are also rabidly anti-Jewish.

What follows is truly "far-side" material—bizarre, yet it is completely factual and distinctly frightening.

According to Middle East Media Research Institute (MEMRI), *Jaam-E-Jam 1*, the Iranian government television channel directed toward Europe, broadcast on June 1, 2004, a program advancing the clearly anti-Jewish theory that the Jews were responsible for the 9/11 hijacking. As proof the program claimed that five Israelis were arrested while they were photographing the World Trade Center just hours before the attacks. Then the show advanced the argument that four thousand Jews working in the Twin Towers were not there on 9/11 because they had taken a vacation day, having been warned in advance of the attack that was ordered by World Zionism as defined in the Jewish Protocols.[6]

MEMRI prints the following statement from the program: "Ever since the establishment of the Zionist regime, the American strategy has been under the Zionist lobby's influence. Zionism, as expressed in the Jewish Protocols, nurtures in its mind the dream of taking over the world. With [George W.] Bush's rise to power, it controls the White House with greater force."

As the MEMRI report documents, Iranian government television attempted to pin the 9/11 disaster on Israel: "A while afterwards, a source in American military intelligence raised details pertaining to an intelligence memo regarding Israel's espionage organization, the Mossad, and its role in the events of September 11. In fact, the claim that Israel was involved in the blasts of September 11 and used it as a basis of America's new strategy for fighting the world of Islam, disappeared in the media coverage, but world public opinion still believes this possibility." In this twisted Iranian logic, the fact that the American media coverage of the 9/11 disaster did not place blame on Israel proves the U.S. government was complicit with the international Jewish conspiracy; in other words, there was a coverup. Forget the more realistic conclusion, namely that the whole conspiracy theory was preposterous to begin with.

This begins to sound like a time warp, the 1930s all over again. But the anti-Jewish lies are being broadcast again, only today the transmissions emanate from Iran. The Iranians' rabid hatred of the Jews has revived once more the mental sickness the world rejected decades ago when Henry Ford and Hitler propagated the same anti-Jewish trash in virtually the same form. Has the world learned nothing since the Holocaust?

In this upside-down world that is the mullah's Iran, the Holocaust is a myth, a story the Jews concocted to blame the Germans (the real victims of World War II) and to steal Palestine away from the Muslim Arabs (the rightful landowners). The decision by President Harry S. Truman in 1948 to listen to Abba Eban and to support David Ben-Gurion, to accept the U.N. partition of Palestine, even to recognize the new State of Israel—according to the mad Jewish-hatred being propagated in Iran—never really happened, except as part of a Jewish conspiracy to grab land and dominate the world. This conspiracy succeeded only because the United States was a Jew-dominated, willing party to the conspiracy.

This would all be worthy of a Lewis Carroll story, except this "wonderland" of Jew-hating is happening all over again, today with the Iranian mullahs at center stage, beating the drums. Does anyone wonder why we might not want these particular madmen to get their hands on nuclear weapons? Does anyone doubt that the 9/11 hijackers would have used nuclear weapons to take down the World Trade Center and the Pentagon if they had possessed them?

In the world inhabited by the clerics who rule Iran, Zionism and the Jewish Protocols are real, living demons. Consider one more shocking example: MEMRI reported on a documentary broadcast by the Iranian television station *Al-Alam* during the first two weeks of April 2004 that argued the Jews controlled Hollywood according to the directives set out in the Protocols of the Elders of Zion. Consider this: "The most important film produced under Zionist guidance in the '60s was called *Operation Eichmann*. This film completed the false myth about the murder of six million Jews at the hands of the Nazis."

The Iranian propaganda circle is complete. We start with the worldwide Jewish conspiracy as articulated in the famously fictitious "Protocols of the Elders of Zion," we proceed to America's establishing and then defending Israel, and we circle back to make sure we attack the "myth" that the Nazis ever committed genocide against any Jews. The Iranian Islamic radicals see the worldwide Jewish conspiracy as behind all the evils of the world, just as the Nazis did almost seventy-five years ago.

MEMRI summarized the documentary's analysis of *Operation Eichmann*:

> But the film did not mention his provocative trial on December 17, 1961. This is because of what [Adolf] Eichmann said about the German Jews' expulsion and killing: "I was only carrying out the orders of the Zionists. They asked me to gather the Jews in a specific place in the world, using expulsion or murder. First, their target was Poland, then Madagascar, but in the end they chose the Middle East. If I am guilty of the so-called killing of 6 million Jews then the Zionist

leaders are much guiltier than I am. This is because they wanted to silence the world under the pretext that if they had stayed in Germany they would have been killed. Because they don't have a country they are forced to occupy other people's land. And that is what they did." The Zionist authorities finished the trial quickly to avoid further commotion. They hanged Adolf Eichmann in 1962 so the secrets of the collaboration between the Zionists and the Nazis would remain hidden.[7]

So now we have the story of the Holocaust according to Iranian television: the Jews themselves caused the Holocaust, which was all a lie anyway, since it never happened. The Jews invented the Holocaust to justify the theft of Palestine from the rightful occupants of the land—the Palestinians. What could be more simple or easier to understand? And U.S. President Harry S. Truman was one of the conspirators.

Critics may argue that this rabid anti-Jewish hatred is not unique to Iran, that enmity toward Jews is rampant in the Middle East. That may be so, but where are the mullahs in Iran, the religious clerics in positions of authority, who have spoken out against this anti-Jewish, anti-Israel hatred? Anti-Judaism is not at the heart of true Islam; this thesis is not central to the genuine religion of Islam. But hatred of Jews is alive within the hearts of the radical Iranian mullahs who have hijacked their religion to serve their terrorist ends. The hatred the radical mullahs express toward Jews is every bit as real and every bit as dangerous as was every sentence Hitler wrote in Mein Kampf and repeated in countless Jew-hating speeches he delivered in the ramp-up to World War II.

On December 15, 2004, Iranian Foreign Minister Kamal Kharrazi announced that Iran would like to have direct discussions with the United States by including the Americans in the negotiations under way with the EU-3 and the IAEA, provided that Washington was willing to treat Tehran as an equal.

Kharrazi seems to have overlooked that the United States has designated Iran a rogue state, that the United States does not have diplomatic relations with Iran, and that the United States has imposed economic sanctions on Iran. No, Kharrazi didn't forget. He is deeply involved in a strange language called "U.N.-speak." All nations are equal in the U.N. General Assembly, regardless of their size, their legitimacy, their dedication to peace, or whether they are actively protecting genocidal maniacs within their borders. Actually a few of the countries appear to have genocidal maniacs as their leaders, but that doesn't bother the United Nations. All countries participating in the General Assembly are equal and each have the same one vote.

So as far as Kharrazi is concerned, Iran and the United States are equals, and he can demand the United States treat Iran as such, or else he won't talk to us. What Kharrazi and others who urge dialogue with Iran forget is that the United States doesn't have diplomatic relations with Iran because it is considered a terror-supporting rogue regime.

Democrats such as John Kerry and organizations such as the EU-3 and the IAEA all seem to have bought Kharrazi's logic. Even when the Iranians insist they need to keep some centrifuges running, the EU-3 and the IAEA don't seem bothered. Iran needs to keep pursuing "research and development," doesn't it? So what if Iran forgets to disclose this clandestine uranium enhancement site or that one? What are a few secret facilities among friends?

If John Kerry had been elected president in 2004, America would now be running to Vienna or Brussels or wherever else Iran wanted to meet, especially if we could find a few Europeans and a multinational organization or two to bring along with us.

The problem is that the Iranians aren't serious about giving up their pursuit of nuclear weapons. We don't need to give the mullahs nuclear fuel to see if they will make bombs. If the Iranians are serious that they don't want nuclear weapons, then all they have to do is give up their centrifuges. The Iranians could then allow open inspection of all their nuclear sites at a time and choosing of the international inspectors. If the Iranians were serious about only pursuing peaceful goals, the mullahs could stop sending insurgents into Iraq to cause trouble. How about Hezbollah? Maybe the Iranians could call off the suicide bombers who are ready to blow themselves up in Israel.

Arieh O'Sullivan, writing in the *Jerusalem Post*, quotes a senior Israeli security source as warning, "History has shown that rogue nations tend to use diplomacy as a cover while they complete their work."[8] The clerics ruling Iran actually do reveal their true intentions in their lunatic diatribes against Israel. Iran remains committed to the destruction of the Jewish state, and there is nothing on the record to contradict that impression.

Once Israel is gone, the mullahs have targeted America. The mullahs hate liberal Western democracy possibly as much as they hate Israel. They despise all that is intrinsic to the freedoms Americans enjoy—our music, our love of life, our businesses, the equal status we grant women, the way we edu-

cate our children, our freedom to worship God as we please. Our minds may
have difficulty grasping this horrible truth, but there is nothing about a return
to the fourteenth century that the mullahs would find objectionable as long as
they could rule with their despotic and perverted form of Islamic radicalism.

Nor would Iran's war against us stop if Israel were wiped from the face of
the earth. The United States, to the Iranian mullahs, remains the "Great
Satan." Their chants have to be taken seriously. "Death to Israel" is not complete unless it is also coupled with "Death to America." Already on the drawing boards is the Shahab-5 with sufficient range to reach the continental
United States. By the time the Shahab-6 is developed, there will be no place
on earth the mad mullahs could not strike with a nuclear weapon on a day
and at a time of their choosing.

Follow the Money: Pro-Mullah Dollars Flow to the Kerry Campaign

As I indicated in the preface, my interest in Iran was rekindled by a telephone
conversation with Aryo Pirouznia. Aryo focused my attention on Hassan Nemazee, one of John Kerry's top fund-raisers in the 2004 presidential campaign.
Nemazee is an Iranian American living in New York City. Going to John
Kerry's campaign Web site, Nemazee is listed in the top tier of Kerry's contributors, one of some sixty people credited with raising one hundred thousand
dollars or more for the campaign, an amount that earned Nemazee the designation of vice chair to Kerry's campaign.[9] We later learned that Nemazee
raised more than five hundred thousand dollars for Kerry's 2004 presidential
candidacy, an amount that elevated Nemazee to a very rarified fund-raising
plateau, even for the Kerry campaign. There was no doubt that Hassan Nemazee was a dedicated Kerry fund-raiser of the highest magnitude.

During the campaign, Aryo Pirouznia and his attorney, Bob Jenevein,
traveled to Washington DC, where we met. As I indicated in the preface, Nemazee had sued Aryo for libel, charging that Aryo had defamed him by calling
him an agent for the mullahs. Aryo is a leader in the United States of a group
known as the Student Movement Coordination Committee for Democracy in
Iran (SMCCDI).[10] The group is a strong advocate for freedom and democracy
in Iran.

Basically, Aryo had referred to Nemazee as an "agent" of the mullahs ruling Iran. Nemazee, a New York investor in charge of Nemazee Capital Management, felt that charge defamed him. He contended that he had no ties or
affiliations to the Islamic Republic of Iran, nor was he an agent of the mullahs.

He denied Aryo's allegation that he was funneling money from Iran into the U.S. presidential election to support John Kerry. But Aryo suggested that the mullahs were contributing to Kerry's campaign to influence him to support the mullahs' efforts to gain their political objectives and, most importantly, full diplomatic and economic recognition from the United States, entry into the World Trade Organization, and access to nuclear fuel for peaceful purposes.

My advice to Aryo and his attorney was to countersue Nemazee to see if Jenevein could lock in a deposition with Nemazee prior to the November election. This strategy succeeded and Jenevein took Nemazee's deposition in New York City on October 18, 2004. I attended the deposition as a consultant to Aryo. We will fully discuss the deposition in chapter 4.

As I researched Nemazee, I realized that he had been funding Democratic Party candidates since the early 1990s. Bill Clinton had received substantial contributions from Nemazee and had nominated Nemazee in 1998 to be the U.S. ambassador to Argentina. This nomination was withdrawn after *Forbes* magazine published an extremely damaging review of Nemazee's career.[11]

Forbes characterized Nemazee as a "polished socialite" with "a Harvard degree, a position on one of the university's prestigious visiting committees and a lot of well-connected friends." The article went on to note that in November 1995 Nemazee hosted a dinner featuring Al Gore, raising $250,000 for the Democratic National Committee (DNC) that evening. "Over the past four years Nemazee and his family have given more than $150,000 to Democratic politicians and the DNC. Six of Nemazee's friends and relatives have given $10,000 apiece—the maximum allowable per year—to Bill Clinton's legal defense fund."[12] Among these donors was the caretaker of Nemazee's twelve-acre estate in Katonah, New York.

Nemazee, according to *Forbes*, was born in Washington DC, the son of an Iranian shipping magnate who was then a commercial attaché to the United States for Shah Mohammad Reza Pahlavi's government. After college, Nemazee formed a joint venture in Iran with New York–based insurance conglomerate American International Group (AIG). This venture "fell victim to the Iranian revolution. Nemazee, on a business trip to the U.S. when the Shah was overthrown, escaped with his wife and a fair amount of wealth outside of the homeland, including property in the Washington area that his father had given him." Nemazee then teamed up with a friend from Harvard, J. C. Helms, to develop the tract of land that became the Galleria in Houston, Texas.

The *Forbes* article detailed family feuding and a lawsuit with former partner Helms, all of which occurred in a real estate downturn in the early 1990s. Nemazee evidently exited with some four million dollars from the land sale, money that his family had obtained from Nemazee's Alzheimer's-afflicted father. The article also detailed a money management venture, First Capital Advisors (FCA), that Nemazee entered into with stock picker Gerry Angulo, who had managed money for one of Ivan Boesky's partnerships. Boesky achieved notoriety in 1986 when the Securities and Exchange Commission charged him with illegal stock manipulation based on insider information; he was ordered to pay one hundred million dollars in penalties and was sentenced to prison.

In 1990 Angulo had FCA apply as a "Hispanic-owned firm" to manage money for the huge California Public Employees' Retirement System (CalPERS). Angulo is a Cuban American, but how was Nemazee Hispanic? Evidently Nemazee applied for Venezuelan citizenship, relying on a family connection to the wealthy Cisneros clan of Venezuela.

In a separate instance, Nemazee's status as a minority money manager was challenged when Nemazee claimed to be an Asian American because his father had been born in Bombay, India. The *Forbes* article detailed questionable transactions and lawsuits that colored FCA's history. Then Angulo and Nemazee tried to take control of Puerto Rico's troubled newspaper, the *San Juan Star*. There were more lawsuits. Nemazee hired David Boies, the famous lawyer who later represented Al Gore in the 2000 presidential election vote recount battle in Florida. Boies lost the suit. And Nemazee, according to *Forbes*, did not himself obtain U.S. citizenship until 1996.

Once the *Forbes* article was on the streets, Clinton, a president not known for thin skin—even when it comes to pardoning people of questionable character—decided the best course of action was to find somebody else to become ambassador to Argentina.

Aryo was particularly upset with Nemazee because of a speech Nemazee gave on June 1, 2002, to the American Iranian Council (AIC). On this day the AIC was holding a conference at the Ritz-Carlton hotel in San Francisco, a conference that keynote speaker Senator John Kerry attended in person. The AIC is a nonprofit group that is supposed to be nonpartisan, according to its charter, though the AIC was proud to boast that support for the San Francisco Conference had come from the Open Society Institute funded by George Soros. Earlier in 2001, Nemazee joined the board of AIC.

Aryo and many others in the pro-democracy for Iran movement in the United States considered the AIC to be dedicated to legitimizing the mullahs, pushing for the mullahs to obtain normal diplomatic relations with the United States, and ending all international economic sanctions, including those imposed through the United Nations. Nemazee's speech to the AIC meeting in San Francisco was on those themes. He urged the group to remember that its goal was to "attempt to establish the basis and the vehicle for a dialogue which will ultimately lead to a resumption of relations" between the United States and the Islamic regime in Iran.[13] A large part of Nemazee's speech focused on attacking the Enhanced Border Security and Visa Entry Reform Act of 2002, which in the wake of 9/11 made entry into the United States by Iranians more difficult.

Meanwhile, Senator Kerry's speech to the AIC in San Francisco was supportive of engaging the terror-supporting mullahs in dialogue: "We wish that Iran were not funding Hezbollah. We wish that Iran were not as intent as it appears to be on seeking weapons of mass destruction. We wish that Iran were more fully in compliance with the chemical weapons treaty. We wish that Iran were not cozying up to some of Hamid Karzai's enemies in Afghanistan, as we try to go forward." Yet Kerry was willing to overlook all these terror-supporting tendencies of the mad mullahs. What he lamented was what he considered President Bush's bad judgment to label Iran as part of the "Axis of Evil," calling President Bush's decision "a silly thing to do." Kerry argued that if China and Vietnam were in the WTO, then Iran should also be in the WTO.

In his June 1, 2002 speech to the AIC at the Ritz-Carlton, Kerry characteristically went back to Vietnam to explain his current understanding of Iran. Kerry mentioned his family home in France that his grandfather rebuilt after it was destroyed in World War II. One thought led to another, and pretty soon Kerry, as usual, was back in Vietnam. The "images" Kerry refers to here are the mental images he has of that house in France:

> These images were vital to me later on when I became a young man and went to Vietnam, because I began to see the impressions that I'd learned about and the lessons I'd drawn from the books that I read about the war suddenly thrust on me as a role that I was playing, as I watched the Vietnamese look on me as an occupier. And I learned that the realities of the efforts to advance your interests through the muzzle of a gun in a far-off part of the world with people who

didn't look like you, who didn't speak a language you spoke, and for whom there were very few cultural connections.

Kerry rambled on about how foreign policy is, after all, "the art of bringing people together, how to find cultural common ground, and advance the interests of your country." He maintained that everything international is still "mainstream American policy, main street 'any capital in the world that you want to select' policy" because of "the extraordinary interconnectedness of our economies." So "we are all bound together," and American foreign policy that starts out with good intentions ends up going wrong because "Americans have a bad habit of only seeing the history and culture of other countries through our own eyes, through our own culture, and through our own history." Then Kerry worked himself back to Vietnam:

> And we have always had a rather isolationist, xenophobic, self-interest definitional problem in trying to do that properly. It's one of the reasons we did what we did in Vietnam. It is one of the reasons why we have trouble today dealing more effectively in the Middle East, particularly the Arab world, and needless to say, of course, Iran.

Kerry claimed that U.S. foreign policy is failing in Iran because America doesn't know how to see the world through the eyes of the Iranians. That thought must have had some of the mad mullahs in Tehran laughing. Translated into how a terrorist might interpret what Kerry said, Kerry had just affirmed that not only was the United States weak, we were also confused. Maybe if we just learned to see the world their way, we would be happy to let them kill all the Jews and send their sleeper cells across our borders to kill us here at home.

The remarkable thing about Kerry's speech to the AIC is that it was given after 9/11, and yet Kerry seems to have no deep appreciation whatsoever that this regime in Iran was paying insurgents to go across the border to fight U.S. troops in Iraq and funding Hezbollah to send suicide bombers to Jerusalem and Tel Aviv. Yes, Kerry lamented those facts, but almost as an afterthought, as inconvenient nuisances that needed to be mentioned, but still, Kerry does not seem to understand fully that the mullahs ruling Iran are enemies of the United States, set on our death and destruction as well as the death and destruction of Israel.

Kerry has always had a proclivity to work with America's enemies. Not only had he met with the enemy in Paris, in the person of Nguyen Thi Madame Binh, with whom he had unauthorized private discussions while he was yet in the naval reserve, but during the 2004 campaign I received dozens of e-mails in which Kerry opponents attached a photograph of Kerry and Senator Tom Harkin (D-IA) shaking hands with our Communist enemy from Nicaragua, Daniel Ortega.

Looking closely at Kerry's speech to the AIC in San Francisco in June 2002, it was clear that Kerry had no reservations about going to Tehran and meeting with these mullahs as if they were the rightful rulers of a legitimate state. Kerry's 2002 speech was an exact prelude to the position he and John Edwards took regarding Iran during the 2004 presidential campaign.

No wonder Aryo was upset. As far as Aryo was concerned, Nemazee was an "agent" of the mullahs because he did the mullahs bidding, whether Nemazee was on the payroll of the mullahs or not, regardless of whether a cent of Nemazee's campaign contributions to Kerry could be tracked back to the mullah's oil money in Iran. Nemazee not only had Kerry speak to the AIC in San Francisco as his guest, he also sat next to Kerry and had lunch with him during the afternoon session.

Kerry's speech is the type of speech that sticks in the craw of Aryo and millions of others who support freedom in Iran. Kerry's speech emphasized how wrong it would be if terrorist profiling singled out Middle Easterners, but he devoted not a single word to discussing the daily abuse of basic human rights or the fundamental intolerance of religious freedom that are standard operating procedures for the mullahs in Iran.

Reporting on the Iranian connection to Kerry, seasoned investigative reporter Ken Timmerman drew the conclusion that the Kerry-Edwards campaign was "headed toward a campaign finance scandal involving contributions on behalf of a foreign power, similar to allegations that plagued Bill Clinton's reelection in 1996. Instead of Communist China, this time the foreign power seeking to influence a U.S. presidential candidate is the Islamic Republic of Iran, the world's premier state sponsor of international terror."[14] In 1996 the Chinese were seeking military technology to enhance their nuclear missiles. The record shows, as Timmerman noted, that the Clinton administration was happy to provide all the assistance the Chinese wanted. What the Islamic Republic of Iran wanted from a potential Kerry administration was equally clear: "a series of concessions that would allow them to become a nuclear weapons power and circumvent the restrictions of the USA Patriot Act to infiltrate intelligence agents and potential terrorists into the United States."[15]

Then Timmerman turned his attention to the political contributions of Susan Akbarpour, an Iranian exile who attended the San Francisco AIC Conference where Kerry and Nemazee spoke. Akbarpour came to the United States in 1997, supposedly a penniless refugee. Timmerman noted her rapid advance in America. "In just seven years, she has started a newspaper, two consulting companies, and a glitzy magazine called *SiliconIran* that boasted some of Silicon Valley's top executives as its patrons during its brief existence."[16] She recently married Silicon Valley entrepreneur Faraj Aalaei, who is the CEO of the NASDAQ-listed firm Centillium Communications. Aalaei began dating Akbarpour in November 2000, and he became a financier for her various business and philanthropic activities. Akbarpour and her husband are credited with raising between fifty thousand and one hundred thousand dollars for the Kerry-Edwards 2004 presidential campaign.

Akbarpour became a controversial figure in the Iranian American community in California because of her outspoken support of the mullahs. Timmerman reported: "Akbarpour's advocacy on behalf of Tehran—odd enough for someone claiming political asylum from the regime—dances around the fringes of U.S. sanctions law and export control violations."[17] In spring 2002, *SiliconIran* funded an investment conference in Dubai to connect venture capital investors from the United States with high-tech opportunities in Iran, even though it is currently illegal for U.S. citizens to invest in Iran—evidently a small detail as far as Akbarpour was concerned. She also raised money for charities in the United States that send money, computers, and software to Iran, even though the U.S. government trade ban currently in force for Iran places severe restrictions on high-technology gifts to the country. Nor is it clear that Akbarpour, who is not a U.S. citizen, is within the bounds of U.S. campaign finance laws that typically prohibit contributions from foreigners.

When the Clinton administration, in one of its many attempts to court favor with Iran, brought Iranian Foreign Minister Kamal Kharrazi to the United States, he was met with protests. At UCLA more than two hundred protesters held up pictures of relatives who had been killed or jailed by the mullahs. Susan Akbarpour managed to join a select list of regime supporters who braved the university protest crowd to join a closed door meeting with Kharrazi. When she came out, she confronted the demonstrators, swearing at them in loud, abusive language, castigating them for not supporting the Islamic regime in Iran. This was again hardly the expected behavior of a political refugee fleeing the mullahs. No wonder the pro-mullah Iranian supporters in the United States want visa limitations and Patriot Act restrictions eased. The goal is clear: to get as many of their pro-mullah allies here as possible, regardless of whether sleeper-cell terrorists enter with the immigrants or not.

In writing about Akbarpour, Timmerman exposed the duplicitous world in which many mullah-supporting Iranians live. He also looked into a 1997 lawsuit that Akbarpour had filed against the California-based Persian-language newspaper *Andisheh*. The lawsuit developed out of a labor complaint in which Akbarpour claimed she was owed $47,255 in back pay, overtime, commissions, and bonuses. Akbarpour sued Shayna Barghi, the owner of the newspaper, claiming that Barghi had defamed her reputation by alleging in a February 1999 newspaper article that Akbarpour came to the United States, not to escape the regime as she had claimed, but to serve within the United States as an agent for the Islamic Republic.

In his defense of the suit, Barghi produced a letter from the director of the *Khorasan* daily newspaper in Iran that addressed Akbarpour as the "director of the Satellite Section" of the newspaper, charging that she was employed by the Martyrs Foundation of the Islamic Republic, a paramilitary governmental agency that the mullahs had been using to funnel money to foreign terrorist operations as defined by U.S. law-enforcement authorities.

A tangled web of conflicting stories surrounds Akbarpour. Much remains unclear. Timmerman revealed accusations that she fled Iran not to escape political persecution but to run away from a husband of some thirteen years. More lawsuits and conflicting e-mails raised questions about whether Akbarpour had ever received a journalism award, as she had claimed, or whether her parents had ever owned a newspaper for which she claimed she had worked. Timmerman concluded: "Iranian-Americans are acutely aware of attempts by the regime in Tehran to infiltrate their community and to create discord and false disputes, demoralize exile opposition groups, and discredit defectors from the Iranian intelligence services who have hard information on Iranian government misdeeds."[18]

The Mullahs Endorse Bush-Cheney '04

SO AFTER all this effort to reach out to the Iranians, one should assume the mullahs endorsed Kerry in 2004. Well, they endorsed George W. Bush.

Rational observers fully predicted that the mullahs would be advocates for Kerry-Edwards '04. Just before the election, Tehran-based political analyst Mahmoud Alinejad said, "Logically speaking everything points to Iran supporting Kerry. If Bush is re-elected it will be on a platform of a radical strategy to democratize the Middle East, if necessary by force. At least what Kerry has hinted at provides the possibility for Iran to get out of this deadlock, to buy some more time."[19] Conservative strategist Amir Mohebian, who advises some of the top policy makers in Iran, was of the same opinion. Mohebian told Reuters: "We prefer Kerry because he favors diplomatic methods rather than pressure. Iran is better off if he wins."[20]

Yet the mullahs went Republican, coming out in favor of Bush-Cheney '04. Reuters reported that Hassan Rohani, the head of Iran's Supreme National Security Council, announced on state television in late October 2004: "We haven't seen anything good from the Democrats. We should not forget that most sanctions were imposed on Iran during the time of Clinton. And we should not forget that during Bush's era, despite his hard-line and baseless rhetoric against Iran, he did not take, in practical terms, any dangerous measures against Iran."[21]

Surprising? Not really. President Bush took out Saddam Hussein, one of Iran's greatest enemies, their neighbor on their eastern border against whom they fought a deadlocked ten-year war in the 1980s. The mullahs were happy to see Saddam gone, even if it took the United States to do so.

Never assume that the Islamic countries in the Middle East all move in unison because they are all Muslims. Iranians are Persians by nationality, not Arabs. Iranians speak Farsi, not Arabian. Even Iranian-born religious leaders, such as the Shi'ite leader Grand Ayatollah Sayyid Ali Husayni Sistani now living in Iraq, fail to drop their Persian accents despite living in Iraq and speaking Arabic fluently for more than two decades.

Nor do Iranian Shi'ites naturally identify with Iraqi Shi'ites. Yes, they both belong to the same sect of Islam. Yet each country has its own identity, distinct language, and national goals. In the Middle East, tribe is probably the primary identifier, followed by nationality. Religious identity, even for Muslims, comes in a distinct third in importance—unless of course there is a common enemy.

Enemy Number One remains Israel, and the various Middle Eastern countries can generally unite in their hatred of Jews. Enemy Number Two is the United States. Without Enemy Number One or Enemy Number Two to unite against, the countries in this part of the world tend to fight each other over nationalistic questions. When Middle Eastern countries are not fighting each other, tribal divisions and tribal warlords within the countries may spark a internal conflict or even civil war.

In the mind of the terror masters ruling Iran, George W. Bush had not only done them a favor by eliminating Saddam Hussein, he was also the devil they knew. Yes, logic would dictate that a President Kerry would more easily give the mullahs what they want. Still, just in case Kerry lost, which he did, the mullahs wanted to hedge their bet.

Besides, Bush talked and acted like the tough guy in this race, and terrorist mentalities generally identify with tough guys, even if they are planning to kill them in the end.

3

Pro-Mullah Democrats, Pro-Mullah Lobbies

JOHN KERRY IS JOINED by a large list of Democrats who have favored working with the mullahs. But President Clinton was not necessarily one of them. His policy in the Middle East was dominated by his passion to negotiate an agreement between the Palestinians and the Israelis. Watching the drama unfold, you could sense Clinton's desperation in the last days of his administration to force an agreement between Ehud Barak and Yasser Arafat.

Clinton could almost taste the Nobel Peace Price he coveted as a talisman to ward off the mortal blow caused to his legacy by his lying under oath in the Monica Lewinsky affair and his impeachment that followed. Huddled away at Camp David, Clinton had pressured Prime Minister Barak to offer the almost unimaginable, namely that Israel would divide Jerusalem and share control of the holy city with the Palestinians.

When Arafat rejected this offer—the most generous any Palestinian had ever been offered—the Palestinian leader made clear to the world that the Oslo Agreements had always been a facade. Instead he not only demanded full control of the Temple Mount, with the Dome of the Rock and the Al-Aqsa

Mosque permanently protected, he virtually refused to allow Jews to pray there. A terrorist at heart, Arafat betrayed the true agenda of the Palestinian movement, which was not to come to an agreement with the State of Israel but to set the conditions where Israel would ultimately be wiped from the face of the earth.

Clinton left Camp David dejected. In his view, he had failed. Yet those dedicated to the survival of Israel around the world were relieved. Israel had dodged a bullet aimed at its heart. If only Arafat had agreed, the clock would have been ticking down to the point at which the extreme Left and the extreme Right in America would be willing to abandon the troublesome question of Israel and the irascible Jews who consider Israel their true and rightful homeland.

But while he focused on Israel, Clinton neglected most of the rest of the Middle East—including Iran. With a policy of "dual containment," he sought to keep both Iraq and Iran within their borders.[1] He lost sight of Iran's exporting terrorism, not seeing the urgency to retaliate for the bombing of the Khobar Towers in 1996, even when he had strongly convincing evidence that Iran was behind the plot that killed nineteen U.S. servicemen. Clinton maintained sanctions on Iran throughout his administration, though he and Vice President Gore accepted generous campaign contributions from Hassan Nemazee and danced with the pro-mullah lobby in the United States as a consequence.

Clinton's secretary of state, Madeleine Albright, in a move typical for the inconsistent administration, made a strong effort to appeal directly to the mullahs in her famous 2002 address to the American Iranian Council (AIC), on whose board of directors was Hassan Nemazee.

Secretary of State Albright Apologizes to the Mullahs

ON ST. Patrick's Day in 2000, Madeleine Albright addressed an AIC conference meeting in Washington DC. In a key part of her speech, the secretary of state apologized for U.S. involvement in the 1953 overthrow of Iranian Prime Minister Mohammed Mossadegh. While the role of the CIA in Mossadegh's ouster had been widely known for decades, never had the United States apologized for this action. She said:

> The Eisenhower Administration believed its actions were justified for strategic reasons; but the coup was clearly a setback for Iran's political development. And it is easy to see now why many Iranians continue to resent this intervention by

America in their internal affairs. Moreover, during the next quarter century, the United States and the West gave sustained backing to the Shah's regime. Although it did much to develop the country economically, the Shah's government also brutally repressed political dissent. As President Clinton has said, the United States must bear its fair share of responsibility for the problems that have arisen in U.S.-Iranian relations. Even in more recent years, aspects of U.S. policy toward Iraq during its conflict with Iran appear now to have been regrettably shortsighted, especially in light of our subsequent adventures with Saddam Hussein.[2]

She went on to suggest that U.S. support for Iraq in the decade-long war between Iraq and Iran in the 1980s might have also been a mistake. No terrorist mullah would have missed the point: here was the most powerful nation in the world saying it was sorry for exercising power when the mullahs themselves had paid no price when the world knew they were behind the bombing of the Khobar Towers and the murder of American servicemen. But that was only one act of terror the mullahs knew they had calculated and pulled off to the severe disadvantage of the United States of America.

Albright's speech represented historical revisionism in the extreme, a one-sided rewriting of history in favor of Iran, delivered by a U.S. secretary of state to a forum whose public purpose is to reestablish diplomatic and economic relationships with the mullahs. How about Hezbollah and the suicide bombers attacking Israel? The justifying comment circulating at the time in the corridors of the State Department was that if Franklin Roosevelt could make a deal with Joseph Stalin, Clinton could work with the mullahs.

Albright offered a litany of small steps toward normalization: allowing the import of carpets and food products from Iran, including dried fruits, nuts, and caviar; encouraging increased contact between American and Iranian scholars, professionals, artists, athletes, and nongovernmental agencies; and increasing efforts to settle outstanding legal claims between the two countries, including possibly a discussion of Iran's assets in the United States that had been frozen since the 1979 embassy hostage crisis. As the adviser for Gulf affairs to the National Security Council at the time admitted, the "United States was making a gesture, not giving away the farm."[3]

The response from Iran was considerably less than Albright had hoped. The following month Ayatollah Khamenei launched an even more repressive crackdown on dissidents within Iran. Yes, Albright's speech had been enthusiastically welcomed at the AIC and by those who supported the mullahs around the world, but no, the Iranian mullahs were not prepared to make any fundamental changes in order to win U.S. friendship, not if it meant abandoning their support of terror, their hatred of Israel, or their determination to crush any movement for freedom that looked like it make take root within their borders.

All that was accomplished by Albright's concessions was that now the mullahs had a way to get pro-mullah money into the United States. Carpets and food goods could easily be subsidized by the mullahs so the difference between the cost on imports and the proceeds from U.S. sales could reward their faithful supporters who had managed to immigrate, thus providing a ready slush fund to reward those willing to do their bidding in prestigious universities and prominent think tanks. Any relaxation in immigration or visitation rights provided the mullahs additional opportunities to place sleeper agents and supporters within U.S. borders. All this and an apology too—the mullahs had to be overwhelmed at how easily Albright and the Clinton administration could be fooled.

Senator Biden Jumps on the Pro-Mullah Bandwagon

ON FEBRUARY 19, 2004, Senator Joseph Biden (D-DE), chairman of the Senate Foreign Relations Committee, raised eyebrows among pro-democracy Iranians living in the United States by attending a California fund-raising dinner at the home of prominent dentist Sadegh Namazikhah, who reputedly was well known in the Los Angeles Iranian community as a strong supporter of the mullahs.[4] Namazikhah had been the chairman of the endodontics department at the University of Southern California and also served on the board of directors of the AIC, along with Hassan Nemazee.

Biden reportedly stayed for three hours, from 8:00 p.m. until 11:00 p.m., made comments that amounted to a "sweeping condemnation" of President Bush's inclusion of Iran in his "Axis of Evil" speech, and left after collecting thirty thousand dollars for his reelection campaign. "He really impressed us by his grasp of world affairs," Namazikhah explained to investigative reporter Ken Timmerman. "He encouraged us to make our views known and to get more involved in American politics."[5]

At the fund-raiser, Biden impressed the guests as being very favorable toward the mullahs. Houshang Dadgostar, a prominent attorney present at the dinner, quoted Biden as saying, "Iran always wanted to be an ally of the United States and to have good relations with the U.S." Another contributor present at the event, Mohsen Movaghar, a Los Angeles businessman, explained to Timmerman: "As Iranian-Americans, we don't want anything to happen to the Iranian government or to the Iranian people as a result of this war on terrorism." Both Dadgostar and Movaghar were reported to be on the seventy-member board of directors of Namazikhah's Iranian Muslim Association of North America (which reduces to the convenient acronym IMAM), a group credited with being supportive of the Islamic Republic of Iran and the mullahs.

Namazikhah denied any official contact with the Iranian government but did tell Timmerman that he regularly travels to Iran and actively supports the moderates within the Iranian ruling clergy. Also, Namazikhah indicated that he would like to see the sanctions on Iran lifted, but he insisted that IMAM was a religious and cultural group that did not pursue political objectives. Researching further, Timmerman determined that IMAM was registered in California as a "church" and, as such, was exempt from financial disclosure. One IMAM board member told Timmerman that the group raises between $300,000 to $400,000 per year from members and that the group had purchased a building in Los Angeles in August 1995 for $935,000, spending many thousands more to build auditoriums and meeting rooms for religious services. Timmerman could not determine where the funds to make these purchases came from.

Examining a calendar for the Persian year 1379 (March 2000–March 2001) that was circulated by the Iranian government, Timmerman found a reference suggesting that IMAM was a pro-regime group. An FBI spokesperson noted that if IMAM were lobbying directly on behalf of the Islamic Republic of Iran, the group might run afoul of U.S. laws prohibiting such activity.

Yet since it hovered in the shadows between being defined as a religion and simply a group interested in the advancement of Iranians, proof that IMAM is a full-scale lobbyist for the mullahs would not likely be obtained. What so bothers pro-democracy Iranians in the United States is that groups like IMAM can engage in what seems like direct pro-mullah fund-raising and lobbying, but the proof required by law to question the group seems to be so demanding that the group is protected, even when the pro-mullah group can go so far as to fund-raise for politicians believed to be favorable to the regime.

Everett Moore, the state Republican Party chairman of California, spoke to reporters after the fund-raiser and demanded that Biden give back the money. "I can't believe that Senator Biden would have a fund-raiser at the home of a pro-Tehran lobbyist two weeks after the White House made it

abundantly clear that Iran was aiding the al-Qaida forces in Afghanistan,"
Moore said. "Frankly, I am appalled that Senator Biden would have the au-
dacity . . . to take money from a lobbyist supporting a country that brutalizes
women, ignores human rights, and endorses terrorism."[6]

Biden objected that IMAM does not support terrorism or religious extremism. "The people I was talking to are opposed to al-Qaeda. They think it
is in the best interests of Iran to build a better relationship with the United
States," Biden explained. "This just shows that the local Republican Party
isn't aware of everything that's going on in U.S. foreign policy—not that they
should be."

Aryo Pirouznia strongly objected to the Biden fund-raising event, seeing
it as yet another example of how the AIC was working to penetrate U.S. politics in support of the mullahs. Aryo objected to IMAM as well, claiming the
group was simply trying to polish the image of "one of the most despotic
regimes in the world."

Biden, however, had no objection to the AIC. On March 13, 2002, he
spoke at an AIC event in Washington DC. The senator had recently charged
that the United States might be viewed as a "high-tech bully" for attacking
terrorists in Afghanistan. He now told the AIC that Tehran had his support
for entry into the World Trade Organization.[7] Add these insights to Biden's
earlier condemnation of President Bush's "Axis of Evil" remarks, and the
chairman of the Senate Foreign Relations Committee looked very pro-mullah.
The Federal Election Commission on-line database indicates that Hassan Nemazee or members of his family contributed twelve thousand dollars to Biden's
campaigns between 2000 and 2004.

Appearing on NBC's *Today Show* on May 27, 2003, Biden objected that
Iran should be the next country in the Bush administration's cross hairs in the
war against terrorism. Responding to Katie Couric, he indicated that Iraq was
his key focus: "You just had a five-minute or three-minute report on the situation in Iraq. We've got a long way to go there, Katie. Billions of dollars, hundreds—tens of thousands of forces for a long, long time to stay in place. I don't
think we should be biting off more then we can chew right now."[8]

When Couric questioned that Iran could not be ignored because the
country is harboring high-ranking al-Qaeda figures and developing nuclear
weapons, Biden was happy to rely on the IAEA: "Well, we know they are developing a nuclear weapons program. They've been doing that for the last ten
years. Although the IAEA is in there. They just investigated, inspected a new

facility where it looks like they're further along. Whether they've violated the international rules, the IAEA rules, the International Atomic Energy Commission rules will, remains to be seen. I think we should be working with and supporting the civilian leadership in there that's been taking on the clerical leadership. But in terms of going in there with force now and going in there to take down, quote, 'that regime' or form any revolution, we should be a little bit careful now."

On January 23, 2004, Senator Biden, in Davos, Switzerland, for a meeting of the World Economic Forum, held a ninety-minute private meeting with Iran's Foreign Minister Kamal Kharrazi, a rare high-level contact between Tehran and Washington. Biden now was the ranking Democrat on the Senate Foreign Relations Committee. The meeting was held in a lounge in full view of reporters. While neither Biden nor Kharrazi answered reporters' questions after the meeting, the press noted that Biden expressed views critical of the Bush administration and offered economic aid, possibly tied to disaster relief for the victims of a December 2003 earthquake, all with a view toward improving relations between the United States and Iran.[9] Shortly after the discussion with Biden, however, Tehran rejected a U.S. proposal to send humanitarian aid.

Just before the 2004 election, reports circulated that John Kerry had decided he would name Biden to be his secretary of state should he win the election. This came as a surprise to many. Biden would have beaten out several top contenders for the position, including Kerry foreign policy adviser Richard Holbrooke, who had been U.N. ambassador during the Clinton administration In Biden, Kerry would have found someone sympathetic to his views on working more closely with the mullahs.

Senator Robert Torricelli Gets Close to the Mujahedeen Khalq

SENATOR ROBERT "the Torch" Torricelli (D-NJ) also spoke at the same March 13, 2002, AIC meeting at which Senator Biden spoke. Torricelli, a member of the Senate Foreign Relations Committee who added his voice to Biden's criticism of President Bush's "Axis of Evil" characterization of Iran, drew fire not so much for his remarks but for the financial support he had drawn from the National Council for Resistance in Iran (NCRI). As was noted earlier, the NCRI, a strong critic of the mullahs, has been distinguished for a series of accurate disclosures regarding Iran's clandestine nuclear weapons program. The problem, however, is that the NCRI has a politically difficult history.

The NCRI has been identified by the U.S. State Department as a front group for the People's Mujahedin of Iran (also known as the Mujahedeen Khalq or the People's Mujahedin, MEK). Thus the State Department classifies the NCRI (in all its various designations) as a terrorist organization. Formed in the 1960s, the group was one of a series of anti-imperialist organizations dedicated to the overthrow of the Shah, a struggle in which the group gained notoriety for its killing of dozens of the Shah's associates and supporters as well as several U.S. soldiers and U.S. contractors in Iran at the time.[10]

During the 1970s the group operated underground within Iran and reputedly conducted assassination campaigns against the mullahs and various officials of the Islamic Republic of Iran. The MEK was part of the 1979 revolution, but the mullahs moved to close the group down because of its communist orientation, its close ties to the Soviet Union, and because the group was gaining too much power.

In the United States during the 1970s the Mujahedin could be seen in the streets of New York City or on various college campuses, raising money and displaying photographs supposedly of torture victims from the Shah's regime. In the 1980s and 1990s the group's leaders fled Iran to seek refuge in Iraq under the protection of Saddam Hussein. Now the photographs displayed in the United States by the group changed to show women mangled and tortured by the mullahs.

The group was led by the husband-and-wife team of Maryam and Massoud Rajavi.[11] Their followers transformed into a quasi-military organization that portrayed photographs of women in military uniforms, brandishing guns and driving tanks, and sworn to displace the Islamic regime in Iran. Largely displaced from Iraq as a result of the U.S.-led invasion, the body of MEK fighters who remained in Iraq are in camps under the watchful eye of U.S. military forces. The MEK has been on the State Department list of terrorist organizations since 1997. The NCRI, as the political arm of the MEK, continues to undertake various publicity and lobbying activities in France and Washington DC, punctuated by occasional public marches and rallies. In June 2003 French authorities soured on the Mujahedin, with 1,300 French police descending on the group's headquarters in Auvers-sur-Oise and arresting some 160 Mujahedin, along with Maryam Rajavi. Protesting this raid, Mujahedin followers in Paris, London, and Rome staged hunger strikes and several set themselves ablaze.

Founded in Tehran in 1965, the MEK has professed a unique blend of radical Marxism and Islamic theology as their unique political-theological signature. In the view of the U.S. State Department, the MEK has been involved in a number of attacks on U.S. interests abroad, including several murders of U.S. servicemen and civilians plus bombings of U.S. business offices abroad. Despite all this, the MEK likes to present itself as the legitimate Iranian government in exile. But in the final analysis, the MEK is a seriously dangerous organization that will not hesitate to use terrorism in pursuit of its narrow goals. Even within Iran, opposition groups today continue to express strong disapproval of the MEK. Even though the NCRI has presented accurate information about Iran's clandestine nuclear weapons activities, the MEK itself remains characterized as a terrorist group.[12]

After the AIC speech, Senator Torricelli's office acknowledged the senator's ties to the MEK. Torricelli reportedly accepted more than $140,000 in campaign contributions from groups related to the MEK.[13] More than once, Torricelli petitioned the State Department to redesignate the group more favorably, something the State Department has yet to do. Federal Election Commission records also indicate that in 2002, Torricelli received some $10,000 in campaign contributions from Hassan Nemazee and Nemazee family members.

But Torricelli's colorful Senate career came to an end in 2002, predictably over campaign financing scandals. In addition to taking funds from the MEK, Torricelli had also received funds from a long list of questionable figures, including a variety of Mafia-related figures and David Chang, a businessman born in Communist China who had a long history of transactions with Communist North Korea.

In the final analysis it would be hard to say if Torricelli was really pro-mullah or if Torricelli simply never met a shady campaign contribution he didn't like. What is clear is that in the confused world of expatriate Iranian relationships, finding an Iran-related group with an open pocketbook and questionable ties to Iran was something Torricelli had the skills to accomplish.

The MEK highlights how complicated the Iranian community is within the United States. On the one hand, the MEK are anti-mullahs, as evidenced by the group's willingness to expose to the world the mullahs' determination to develop nuclear weapons. Yet the MEK uses a political front, the NCRI, to make these inflammatory press releases, carefully holding out the NCRI as the group's anti-regime facade. These press releases appeal to the pro-freedom

Iranians in the United States and their supporters. Saddam Hussein supported the MEK not because he was a Marxist but because he shared the MEK's hatred of the mullahs, even though they all were Muslims.

Still, the MEK itself remains problematic. The group at its core remains cultist and dedicated to Marxist principles. Should the MEK ever come to power in Iran, the vast majority of the freedom fighters among the Iranian community would be dismayed. Freedom would again be set back, not by the theocracy of the Muslims, but by the communism of the MEK. The Bush administration cannot embrace the group, despite the group's strong opposition to the mullahs.

Perhaps most of all, the MEK demonstrates how skillful the Iranian expatriates are at working within Western political systems. The group can mask its ideology and find politicians to fund while trying to advance a specific political agenda, even if the politicians accepting the group's campaign financing do not fully understand the group or its goals. As we have noted before, Persians have a historically close affinity for Americans. The Persians are well educated and cultured; Persians who emigrate to the United States generally are economically and professionally successful, finding little or no difficulty in integrating with American society. In comparison, the Afghan and Iraqi communities in the United States are relatively small, and as a consequence their presence on the American domestic political scene is considerably less than the diversified and complex presence of Persians.

Which Persian group is on what side of the political spectrum and what exactly is the nature of the group's relationship to or opposition to the mullahs are questions not easily answered. American politicians entering this political landscape may be entering a minefield where supporting the wrong group for the right reason or the right group for the wrong reason are choices to avoid. As Senator Torricelli's case demonstrates, picking a group in this arena or accepting campaign contributions from one of these groups can be a formula for political embarrassment—or worse.

The Alavi Foundation: A Pro-Mullah Slush Fund?

THE ALAVI Foundation in New York City has been a controversial subject for twenty-five years. The original foundation, established by the Shah in 1975, was controlled by the Iranian government and named for the Shah: the Palahvi Foundation. But in 1979 the massive holdings of the Palahvi Foundation in New York, as well as the parent Palahvi Foundation in

Tehran, were taken over by the revolutionary government of Ayatollah Ruhollah Khomeini.[14]

The Shah's massive assets were transferred to the legal control of the ayatollah to be managed for the "oppressed" and needy. Thus the Mostazafan Foundation was formed in Tehran as well as the Mostazafan Foundation of New York. *Mostazafan* means "oppressed" in Farsi.[15] In Iran, the Mostazafan has grown to a multibillion industrial conglomeration that is involved in a wide range of businesses including food and beverage, farming, chemicals, petrochemicals, construction materials, dams, finance, and defense industries. The connection with "oppressed" seems to be the idea that the mullahs are seeking to employ and otherwise benefit the people of Iran who were downtrodden under the Shah's supposedly repressive regime. For the moment, let's not focus on the control the Revolutionary Guard exerts over the Mostazafan Foundation in Iran or on the funds the Revolutionary Guard regularly funnels to Iran's surrogate terrorist organization, Hezbollah, in Lebanon.

The purpose here is to track down what is now known as the Alavi Foundation in New York whose primary asset is a thirty-six-floor office building at 650 Fifth Avenue, at Fifty-second and Fifth Avenue, right in the heart of Midtown Manhattan. Built in 1970 with Iranian government money, 650 Fifth Avenue had an estimated 1979 value of $50 million and has a current estimated value in the range of $250 million. The building, by anyone's definition, is prime real estate.

The foundation claims approximately $4.5 million per year in revenue, realized from rentals at this property. Critics claim that figure is intentionally sandbagged, understated so unaccounted-for funds can be channeled into clandestine purposes. The foundation, however, sticks by its audited tax returns, although 2002 is the last federal income tax form listed on the foundation's Web site. Also, the Web site indicates that Alavi Foundation currently owns only 50 percent of the building. Critics charge that half the business was sold in a scheme that allowed the proceeds to return to the mullahs' control via the Cayman Islands. Inevitably, a series of Iranian-controlled international banks are listed when investigative reporters trace the foundation's financial schemes.[16]

The Alavi Foundation's pro-Shah board of directors was forced out in 1979 and replaced by a board favorable to the ayatollah. Mohammad Hadi Nejad-Hosseinian assumed control of the foundation on August 27, 1979. During the Clinton administration, Nejad-Hosseinian served as Iran's ambassador to the United Nations. Today he serves as the deputy oil minister in Tehran.

According to the Alavi Foundation's Web site, the group "provides financial assistance to not-for-profit organizations that are involved in the teaching of Islamic culture and the Persian language."[17] For the past twenty-five years pro-freedom Iranians have charged that the Alavi Foundation is a front, part of the pro-mullah lobby in the United States, with direct links to Tehran. The foundation claims its activities are religious and educational, noting, for instance, that over the past twenty-five years millions have been placed into various "Islamic Education Centers." Critics expectedly charge that these "centers" serve propaganda purposes by providing a home for regime-sympathetic clerics to preach the mullahs' particular breed of anti-Jewish and anti-American hate.

A major controversy involves the Alavi Foundation's funding of the Islamic Education Center in Potomac, Maryland. This center is operated by Mohammad Asi, an Islamic cleric known for various hate speeches. For example, seven weeks after the 9/11 attacks, Asi made a speech at the National Press Club in Washington DC in which he called the attacks "a grand strike against New York and Washington" launched by "Israeli Zionist Jews" who had warned in advance some five thousand Jews working in the World Trade Center to stay away from work on 9/11. Asi also warned America that if it continued to offend Islam, "the day of reckoning is approaching."[18]

On December 11, 2004, Mohammad Asi traveled to Irving, Texas, for a "Tribute Conference" honoring the late Ayatollah Khomeini as the "Great Islamic Visionary." The Metroplex Organization of Muslims in North Texas, a Shi'a group, organized a full-day seminar with national speakers. The tag line on Asi whenever he appears always seems to refer to him as a radical Muslim who has been monitored by U.S. law-enforcement agencies for his suspected ties to Tehran's mullahs.[19]

Critical articles written about Alavi typically find a former governmental anti-terrorism official who will claim that the Alavi Foundation is controlled by the Iranian government. Whenever such charges are made, the foundation relies on legal counsel to file motions and ward off criticism.

For instance, in December 2004 the New York City Police Department tried to loosen federal restrictions on the surveillance of political groups, with the intention of going after the Alavi Foundation. David Cohen, the NYPD's deputy commissioner of intelligence, wanted to investigate further a claim that the Alavi Foundation, a group "totally controlled by the Iranian government," in 1997 gave $1.4 million to the Al-Farouq Mosque in Brooklyn, whose former imam is Sheik Omar Abdul Rahman. The key here is that Rahman, the spiritual leader of many of the defendants in the 1993 bombing of the World Trade Center, is currently serving a life sentence for his role in a plot to bomb New York landmarks.

In response, Alavi's attorney, John Winter of Patterson, Belknap, Webb and Tyler, filed an eleven-page letter with the court, responding that the foundation never gave money to the Al-Farouq Mosque and that the Foundation's tax returns show total charitable contributions for 1997 were under $1 million in total. Counsel for the NYPD responded by claiming that Cohen made a mistake and the contributions to the Al-Farouq Mosque were made from 1988 to 1982 under the name of the Mostazafan Foundation.[20] This controversy was the typical claim-counterclaim that never fully established the basic charge—that the Alavi Foundation was controlled by the mullahs—but at the same time never quite lifted the cloud that always seemed to hang over the foundation and its activities.

The Alavi Foundation also funds a considerable number of universities with Persian studies programs, including Harvard, Rutgers, the University of Virginia, the University of Wisconsin-Madison, Drew University, and Hunter College, to name a few. Critics see this as a plot by the foundation to cast a large web throughout the United States, recruiting academics and intellectuals who will write favorably about the mullahs and include courses and lectures aimed at supporting the regime. The foundation, of course, countercharges that the critics are paranoid and that all the activities of the foundation are only aimed at a greater understanding and acceptance within America of Islamic views. The Alavi Foundation has always argued that its only goal is tolerance and education, not politics or support of the mullah's radical revolutionary agenda.

With the Iranian community in the United States totaling nearly one million, there are hundreds of suspect Iranian organizations and Web sites that get accused of doing pro-mullah work. Many Iranian Americans were born after 1979 or are too young to have any personal memories of 1979. Still, concerns about sleeper cells are certain to circulate when Islamic groups supported by the Alavi Foundation decide to bring inflammatory speakers like Mohammad Asi into the heart of Texas to give daylong tributes to "The Great Visionary," Ayatollah Khomeini.

Were it not for radicals like Mohammad Asi, whom the foundation has so openly supported, it would be easy to dismiss the foundation's critics as religious bigots. Ken Timmerman, an investigative reporter who has dogged the pro-mullah Iranians in the United States for years, claims that the centers funded by the Alavi Foundation "have become a magnet for the Iranian community by offering Farsi-language primary school classes that are fully accredited within the Iranian national educational system. But they continue to spread virulent anti-American and anti-Semitic propaganda, including videotaped speeches of neo-Nazis such as Ahmed Huber, who praises [the] Ayatollah as the living embodiment of Adolf Hitler."[21]

Albright Supports the Mullahs Again

AFTER THE defeat of John Kerry in the 2004 presidential election, former Secretary of State Madeleine Albright stayed on theme. On December 13, 2004, she and seven former foreign ministers (from England, France, Italy, Canada, Denmark, Spain, and the Netherlands) published a letter in the *Washington Post* urging even more concessions be made to Iran to induce the mullahs to keep their word that they would stop enriching uranium.[22] They wrote: "As people who have experienced firsthand the challenge of balancing carrots and sticks in these sorts of delicate and serious negotiations, we offer the following ideas on obtaining full cooperation from the Iranians."

What are their ideas? First, the United States and Europe had to make sure the world knew they stood together, united in a collective purpose. Translated, this was a repeat of John Kerry's campaign criticism that President Bush did not know how to make enough concessions to the Europeans to form a "coalition." America and the Europeans should make it clear to Iran that, under the terms of the Nuclear Proliferation Treaty, it would be wrong for Iran to make nuclear weapons. This was a reprimand that was unlikely to disturb the terror-loving mullahs. Still, the ministers wanted to soften the "bite" of even that gentle reminder: "In the same breath, American and European heads of state must emphasize that the West does not seek to deny Iran the right to a peaceful civilian nuclear energy program under the necessary safeguards."

So the mullahs have won at least one critical point. Madeleine Albright is leading the charge to make the mullahs' desire for nuclear power look justified, conceding the mullahs' argument that they are a legitimate state and that nuclear power is a legitimate right of a legitimate state. Where was the argument that Iran has more than abundant nonnuclear resources (oil and natural gas) to produce electricity?

Second, Albright and the foreign ministers wanted to "provide a firm guarantee to supply fresh reactor fuel for civilian purposes and to retrieve and dispose of spent fuel in exchange for Iran's agreement to permanently forswear its own nuclear fuel-cycle capabilities, including enrichment, reprocessing, uranium conversion and heavy-water conversion." So Iran would get all the nuclear fuel it wanted, fuel already enriched to about half the grade needed for weapons grade. Albright was as ready to trust the mullahs as she had been to take the word of Kim Jong Il years before. Had she learned nothing?

Third, the United States should make sure the world knows we are solidly behind the agreement just negotiated by the EU-3 and the IAEA with the mullahs. "While it is unclear whether this deal will ultimately halt Iran's nuclear ambitions, only a unified approach will enable Europe and the United States to find out." Sounds precisely like the test Kerry proposed in the first presidential debate with President Bush. What is there to find out? The mullahs have made it abundantly clear that they feel it is their right to have nuclear weapons, and we know they have run an ambitious clandestine program to accomplish that goal. Evidently Albright and the other foreign ministers were not paying attention. There is no test needed; we already know what the mullahs are going to do. The mullahs are going to do exactly what Kim Jong Il did—they are going to make atomic bombs that they can deliver on their Shahab missiles to attack the United States and Israel.

But Albright and the other foreign ministers had in mind more bribes: "Washington should put its full support behind this diplomatic effort and consider launching commercial and diplomatic engagement with Iran." Translated, this recommendation is that the United States should reestablish full diplomatic relations with Iran, drop all sanctions, and support Iran's entry into the World Trade Organization. In other words, we should reward Iran for getting to the brink of having deliverable nuclear weapons. We should simply concede the progress Iran has already made—a fait accompli, nothing we can do about their lying and cheating to date.

Albright and the former foreign ministers continued: "That country's political leadership and culture have changed dramatically over the past two decades and are much more complex than many realize. Understanding the various operatives inside Iran and their motivations require the United States to instigate face-to-face interaction." Yes, direct talks and a "nuanced" approach—as Kerry would have liked to phrase it—to divide factions within Iran by producing one policy with both good-guy and bad-guy elements wrapped together.

Sounds good, but to the mullahs the formula should look like one to prop up their regime by pumping more economic stimulation into their already politically repressed home front. The former Western diplomats also held out the possibility that these direct discussions offering more economic and diplomatic benefits to the mullahs might engage them in helping us to solve other problems, such as narcotics enforcement, Iraq, the fight against terrorism, and peace in the Middle East.

Albright had the eight years of the two Clinton administrations to make her "let us reason together" approach work. The result we got from her service to the nation as secretary of state was the strengthening of world terrorism, including allowing the mullahs to tighten their grip on Iran, while every attempt to retaliate or defend ourselves was restrained, lest we take the law-enforcement approach to fighting terrorism too far into territory where we might not have proof positive, or where we might inflict too much collateral damage in our effort to kill these dedicated enemies of freedom.

Suppose all these proposed diplomatic and economic carrots failed? Suppose the mullahs took every concession offered and continued to develop nuclear weapons secretly? What did Albright suggest might be our "stick"? Simple, as a last recourse, the "Europeans should be ready for alternative courses of action, including going to the U.N. Security Council, and they should repeatedly stress their willingness to act." Her suggestion carefully left the United States out of the move to go to the Security Council. She implied that the United States wouldn't want to appear too aggressive to anyone, since we need to make sure the world knows we are downplaying our superpower status. Be modest always, that was Albright's watchword. One begins to wonder if the Democrats have an inherent aversion to American military power.

Or is their aversion to using military force against Islamic terrorists simply a version of the argument developed three decades ago by the Soviet Union's KGB that charged U.S. troops with war crimes in Vietnam? Bertrand Russell's Stockholm War Tribunals in the late 1960s picked up a Russian-manufactured lie, adding an innovation to formalize the process of taking testimony, to make a show of what could be billed as an "investigation." John Kerry's Vietnam Veterans Against the War echoed the KGB-created charge in their infamous "Winter Soldier Investigations" held in Detroit, Michigan, in early 1971, following Russell's tribunal methodology. Here was the core "proof" Kerry used when he made the same unsubstantiated charge to Senator J. William Fulbright's Foreign Relations Committee in his April 1971 testimony charging that the American military was committing war crimes on a daily basis, crimes that were fully approved up and down the chain of command.[23]

So given the political left's aversion to military action, how exactly were the Europeans willing to act? Would they stamp their feet harder the more the Iranians lied to them? "The transatlantic community should not be trying to force a confrontation with Iran, but we must not fear one if that's what is necessary to prevent the introduction of another nuclear weapons program into the combustible Middle East." No wonder Saddam Hussein defied so many countless U.N. resolutions. Tough talk does not impress dictators. The mullahs have heard plenty of tough talk over the years.

There is ample proof that the mullahs are not to be trusted, no matter how many times they give their word. The EU-3 and the IAEA finalized their agreement with Iran at the end of November 2004, before the deadline that would have forced the issue to the Security Council. And before the end of November 2004, the Iranians had already found exceptions from the agreement that would allow them to continue enriching uranium.

First, the Iranians insisted they needed to keep some twenty or thirty centrifuges running, for "research purposes."[24] Besides, the centrifuges wouldn't have any uranium in them, or if the centrifuges had some low-grade uranium, that would be the uranium already in the pipeline, not new uranium. Not to worry, the IAEA could run cameras on a twenty-four-hour basis to watch the centrifuges real-time, just to make sure nobody cheated. The IAEA bought it. Why not? Sounds fully verifiable, doesn't it?

Sure, but what was the real point the Iranians were after?[25] Intelligence specialists in the United States pointed out that our satellites are able to detect the unique sound centrifuges make. The Iranians needed to keep some centrifuges running somewhere, somehow—just so they could keep the secret ones going, the ones they had always planned to keep running, no matter what the agreement said, to enrich the uranium they hadn't disclosed.

The "research" centrifuges would "mask" the signature noise of the clandestine centrifuges, and the Iranians would have an excuse to throw everybody off track. By the time the IAEA figured it out, a lot more uranium would be enriched to weapons grade. The whole proposition was an elaborate ploy, and the EU-3 and the IAEA fell for it. The mullahs got proof once again that they are smarter than the EU-3 and the IAEA, something that as terrorists they pretty much started out believing.

The latest ploy came in the final weeks of 2004 when the Iranians told the IAEA that they had decided to continue UF4 production (uranium tetra-fluoride) until the end of February. UF4 is the precursor to uranium hexafluo-ride (UF6), the gas that is fed into the centrifuges that spin at supersonic speeds to purify the fuel that is used in peaceful power plants to the richer grade of uranium that is used in bombs.[26]

Somehow the Iranians didn't believe this exception violated the IAEA agreement reached at the end of November. Nobody said anything about UF4. What's the problem? Since you can't do anything harmful with UF4, there's no problem if the Iranians produce some. But the IAEA is watching the empty centrifuges with real-time television. So how could the mullahs cheat? They can't, unless they put the UF4 in the clandestine centrifuges, whose sound is being masked by the empty ones being watched. Pretty clever, huh? The mullahs probably think so.

Then there's the thirty-seven-ton exception. Before the November agree-ment was reached, the Iranians reminded the IAEA that they were already en-riching a thirty-seven-ton quantity of yellowcake uranium. The agreement focused on not enriching any *new* uranium, they argued. Nobody said anything about stopping the enrichment of what they already had. This, it turns out, is enough uranium to make five nuclear warheads.[27] Sounds like enough to take out Israel, doesn't it? Maybe there would be one or two weapons left to drop on some U.S. troops in Iraq or in Afghanistan, maybe both.

The Iranians are playing the world for a fool. As was noted in the intro-duction to this book, Ayatollah Khamenei last July told a group of mullahs meeting in Hamadan, "We are at war with the enemy [meaning the United States]. The central battlefield is Iraq." At present, Iran is funding insurgents in Iraq to destabilize and disrupt the rebuilding process and to obstruct the scheduled January 2005 elections. "We must have two bombs ready to go in January," the ayatollah told the gathering, "or you are not Muslims."[28]

In August 2004 photographs of Shahab-3 missiles indicated that the Ira-nians successfully had modified the missile's warhead to accommodate nuclear weapons. Experts surmised that the Iranians were assisted by experts from the former Soviet Union hired by Iran under personal contracts or by experts from North Korea. The photographs also indicated that various "short wings" had also been added to the warhead, very likely as an aid to reentry.[29]

U.S. officials also announced that Iran had demonstrated an ability to launch Shahab-3 missiles within hours of receiving the order to fire. On October 20 the Iranian Revolutionary Guard successfully test-fired a Shahab-3 under battlefield conditions, launching the missile 1,990 kilometers, more than enough to reach Tel Aviv. Iranian Defense Ministry sources also detailed a five-stage program to develop chemical, biological, and nuclear warheads. The $1.5 billion cost of the warhead program was financed from oil money, according to the London-based Arabic-language newspaper *Asharq Al Awsat*.[30]

How close are the Iranians to having a deliverable nuclear weapon? From the sound of their threats and the reports coming from intelligence sources, the mullahs may be very close. What will the mad mullahs do when they get an atomic bomb? They will use it. Terrorists don't like to warehouse weapons. Terrorists like to use all available weapons now, as soon as they are ready, before somebody comes along and takes them away from them. To calculate that terrorists will do otherwise is a dangerous strategy predicated on the questionable assumption that the terrorists can be reasonable.

Why Not Just Work with the Mullahs?

THE INTERNATIONAL Atomic Energy Agency (IAEA) had just concluded at the end of November 2004 a new agreement that Iran would stop enriching uranium, and almost immediately the Europeans moved in to profit and to begin rewarding the Iranians economically. On December 29, 2004, the European Union (EU) in Austria announced that economic negotiations with Iran would resume on January 12, 2005, with the prospect of generating some twenty billion dollars in new trade ties.[31]

On November 27, 2004, representatives from the Russian Aviastar company announced that a delegation of aircraft manufacturers was traveling to Tehran for a three-day negotiation to conclude Iran's planned purchase of ten Tupolev-100-204 passenger airplanes to Iran.[32] From London, Iran's ambassador to Belgium announced that direct flights between Brussels and Tehran would begin soon. Prior to this, Iranians wishing to travel to Brussels were forced to take connecting flights from Frankfort, Amsterdam, Paris, or London. Twelve thousand Iranians are estimated to be living currently in Brussels, most in skilled jobs, business, or various professions.[33]

Almost as soon as the November 2004 negotiations ended, officials in the Iranian government began privately to boast that they have pulled a big one over on the world—a political and diplomatic victory. Iranian President

Khatami said, "The fact that we prevented our nuclear dossier from being transferred to the U.N. Security Council is a victory for us." The agreement to stop enriching uranium is only temporary and calls for even the temporary cessation to be voluntary. There is no legally binding commitment in the agreement; that was negotiated out in the last hours of wrangling.[34]

Moreover, the mullahs feel the IAEA agreement announces to the world that Iran has a right to pursue nuclear technology. This not only amounts to a significant boost in national pride, the agreement gives further credence to the mullahs as legitimate rulers of Iran—a considerable distance from the U.S. designation of Iran as a rogue state, part of the "Axis of Evil." Tehran also is taking great glee that the agreement further isolates the United States from the world diplomatic community while serving to drive even further the wedge that is separating the United States from the EU.

Oil was the focus of the planned January 2005 economic talks with the EU. Iran has made a concerted effort in the last few years to conduct explorations for oil. As recently as 2000, Iran's reserves amounted to 96.4 billion barrels of oil; today that total exceeds 130 billion barrels of oil. There is no danger looming on the horizon that Iran will soon run out of oil. With current production hovering around 3 million barrels a day, Iran at that rate has about 130 years of reserves with what's been found to date.[35]

The economics compel the politics in Iran's relationship with the EU. More than 80 percent of all Iranian exports to the EU are oil. In 2003 oil was averaging around $26 per barrel.[36] As 2004 comes to an end, the average price for a barrel of crude has held at around $45 per barrel. Let's roughly estimate that Iran has $150 million a day in gross oil proceeds. With Japan, China, and the EU buying increasing quantities of oil from Iran, those windfall profits will probably stay high. Oil companies in the United States are screaming that the only impact of our sanctions is to keep the United States out of the Iranian oil bonanza. Representatives of oil companies such as ChevronTexaco and Conoco are currently listed as serving on the board of directors of the American Iranian Council (AIC) for years, the group with which Hassan Nemazee was associated, a group that has pushed for the United States to normalize economic and diplomatic relations with Iran.

Based on analyzing Iran's trading relations with its five major international partners in 2002 (Germany, France, Italy, China, and South Korea), U.S. companies are losing $6.2 billion in export trade annually by retaining U.S. sanctions against the mullahs.[37] The lost trade impacts various sectors of the U.S. economy, including wheat producers in the heartland, aircraft manufacturers such as Boeing and McDonnell Douglas, power generation companies such as GE, and major insurance companies. Also prominent in the AIC's leadership are representatives of ExxonMobil, Halliburton, and AIG, one of the largest U.S. insurers.

As Iran's oil profits surge, international banks are certain to hover around. Some two dozen European, Asian, and African banks announced in December 2004 that they planed to arrange an estimated $50 billion in corporate loans to Iran.[38] One of the banks moving in to participate is BNP Paribas, infamous recently for its role in moving money around for the nations involved in the oil-for-food scandal at the U.N. Once again, three of the world's biggest lenders—Bank of America, Citigroup, and JPMorgan Chase—are shut out of the action because of U.S. sanctions—something these three are certain to resent.

The pressure on the United States to eliminate sanctions on Iran is certain to build in 2005. So why don't we just give up and join the world party? We could easily conclude that warmongering against the Iranians is counterproductive, moreover that the Iranians are Persians with a long history of productive economic activity. We could even hope that by extending renewed diplomatic and economic ties to the Iranians, we might encourage the mullahs to moderate, or even more hopefully, that a peaceful movement for regime change would be encouraged to emerge from within, through the energizing of the existing opposition groups that have been stirring in Iran for twenty-five years. Isn't this the hope of Democrats like John Kerry who want to work with the mullahs? The hope of Madeleine Albright? The hope of the EU-3?

The problem is that the mullahs are still in charge, and any economic relief they get may well only further strengthen their grip on the government. Also, the mullahs are certain to continue building nuclear weapons clandestinely unless we are to believe that carrots of economic incentives will be sufficiently strong to get them to abandon their dreams of nuclear warheads.

Once Iran possesses nuclear weapons, the terrorist mullahs will gain even more power. Oil plus nukes is a formula certain to appeal to the mullahs who support Hezbollah and the suicide bombers who continue to represent a threat to Israel.

Even here, however, much of the world doesn't care. The U.N. passes or threatens to pass resolution after resolution that favors the Palestinian Liberation Organization. Besides, Israel doesn't have any oil. So why don't we just give in and abandon Israel? The pressure to give up on Israel will intensify. How hard, many ask, is it to maintain this little pocket of Jews on land that the overwhelming numbers of Arabs are constantly pushing to take over?

If John Kerry had been elected president, we would most likely have moved in the direction of appeasing the mullahs, taking the easy path, the popular path the Europeans and the Muslim world is begging us to take. We would be urged to forget that the formula didn't work for North Korea. After all, it was President Clinton and Secretary of State Albright who came up with the idea that rogue nations like North Korea could be trusted with nuclear fuel. Yet even the failure to appease North Korea didn't seem to change the mind-set of the Democratic Party.

Has everybody forgotten how the mullahs like to chant "Death to America" and "Death to Israel"? Or do we just think they're kidding? Terrorists don't make jokes. Take a look at pages 240–41 of the *9/11 Commission Report* and read the text under the heading "Assistance from Hezbollah and Iran to al-Qaeda." The commission was very clear that eight of the ten "muscle terrorists" who flew the hijacked airplanes into the World Trade Center and the Pentagon had traveled freely in and out of Iran between October 2002 and February 2001.

We are in for a crisis over Iran. Israel cannot be expected to sit tight while its sworn enemy places nuclear warheads on its Shahab-3 missiles. For twenty-five years we have been hearing that a freedom movement is building in Iran and that the mullahs are increasingly unpopular. That may well be true, but the mullahs still know how to use terror tactics to suppress dissidents within as well as attack enemies without.

President Bush will need understanding from the American people if he is to continue a hard-line approach toward the mullahs. He won't get any support from U.S. banks, oil companies, or Democrats. If President Bush follows Democrats' advice and drops sanctions on Iran, he will be blamed for any terrorist attack that hits us from Iran. The 9/11 Commission tried hard to excuse the eight years of the Clinton administration and pin all the blame on Bush, despite his being in office for less than one year when the attacks came.

The Democrats are poised to play the blame game. The president has no choice but to protect the United States, even if he has to stand alone to do so.

4

The Nemazee Double Take

ON OCTOBER 18, 2004, Hassan Nemazee, one of John Kerry's top fund-raisers, was deposed in relation to a defamation suit he filed against Aryo Pirouznia, a pro-freedom Iranian who is the head of the Student Movement Coordination Committee for Democracy in Iran (SMCCDI). Bob Jenevein, Aryo's attorney, conducted the deposition. I attended as a consultant to Aryo.[1]

Atomic Iran: How the Theme Fit In

THE BACKDROP for Nemazee's testimony was the 2004 presidential campaign, with Election Day, November 2, coming up in exactly two weeks and two days. Iran was simmering as a possible election issue after Kerry had said in the first presidential debate that he favored giving nuclear fuel to Iran to produce electricity as a test of their true intentions. We would know Iran had evil intents if it proceeded to build atomic bombs, otherwise we could not prove beyond a shadow of a doubt that its intentions were anything but peaceful. As has been discussed earlier, Kerry tended to frame the matter legalistically, as had his Democratic predecessors. Terrorism, to Kerry and those of his ilk, was predominately a law-enforcement problem, not a war. The EU-3 and the IAEA were working feverishly to produce a new agreement with Iran, and their methods reflect Kerry's wrongheaded approach.

Depending upon the outcome of the Nemazee deposition, I anticipated we might have sufficient controversy to fuel a campaign issue. The issue of Iran's developing atomic weapons was an important issue for those voters who were committed to the survival of Israel. Israel supporters came from important segments of both the Christian and Jewish communities throughout the United States. There was a reasonable chance that the issue of Iran would be particularly important in several battleground states, such as Ohio and Florida. The vote tallies in these states were likely to be so close that only a small margin of voters might be influenced here or there to make a critical difference in the outcome of the national election.

Hassan Nemazee Turns on the Mullahs

ARYO PIROUZNIA had called Hassan Nemazee an "agent" of the Islamic Republic of Iran because of what he perceived to be Nemazee's strong support for the mullahs. Nemazee was a member of the board of directors of the American Iranian Council (AIC), a group that had been an outspoken advocate for Iran, arguing that the United States should reestablish diplomatic and economic relations with the mullahs. As was discussed earlier, Nemazee hosted John Kerry when the senator spoke at an AIC conference in San Francisco on June 1, 2002. Nemazee was widely known to be a top fund-raiser for Kerry's presidential campaign in 2004, and Kerry had also advocated working with the mullahs. In Aryo's view, Nemazee was utilizing his resources, including resources Nemazee managed in his New York investment firm, Nemazee Capital, to advance the same agenda the mullahs in Tehran wanted advanced in the United States. This was the basis of the ten-million-dollar libel suit Nemazee had filed against Aryo.

From the beginning of the deposition, Nemazee took a position strongly against the mullahs. In the first minutes under oath, Nemazee took pains to separate himself from the AIC and to make strong statements against the Islamic Republic of Iran. The first exchange reproduced below is a bit lengthy, but it is important. The quotation comes directly from the deposition's question-and-answer dialogue.

Nemazee: I joined the board of the American-the Iranian American Political Action Committee in order to promote Iranian-American participation in the American political system.

Jenevein: Okay. And that's what I'm getting at. The organization had goals that you supported.

Nemazee: Correct.

Jenevein: Is that also a true statement for the American Iranian Council?

Nemazee: I joined its organization and I supported its goals at the time.

Jenevein: You say "at the time." Does that mean you no longer support its goals?

Nemazee: I am not a member of the board of directors. I resigned in, I believe it was December of 2003.

Jenevein: Object. Nonresponsive. I know that, but I guess to rephrase my question, why did you resign?

Nemazee: I resigned because of issues of corporate governance. We asked for an audit of the financial statements. We never received it.

Jenevein: Okay. Well, then did you ever come to depart from the goals of the AIC?

Nemazee: In a material fashion, no.

Jenevein: The AIC, you would have to concede, held as one of its primary goals, if not its primary goal, the resumption of diplomatic relations between the United States and Iran, correct?

Nemazee: No. My understanding of what the goals were and why I joined the organization—I have no truck with the Islamic Republic of Iran, period, end of quote. It is not a government that I feel has any credibility in the world and

the resumption of relations in and of itself is not something that I ever supported.

Jenevein: Do you support regime change in Iran?

Nemazee: I would like nothing better than to see a regime change in Iran.

Jenevein: When you say regime change, is that in part because you would like
to see a more democratic government there?

Nemazee: I would like to see a democratic government there.

From a legal point of view, attorney Jenevein had established an important point. Nemazee admitted he was on the AIC board and that he never de-
parted from the goals of the AIC in any "material fashion." Aryo was upset
because Nemazee had pushed so hard for the Islamic Republic of Iran to be
given diplomatic recognition, something Nemazee had to support as an AIC
board member. Now Nemazee evidently wanted nothing to do with the AIC
or its stated goals.[2]

Nemazee, however, was uncomfortable with this designation. He stressed
that he had resigned from the AIC board. Then he launched into a strong attack on the mullahs so as to distance himself from them and make it clear he
was supporting regime change. He either took this position because he had
experienced a change of heart, or perhaps he felt the position under oath was
more defensible in the pursuit of his legal action against Aryo. If Nemazee was
opposed to the mullahs, the reasoning might go, then how could Aryo legiti-
mately accuse him of having been a mullahs' agent?

At any rate, the purpose here is neither to read Nemazee's mind nor to lit-
igate the defamation suit. From a political perspective, Nemazee had just con-
tradicted John Kerry on the issue of Iran. Kerry was supporting reestablishing
diplomatic and economic relations with the mullahs, going so far as to pro-
pose giving the mullahs nuclear fuel for peaceful purposes. One of his chief
fund-raisers, however, had just suggested the mullahs were not a legitimate
government. Why then give them nuclear fuel? A few minutes more into the
deposition and the issue of nuclear fuel came forward center stage. This sequence began with another Nemazee denial that he wanted to have anything
to do with the mullahs:

Nemazee: They have accused me of being an agent of the Islamic Republic of Iran. They have accused me of pursuing an agenda that is effectively as a lobbyist of the Islamic Republic of Iran. And I categorically deny vehemently that I have anything to do with the Islamic Republic of Iran, that I am a supporter of, defender of, or desirous of seeing anything happen to the Islamic Republic of Iran other than its demise.

Then, attorney Jenevein turned his attention to Kerry's debate statement that he wanted to give nuclear fuel to the Iranians for peaceful purposes.

Jenevein: You have personally raised close to about half a million dollars for Senator Kerry, correct?

Nemazee: Yes.

Jenevein: Don't you think that if you called, he would pick up the phone?

Nemazee: Yes, he would.

Jenevein: Have you called him to suggest that maybe we should not give a terrorist regime nuclear fuel?

Nemazee: No, I have not.

Jenevein: Why not?

Nemazee: Because that's not an issue that is, in my opinion, something that I have any input in that can have any credibility. I have no knowledge on nuclear policy. The only thing I would tell Senator Kerry, if I had the opportunity, is that I would not trust this regime on the nuclear issue to have any intentions other than a weaponized program.

That was a shocker. Sitting in the room, listening to the deposition, I wanted to suggest, "Would somebody please get Mr. Nemazee a telephone? He needs to call Senator Kerry and tell the senator that the mad mullahs are going to make atomic bombs out of any nuclear fuel he or anybody else gives them."

Untwisting what Nemazee had just said under oath was important in the context of Kerry's campaign. Put directly, Aryo Pirouznia was charging that Kerry had an "Iran-gate" at the center of his campaign. Was Kerry willing to trade access to nuclear technology and nuclear fuel to the Iranians in return for more generous campaign contributions from a top pro-mullah Iranian fund-raiser?

Aryo Pirouznia had suggested that Kerry had been bought—that Kerry had openly associated with the AIC, whose purpose was to normalize relations with Iran. Kerry even gave a speech to the AIC in San Francisco, where he was hosted by Nemazee and mingled with another pro-mullah campaign contributor, Susan Akbarpour. Kerry was ignoring that the United States had imposed sanctions on Iran and that President Bush had labeled Iran as part of the "Axis of Evil." All that was just mistaken policy, another failed instance of Bush diplomacy. Kerry took money from pro-mullah fund-raisers and now he was advocating the mullahs' positions. Aryo spoke out and called Nemazee an "agent" of the mullahs, for which Nemazee slapped him with a defamation suit. Aryo was asking the American public to connect the dots.

Evidently Nemazee did connect the dots. Rather than proclaim support for the mullahs that would have supported Aryo's argument, Nemazee talked tough under oath. He called for regime change in Iran and said that Senator Kerry's policy to provide nuclear fuel was essentially irresponsible. Clearly, Nemazee wanted everyone studying the deposition to conclude that he could not possibly be a mullah agent if he too felt they were so evil.

Or perhaps there is another interpretation. Let's follow the money for a moment and assume that in these investigations the "money talks." If the truth was spoken by Nemazee's money, not the words he uttered at his deposition, then Nemazee (and the mullahs) got the results they wanted when Kerry stated his position on Iran in the first debate. In addition to nuclear accommodation, Kerry's campaign had embraced virtually every key position held by wealthy Iranian Americans lobbying for Tehran, including ending the finger-printing of Iranian visitors to the United States, expanding "family reunion" visas to allow more immigration by Iranians wishing to enter the United States, offering a "dialogue" with the cleric-dominated theocracy in Iran, and helping Iran get quick entry as a full member of the World Trade Organization. Even John Edwards, Kerry's vice presidential candidate, was on record with the *Washington Post* as proposing a "great bargain" for the Iranians if only Kerry-Edwards were to be elected.

Coming out of the deposition, we decided that the best strategy was to quote Nemazee directly and go to the public with the evidence that one of John Kerry's top fund-raisers, an Iranian American financier living in New York, a person who had arranged for more than five hundred thousand dollars to be contributed to Kerry's campaign, was now repudiating Kerry's position on Iran. Here was the new headline we intended to take to the American public in the final days of the campaign: "Hassan Nemazee, a top Kerry fund-raiser, says the mullahs will make atomic bombs with the nuclear fuel Kerry wants to give Iran for peaceful purposes."

How did it tie together with the themes we had already developed in the Swift Boat controversy? "Kerry never met an enemy of the United States he didn't like," would be the unifying theme. Kerry as a radical antiwar activist had supported the enemy so that the United States would withdraw from Vietnam as a loser; now he was advocating giving nuclear fuel to a terror-supporting rogue regime in Iran, when even one of his top Iranian American fund-raisers said the mullahs would use the fuel to make bombs. That was the message resulting from the Nemazee deposition.

The John Kerry Lesson on Iran

HASSAN NEMAZEE is now on record as saying that the mad mullahs cannot be trusted not to make atomic weapons out of any nuclear fuel they are given for peaceful purposes. At the end of the 2004 presidential campaign, I sounded the alarm buzzer over this statement, and I am continuing to do so today.

If, under oath, a wealthy fund-raiser for John Kerry feels he must repudiate Kerry's policy toward Iran, the whole world should take notice.

The story here is no longer focused on John Kerry. Whether John Kerry will ever emerge as a serious contender for the presidency again remains to be seen. Ever since the experience with Adlai Stevenson in the 1950s, the Democratic Party has been reluctant to back a one-time loser in a second try as the party's presidential candidate.

This notwithstanding, John Kerry intends to be a strong voice in the Senate and will likely continue his career as a U.S. senator for years to come. There is an important point to consider before we pass from our focus on him. Many of the nation's top liberals today hold influential positions in politics, in the media, and in our universities. For many of these people, their formative years in politics were centered upon their participation in the Vietnam antiwar movement or their enthusiasm for that movement as observers.

Among the lessons learned by these antiwar liberals are the following:

- The exercise of military power by the United States is usually suspect if not always immoral.

- The United States tends to act like a colonial power, infringing upon the legitimate rights of less powerful sovereign nations.

- Resistance to American political power is required since American politicians (especially Republican politicians) tend to exercise aggressive foreign policies that use military force too easily and are prone to violate the rights of other nations in the process.

As a consequence, liberals are uneasy when U.S. forces are deployed, as they have been in the war against terrorism, even though we were attacked on our own soil on 9/11. The war in Afghanistan and in Iraq has called forth a litany of sins that were first recited by the antiwar movement to attack the war in Vietnam. So inevitably, the Left sees us in another Vietnam quagmire, one that we have entered without a plan to win, one we have fought with war crimes being an everyday occurrence (here substitute "Abu Ghraib" for "My Lai").

A key argument of this book is that the Iranian mullahs are supporting terror internationally. Further, that the mullahs are already at war against both Israel and America, and anything they say to the contrary is subterfuge. When the terrorists control the state and when the terrorists controlling the state are able to develop deliverable nuclear weapons, then all bets are off. We may not have the time left to build international coalitions and pursue diplomatic solutions the way the American Left seems to prefer, not when dealing with this Iranian government.

John Kerry displayed for us precisely how a leading antiwar spokesperson of the Vietnam era would handle the terrorists ruling Iran. Kerry would give them nuclear fuel to see if they would make bombs out of that fuel. We had all better think seriously about what Hassan Nemazee said under oath—the mullahs cannot be trusted to do anything else.

5

Democrats Attack U.S. Intelligence Operations

In THE 2002 MIDTERM elections, the Democratic Party did very poorly. Republicans picked up seats in both the House of Representatives and the Senate, holding majorities in both. Moreover, President Bush's surge in popularity after 9/11 was holding strong, as the war on terror overshadowed the economy and other domestic issues the Democrats had tried to advance in their campaigns.

Resentment intensified. To many Democrats, Bush had never been elected. "Selected, not elected" was sounded as a battle cry. Rather than moving more to the center, the Democratic Party moved further left. "Anybody But Bush" was the new slogan. The decision was made to attack Bush at the core of his foreign policy strengths.

Aided by radical leftist supporters such as George Soros and Moveon.org, a new series of arguments emerged to attack politically the war in Iraq: the Bush administration had been negligent in not anticipating 9/11; Bush's response to 9/11 was to engage in a grudge match against Saddam Hussein, settling the score for his father; Bush lied when he claimed that Saddam Hussein had weapons of mass destruction and in claiming that Iraq was an imminent threat to the security of the United States; Bush fought the war against Iraq for oil, not to defeat terrorism; Bush "took his eye off the ball," allowing Osama bin Laden to escape from Afghanistan; Bush launched the wrong war, against Iraq instead of pursuing al-Qaeda.

Michael Moore's film *Fahrenheit 9/11* reached down into personal attacks against Bush—that he was stupid and slow to respond, confused by the 9/11 attack, maybe even in cahoots with the Saudis, that he let Osama bin Laden's family escape from the United States after 9/11. Then the 9/11 Commission launched a partisan investigation, highlighted when former National Security Council adviser Richard Clarke began his testimony with an apology to the 9/11 families. The constant barrage of Democratic attacks took a toll on Bush's popularity. As the Democratic primaries turned serious, Bush looked vulnerable.

The setup of the "Anybody But Bush" campaign was designed so that no Democratic candidate could lose, no mater how inept. Many Democrats were in shock and disbelief that John Kerry actually lost the election, especially after an effectively waged "Anybody But Bush" campaign had prepared the election battlefield to favor the Democrats.

Though presenting themselves as the champions of national security, the Democrats were carefully planning to secure for the coming decades a leftist bias to the intelligence-gathering capabilities that the nation relied upon to win the war against terrorism. But this was a war the Democrats wanted to abandon as soon as John Kerry won and the Democrats reclaimed the White House. Behind the scenes, the Democrats had launched a major assault on America's intelligence-gathering apparatus.

The "Hannity Memo," or How the Democrats Politicized the Senate Intelligence Committee

IN NOVEMBER 2003 talk-show host Sean Hannity revealed an internal memo written by a staff assistant for Senator Jay Rockefeller (D-WV), the cochairman of the U.S. Senate Committee on Intelligence. The memo had been leaked to Fox News.[1] The Senate Committee on Intelligence is one of the most sensitive committees in Congress. Charged with overseeing U.S. intelligence operations, the Senate Committee on Intelligence often receives classified information that is off-limits even to the senators' aides. This memo was shocking because the Democratic staffer clearly outlined a strategy for politicizing the process and using classified information to damage President Bush in the 2004 election campaign. At the time the memo was written, the committee was investigating the intelligence events leading up to the decision to go to war against Saddam Hussein in Iraq.

The memo outlined a purely political strategy to force "major new disclosures regarding improper or questionable conduct by administration officials." To pursue this goal, Democratic staffers had compiled "all the public statements on Iraq made by senior administration officials. We will identify the most exaggerated claims and contrast them with the intelligence estimates that have been declassified. Our additional views will also, among other things, castigate the majority for seeking to limit the scope of the inquiry. The Democrats will then be in a strong position to reopen the question of establishing an independent commission."

What the Democratic staffers had in mind was not a nonpartisan investigation aimed at improving the nation's security. Instead, their purpose was to conduct a witch-hunt with the goal of hurting President Bush's reelection chances. The Democratic staffers concluded by stressing that "we have an important role to play in revealing the misleading—if not flagrantly dishonest methods and motives—of senior administration officials who made the case for a unilateral, preemptive war. The approach outlined above seems to offer the best prospect for exposing the administration's dubious motives and methods." The language of the memo was inflammatory, arguing that the committee could "pull the trigger" for an independent investigation committee, but since "we can only do so once," it would be better to pull the trigger in 2004, closer to the election. While admitting "we don't know what we will find," the memo still urged "fishing expeditions," wide-open requests for any information they might get.

The liberal Democrats believed that Bush stole the 2000 election; then they argued that as president he launched the country into a needless war against Iraq. The entire tone of the memo was adversarial. The Democrats wanted to expose a warmongering group within the administration that was so predetermined to go to war that available intelligence information would be ignored or distorted to serve that goal.

The committee's chairman, Pat Roberts (R-KS), said he was "stunned" by the memo, calling it a "purely partisan document that appears to be a road map for how the Democrats intend to politicize what should be a nonpartisan objective review of prewar intelligence."[2] Senator Roberts was clear about the danger of making intelligence gathering a political operation: "You can be sure that foreign intelligence services will stop cooperating with our intelligence agencies the first time they see their secret reports in our media."[3]

Senator Rockefeller objected not to the memo but to the memo becoming public, complaining that the memo "was likely taken from a wastebasket or through unauthorized computer access."[4] The only Democratic senator to object to the memo's content was Zell Miller (D-GA) who said: "If this is not treasonous, it's the first cousin of treason. This is one of those committees that you should never, ever have anything politicized because you're dealing with the lives of our soldiers and our citizens. Heads ought to roll."

Washington insider Robert Novak wrote that the memo reflected the thinking of committee member Carl Levin (D-MI): "The memo setting forth a political strategy for Intelligence Committee Democrats cannot be written off, as Democratic senators try to do, as the work of one possibly errant staffer. It represents dominant political thinking inside the committee by Michigan's Sen. Carl Levin, one of the smartest, toughest and more partisan members of the U.S. Senate. The Intelligence Committee is no longer a nonpartisan island in a bitterly partisan legislative ocean."[5]

The memo sounded as if the Democrats on the Senate Intelligence Committee believed that George Bush was a greater threat to the nation than was either Osama bin Laden or Saddam Hussein. The memo was no aberration. From November 2003 until Election Day a year later, prominent Democrats implemented what the memo recommended—a dragnet request that the administration produce internal intelligence files so the Democrats could see if anything embarrassing could be found.

In July 2004 the Senate Intelligence Committee issued a report following the plan laid out in what had become known as the "Hannity Memo." According to the report, most of the key judgments on Iraqi weapons threats were "either overstated or were not supported by the underlying intelligence reporting." The report blamed the process of CIA intelligence gathering for the fault, not the administration. Still, Senator Jay Rockefeller, followed the script and went on NBC's *Meet the Press* with scathing comments: "Cheney, Rice, Rumsfeld, Wolfowitz, etc.—they were putting out these hair-raising, paralyzing, horrifying statements about what was going to happen, was about to come back to the homeland, the mushroom cloud. This is pressure, folks. This is pressure."[6]

Still, the report showed considerable evidence of weapons programs in Iraq, including tons of unenriched uranium at a nuclear weapons plant, dozens of artillery shells containing sarin and mustard gas, a fleet of Iraqi al-Samoud II missiles with a range in excess of that allowed by the first Gulf War cease-fire agreement, and abundant evidence that Iraq had harbored many dangerous terrorists, including Abdul Rahman Yasin, the notorious 1993 bomber of the World Trade Center, and Abu Musab al-Zarqawi, who was treated for leg injuries in a hospital run by Saddam Hussein's son Uday.[7]

As late as October 2004 Senator Levin was still charging that the Pentagon ignored corrections by the CIA on information linking Iraq to al-Qaeda.[8]

Though disappointing for the Democrats, none of this attack inflicted mortal damage on President Bush's reelection chances. Many reputable intelligence agencies around the world, not just those in the United States, had overestimated the threat represented by Saddam Hussein. Moreover, Saddam acted guilty, not complying with dozens of U.N.-passed resolutions over many years. Democratic candidates, including John Kerry, continued to say they would have voted for the Iraq War, even after failures in intelligence operations became recognized.[9] In the final analysis, Americans did feel safer that Saddam Hussein was no longer in power, and no Democrat argued seriously that he should be returned to office.

Democrats Demonize the "Neocons"

THE LIBERAL Democrats attacking Bush did have a conspiracy theory in mind. Basically, the charge was that a small group of "neoconservatives" (generally shortened to "neocons") was dictating foreign policy from within the Pentagon with the assistance of a few influential Washington think tanks. These neocons, so the conspiracy theory went, had gained control of important mechanisms of public policy where they could filter through only intelligence reports that supported going to war with Iraq. These policy directives were then passed through Vice President Dick Cheney's office, since the vice president was the real foreign policy decision maker. The president, who lacked experience in foreign policy, generally did what the vice president told him to do, while National Security Adviser Condoleezza Rice tutored the president so he wouldn't appear at a loss when forced to speak in public.

This foreign policy conspiracy theory was the explanation for the Left's charge that the intelligence in the ramp-up to the Iraq War was manipulated (by the neocons) to fabricate the illusion of a threat that would turn out to be a lie when Saddam Hussein was found to possess no weapons of mass destruction.

What is a "neocon"? The term was coined to describe a movement that began in the late 1960s from within the Democratic Party. Certain intellectuals who had grown up in the tradition of Franklin Roosevelt and the New Deal became disillusioned with the party's move to the Left, especially with Lyndon Johnson's "War on Poverty," which was seen as socialistic in nature, and with the party's embrace of the antiwar movement. The group coalesced over President Reagan's strong stand against communism in which he called the Soviet Union the "evil empire" and called upon Mikhail Gorbachev to take down the Berlin Wall. "Mr. Gorbachev, tear down this wall!" was the phrase that rang true for those who emerged as "neoconservatives." The liberal Left coined the term to distinguish the new conservatives who came from within the Democratic Party from the traditional conservatives (now called "paleo-conservatives) who were typically identified with the Barry Goldwater wing of the Republican Party.[10]

According to liberal Democrats, neocons "envision a world in which the United States is the unchallenged superpower, immune to threats. They believe that the US has a responsibility to act as a 'benevolent global hegemon.' In this capacity, the US would maintain an empire of sorts by helping to create democratic, economically liberal governments in place of 'failed states' or oppressive regimes they deem threatening to the US or its interests."[11] Neocons, so the argument goes, believe the Middle East will remain a breeding ground for terrorism until democracies replace the Islamic tyrannies that now rule those countries. Neocons have a natural disdain for multinational organizations, such as the United Nations, believing that anti-democratic forces whose only goal is to belittle the United States dominate such organizations. Neocons are drawn to support Israel, believing that Israel is an outpost of democracy in the Middle East and that the United States must support the continuing sovereignty of Israel at all costs.

While paleo-conservatives and neoconservatives agree on many issues, especially with regard to foreign policy, liberals would argue that true paleo-conservatives are cautious not to overestimate the military strength of the United States, especially when it comes to questions of nation building. By nature, paleo-conservatives are distrustful of entering any foreign war unless the war is essential to preventing an immediate threat to the United States.

On the question of the war against terrorism, paleo-conservatives and liberals tend to agree, especially as the war against terrorism is expanded beyond the Taliban in Afghanistan or al-Qaeda wherever al-Qaeda is definitely known to be operating. Since the Vietnam War the main philosophical difference is that extreme liberals have tended to be against American wars in general, accepting at face value the long-standing socialist and communist interpretation that the United States is a colonial, imperialistic power that tends to go to war to aggrandize its narrow self-interests, including grabbing available natural resources (such as oil) from weaker nations.

Who are the neocons supposedly involved in the conspiracy? For our purposes here, five individuals are the most important:

1. **Richard Perle.** One of the chief architects of the policy to invade Iraq, Richard Perle served as chairman of the Pentagon's Defense Policy Board until he resigned in March 2003. Opponents argue his determination to invade Iraq was stated in 1996 when he delivered to Israel's right-wing Likud Party a report entitled "A Clean Break: A New Strategy for Securing the Realm." Sometimes called by political opponents "the Prince of Darkness" for his hard-line stance on questions of national security, Richard Perle would be regarded by leftists as the "intellectual godfather" of the Iraq War conspiracy.

2. **Paul Wolfowitz.** Currently the deputy secretary of defense, Paul Wolfowitz is the second in command at the Pentagon under Secretary Donald Rumsfeld. Wolfowitz is regarded as the chief architect of the Iraq war plan in the Pentagon. From 1989 to 1993 he served as undersecretary of defense for policy and was known for advocating preemptive military strikes against countries known to be developing weapons of mass destruction. Paul Wolfowitz would be regarded by leftists as the "war planner" or "chief strategic architect" of the Iraq War conspiracy.

3. **Douglas Feith.** As undersecretary of defense for policy, Douglas Feith is regarded as the number-three civilian in the Pentagon, following only Secretary Rumsfeld and Deputy Secretary Wolfowitz. Feith served in the Reagan administration as deputy assistant secretary of defense for negotiations policy and, prior to that, as special counsel to Richard Perle. Douglas

Feith would be regarded by leftists as "Mr. Inside" of the Iraq War conspiracy, a tribute to the support implementation role he has played for Rumsfeld and Wolfowitz.

4. **Lewis "Scooter" Libby.** Libby is the chief of staff and national security adviser for Vice President Dick Cheney. In the administration of George H. W. Bush, "Scooter" served in the Pentagon as principal deputy undersecretary (strategy and resources) and later as deputy undersecretary of defense for policy. Scooter Libby would be regarded by leftists as "Mr. Go-Between," a reference to his convenient positioning to pass information from the conspiracy within the Pentagon to Vice President Cheney's office, so Cheney could make the key decisions on the Iraq War and prepare the appropriate White House staff (including Condoleezza Rice) to explain the decisions to President Bush.

5. **Michael Ledeen.** Ledeen is currently resident scholar in the Freedom Chair at the American Enterprise Institute, where he works closely with Richard Perle. Prior to this, he served as an adviser to Secretary of State Alexander Haig during the Reagan administration, where he played a role in the infamous Iran-Contra affair. Ledeen has been calling for democratic revolution in Iran for many years. He has supported numerous bills proposed in Congress to support opposition groups in Iran. He would be considered by leftists the "Doctor-Philosopher" of the Iraq War conspiracy, since his writings have provided much of the intellectual justification not only for why the United States needed to attack Saddam Hussein but, more important, why the mullahs must be removed from power. Ledeen was in the lead in predicting the terror war of insurgency that the mullahs would mastermind in Iraq. Arguing consistently that war is a last resort, he has written and argued for years that peaceful democratic change from within is the best solution for Iran.

Far-left Democrats believed that this cabal of neocons is the heart of the enemy. Exposing the neocon conspiracy was a major goal of the Democratic staffers who wrote the infamous Hannity Memo for the Senate Intelligence Committee. What the Democrats desperately wanted to do before the 2004 election was to uncover as many documents as possible so they could prove to voters that this neocon conspiracy had falsified intelligence reports about Iraq so as to exaggerate the threat and provide the justification needed for the United States to launch the preemptive strike against Iraq that this group long ago determined to be necessary.

There was one underlying understanding that liberals were loath to discuss openly: all five of the above-identified neocons are Jews. What many extreme leftists really believe, though they would never admit it, is that here was the international Jewish conspiracy at work, the Zionists embedded within the Pentagon and White House who were plotting to push the United States to war throughout the Middle East in order to protect the State of Israel.

Senator Fritz Hollings (D-SC) just about let the cat out of the bag for the Democratic left when he wrote a May 2004 op-ed piece for the *Charleston Post and Courier,* arguing that President Bush went to war against Iraq to protect Israel and to win support from Jewish voters.[12] Senator Hollings called "ridiculous" the firestorm of criticism that followed the publication of his opinion letter, insisting that he was not anti-Semitic.[13]

Then retired Gen. Anthony Zinni (USMC) broke ranks with the administration and charged that Iraq was the wrong war at the wrong time with the wrong strategy. He blamed the neoconservatives, the small group of senior Jewish policy makers who hijacked the Iraq War decision-making process to serve their own ends. "I think it's the worst kept secret in Washington. That everybody–everybody I talk to in Washington has known and fully knows what their agenda was and what they were trying to do," Zinni told CBS's 60 *Minutes* in late May 2004.[14]

The anti-Jewish accusation was clear: remove Israel from the equation and there was no reason to go to war against Iraq. The battle lines were drawn. Even John Kerry could see the obvious political damage of being so blatantly outspoken. He quickly called Senator Hollings's statement "absurd," adding that comments "such as these lend credence to unacceptable and baseless anti-Semitic stereotypes that have no place in America or anywhere else."[15]

What the Left had failed to calculate is that a great number of the American people remain committed to the survival of Israel. Just as Bush had gained points arguing that America was better off with Saddam Hussein removed from power, the administration was on strong ground arguing that the world was better off with Israel protected. Even John Kerry realized immediately that if the attack launched by the Left on the decision to go to war in Iraq ever reached the question of Israel's survival, the argument was a sure loser.

Hollings and Zinni made a terrible mistake. Yes, anti-Jewish and anti-Israel sentiments did motivate much of the argument from the Left. Yet to articulate this argument openly would mean not only losing the debate, it would also mean losing the election, probably in a landslide.

Still, the demonizing from the Left intensified. President Bush was soundly ridiculed on DemocraticUnderground.com a left-wing Internet forum that accepted posts without deleting any expletives. Here Bush began to be referred to as "Chimpy," an abbreviated form of "chimpanzee." The physical characteristics being mocked were the shape of the President's ears and face, but the obvious slam was on the president's intellect. President Bush might have taken some solace recalling that even a president as revered as Abraham Lincoln was slandered in his lifetime by caricature depictions presenting him as an ape. The extreme Left of the Democratic Party seem so locked in a rabid form of anti-Bush hatred that even extreme and abusive images were not ruled "out of bounds" but actually seemed to be condoned or even found amusing, especially when they came from the mouths of well-known movie stars, such as Whoopi Goldberg when hosting posh New York City fund-raisers for candidate John Kerry.

Douglas Feith and the Controversy over the Office of Special Plans (OSP)

IN SEPTEMBER 2002 Undersecretary of Defense Douglas Feith renamed the Northern Gulf Affairs Office as the "Office of Special Plans" and increased its four-person staff to sixteen. The OSP worked alongside the Near East and South Asia (NESA) bureau in Feith's office to analyze intelligence related to connections between Iraq and al-Qaeda. Almost immediately, the OSP drew fire from left-wing critics who charged that the OSP was set up to be a neocon-dominated propaganda office whose real purpose was to concoct an intelligence case against Saddam Hussein and to feed the information to Vice President Cheney's office to buttress the case for war.

The controversy broke into the mainstream news when Seymour Hersh wrote an article in *The New Yorker* charging that a "small cluster of policy advisors and analysts" that self-mockingly called itself a "cabal," or translated more directly, the neocons, had created the OSP to help shape American public opinion in favor of attacking Iraq.[16] Hersh—who during the Vietnam War seized on the My Lai incident as evidence of what the Left considered ubiquitous American military war crimes—had found a new theme to advance with the OSP. When the Abu Ghraib prison scandal came up, Hersh was once again the journalist on the scene to exploit for maximum political damage another scandal slamming the U.S. military. The OSP and the charge of a private unit within the Pentagon exploring raw intelligence documents and courting intelligence sources outside normal channels was a story Hersh could not resist jumping on.

Hersh reported that the OSP had turned to Ahmad Chalabi, an Iraqi expatriate who led the Iraqi opposition movement, the U.S.-backed Iraqi National Congress (INC). Chalabi had a cloudy past. In 1992 a Jordanian court sentenced him in absentia to twenty-two years of hard-labor prison time for his suspected role in a bank fraud case. In the 1990s the CIA had secretly paid Chalabi and the INC millions of dollars to provide intelligence on Saddam Hussein. Now Hersh argued that Feith and the OSP were paying Chalabi and the INC for exaggerated threat information regarding Saddam Hussein's WMD program and his association with al-Qaeda.

With the publication of Hersh's article, the firestorm over the OSP began. On October 1, 2003, Senator Jay Rockefeller sent a letter to Feith, writing him officially in his capacity as vice chairman of the Senate Intelligence Committee. Rockefeller's letter listed six pages of detailed questions reminiscent of the dragnet strategy outlined in the Hannity Memo. The Democrats were on the warpath against the neocons and their private intelligence office. Question after question was written in the broadest possible terms—"list all," "describe any," "what services were provided and when?" etc. A series of questions specifically addressed whether the OSP had provided any terror-related intelligence to Israeli Prime Minister Ariel Sharon's office, or whether the OSP had accepted any terror-related assignments from the Israelis.

Another set of questions asked for descriptions of meetings Michael Ledeen may have held with Iranians in 2001, asking Feith to "describe contacts between him and any European defense or intelligence officials in connection with those meetings. Please identify any Department of Defense personnel who took part in any of those meetings, and describe their involvement. Were these activities coordinated with CIA, the State Department, or any other part of the United States Government, or anyone outside the U.S. Government? In each case, identify the people involved in the coordination. Please list and provide any documents that describe these matters."[17]

On November 25, 2003, Senator Carl Levin, the ranking Democratic member of the Senate Committee on Armed Services, wrote Undersecretary

Feith an equally broad letter demanding documents. Each of Levin's five separate requests was worded as an all-encompassing search and seizure. Consider, for instance, the first: "All documents relating to the establishment, functions and responsibilities of the office of Special Plans within the Office of the Under Secretary for Policy."

Levin was clearly interested in how the OSP had worked with Chalabi to obtain intelligence on Iraq: "All documents produced by either the Office of Special Plans or the Policy Counter-Terrorism Evaluation Group, including but not limited to all documents related to debriefings by Defense Department personnel of Iraqi defectors assisted or made available by the Iraqi National Congress, and any reviews of or contributions to documents produced by other agencies." Last, Levin wanted to know all communications between the OSP and the CIA, the Defense Intelligence Agency (DIA), the State Department, the National Security Council, the office of the vice president, or the office of the president.[18]

With these two letters by Senators Rockefeller and Levin, the methodology laid out in the Hannity Memo was clearly being implemented. The Democrats were truly not interested in legitimate congressional oversight activities here; what they wanted was dirt that could be used for partisan political gain in the 2004 presidential election.

The dragnet technique also promised to be very detrimental to future intelligence-gathering activities. In the thousands of documents likely to be surfaced, should any one of them prove even slightly damaging politically, that was the document the Democrats would be sure to be parade before the press, even if the results were the destruction of careers and the suppression of legitimate intelligence activity that might well have been productive and necessary. Career intelligence agents have families and mortgages, as do other government workers; threats to their job security are not productive to getting from them a maximum effort to protect national security. This concerned Democrats such as Jay Rockefeller and Carl Levin very little in their pursuit of any politically damaging document their overly broad requests might happen to find.

Then criticism began to flow from Karen Kwiatkowski, a retired U.S. Air Force lieutenant colonel. As a regional analyst within the Pentagon, she was transferred in the spring of 2002 to a post as a desk officer for NESA. There she concluded that the OSP was "a pet project of Vice President Dick Cheney and Defense Secretary Donald Rumsfeld," or as she described the OSP to the

LA Weekly, "a nerve center" for what amounted to a "neoconservatives' coup, a hijacking of the Pentagon."[19] Kwiatkowski charged that the OSP mission was to push the neocon agenda:

> across a network of policymakers—the State Department, with John Bolton; the Vice President's Office, the very close relationship the OSP had with that office. That is not normal, that is a bypassing of normal processes. Then there was the National Security Council, with certain people who had neoconservative views; Scooter Libby, the vice president's chief of staff; a network of think tanks who advocated neoconservative views—the American Enterprise Institute, the Center for Security Policy with Frank Gaffney, the columnist Frank Gaffney—was very reliable. So there was not just a process inside the Pentagon that should have developed good honest policy, but it was instead pushing a particular agenda; this group worked in a coordinated manner, across media and parts of the government, with their conservative agenda."[20]

Kwiatkowski presented herself as a responsible whistle-blower, a career air force officer who had been at the Pentagon for a while, working close enough to the OSP to observe its internal workings. What Kwiatkowski did not make clear to the public was her apparent association with Lyndon LaRouche's Libertarian Party. LaRouche's organization has been described as a bizarre cult. His own political views have gyrated wildly over the years since 1968, when he founded the far-left National Caucus of Labor Committees (NCLC) as an offshoot of the radical student movement. In the 1970s and 1980s Larouche's activities moved to the Far Right; he created an international network for spying and propaganda, with cloudy ties to the intelligence organizations of a variety of countries. In 1980 LaRouche accused George H. W. Bush of being an agent of the "Trilateral Commission," charging that the Trilateral Commission was a shadowy organization secretly dedicated to creating a "new world order." In 1989 LaRouche was sentenced to a fifteen-year prison term for mail fraud, based on fraudulent fund-raising policies as well as tax evasion.

Anti-Jewish hatred is one of LaRouche's few consistent themes over his four decades of political involvement, that and belief in wild-eyed conspiracy theories ranging from a belief that there is an ancient secret society of *Illuminati* controlling history, to a belief in the *Protocols of the Elders of Zion* that all anti-Semites since Hitler feel compelled to cite as proof of the existence of an international Jewish conspiracy. No wonder Kwiatkowski viewed the OSP as a vast neocon conspiracy. Her affinity for LaRouche probably predisposed her to believe just about anything, except that Saddam Hussein might actually be a terror threat to his own citizens and to the world at large.

Still, in many respects, placing Kwiatkowski's criticism of the OSP side by side with criticism coming from liberal Democrats, the arguments of both groups appeared about the same, even in their extremely strident tone. On July 9, 2004, Senator Jay Rockefeller held a press conference in which he charged, "We've done a little bit of work on the Number-three guy in the Defense Department, Douglas Feith, part of his alleged efforts to run intelligence past the intelligence community altogether . . . and was he running private intelligence failure, which is not lawful?"[21] The Democrats, the political kooks, and the political near kooks had each circled the OSP, perhaps going initially in different directions but all still joining together at the same point on the other side.

Outraged at Senator Rockefeller's charge, Powell A. Moore, assistant secretary of defense (legislative affairs), drafted a July 9 letter to the senator pointing out that Undersecretary of Defense Feith and his staff had spent "more than 1800 hours reviewing thousands of pages of documents for relevance and responding to Committee inquiries. They have provided thousands of pages of materials and scores of hours of testimony, including testimony by Secretary Feith before the full Committee and Committee staff interviews with numerous members of his staff. My understanding is that the information thus far collected by the Committee does not support any of the charges of impropriety, much less any unlawful behavior." The Department of Defense demanded any evidence "supporting the serious charge you floated during your press conference" or, "if there is not evidence, then a retraction and apology would be appropriate."[22]

No documentation or apology came forth from Rockefeller's office. The Democratic senator from West Virginia was evidently comfortable about letting the threat of criminal prosecution further dampen legitimate intelligence-gathering activities. Now career agents and officers of departments in the Pentagon and the CIA had to worry not only that they might lose their livelihoods but also might be criminally prosecuted if, in their zeal to uncover real threats to national security, they violated any operating procedures the Democrats had recently defined so narrowly as to restrict their efforts. Senator Rockefeller was only upset at the OSP because journalists with decades of leftist credentials (such as Seymour Hersh) and critics with a history of dubious politics (such as Karen Kwiatkowski) had suggested that the OSP was out to prove the case that Saddam Hussein was a threat. If the OSP had been conducting a propaganda effort aimed at proving that President Bush had lied to the American people by exaggerating intelligence reports about Iraq, Rockefeller probably would have recommended the OSP participants for raises and commendations.

The Democrats Accuse Israel of Spying

ON THE eve of the Republican National Convention, CBS News broke a story that the FBI was investigating whether a Pentagon analyst who worked for Douglas Feith had been passing secret government intelligence documents dealing with Iran to the Israelis. The timing of the story was suspicious, almost as if it were designed to put the OSP controversy back on page one to embarrass President Bush just as he was being renominated for the presidency.

The charge was that Larry Franklin, an officer in the Pentagon's NESA Bureau, had passed classified documents to members of the American Israel Public Affairs Committee (AIPAC), a Jewish advocacy group. CBS played the story in a sensational fashion, suggesting that Israeli intelligence had placed a "mole" within the Pentagon, recalling the infamous case of Jonathan Pollard, the naval intelligence officer who in the mid-1980s was convicted of passing top-secret intelligence documents to the Israelis for pay.

CBS ran the story fully enhanced with images of the U.S. and Israeli flags, a blacked-out silhouette of a man in a brimmed felt hat with a document stamped "classified" in the background, photographs of Douglas Feith and Paul Wolfowitz, and an alarming suggestion that FBI arrests were imminent. Even though the FBI investigation had been ongoing for nearly a year, CBS decided to present the story as a major new scandal, suggesting yet another new and frightening U.S.-Israeli breach of security, a serious threat on the magnitude of the Jonathan Pollard affair. Observers jaundiced by the obvious pro-Democratic bias CBS had shown throughout the 2004 presidential election campaign questioned if CBS had politically orchestrated the story, deciding to flash it as a major news alert when it was really a suspect story that had been simmering on a back burner for a year. What better way to embarrass the president than to have a new U.S.-Israeli spy scandal appear suddenly as "breaking news" on the day the Republican National Convention was opening?[23]

Buried in the CBS breaking reports were denials from Israel. Prime Minister Sharon affirmed that, after the Jonathan Pollard incident, Israel had permanently put an end to all spying activities within the United States. Legislator Ehud Yatom, chairman of Israel's parliamentary committee on covert intelligence, dismissed the story, telling Israeli radio that Israel expected the allegations to be withdrawn quickly: "I imagine that within a few days the United States will come out with an announcement that Israel has no connection whatsoever with the supposed spy and his activities." Uzi Arad, a former official in the Mossad, suggested the allegations were leaked to hurt the pro-Israel lobby in the United States: "The way it was reported, they pointed out in which office [Franklin] worked. They pointed at people like Doug Feith or other defense officials who have long been under attack within the American bureaucracy." Eitan Gilboa, professor of political science at Tel Aviv's Bar Ilan University, questioned the timing of the reports. Writing in the *Yediot Ahronot* daily, Professor Gilboa said directly that the CBS stories were timed to embarrass President Bush as the Republican National Convention was starting.[24]

The outcome of the investigation suggested that CBS was acting in a politically biased manner. Reporter Edwin Black, writing in the *Jerusalem Report,* also commented on the long-term bias of the FBI: "The FBI has never given up the hope that a Pollard clone, commonly referred to as 'Mr. X,' will be found, and maintains that Pollard's pre-computer-era intelligence is still a threat to U.S. security."[25]

Through the end of 2004 Larry Franklin had yet to be arrested or charged with any crime. The case was reduced to the possible misuse of one classified document, not exactly espionage at the highest security levels. Unfortunately, the offense of "mishandling classified documents" is not exceptional in Washington DC, where many government officials over the years have been insufficiently prudent or just plain careless when it comes to not sharing secret documents in their possession.

Still, those individuals anxious to ensure that Israel was pounded in the press exaggerated what was a minor offense at most. Pat Buchanan, appearing on NBC News' *Meet the Press* on September 5, 2004, sounded an alarm bell over the Franklin incident: "We need to investigate whether there is a nest of Pollardites in the Pentagon who have been transmitting American secrets through AIPAC, the Israel lobby, over to Reno Road, the Israeli embassy, to be transferred to Mr. Sharon." Buchanan went so far as to suggest that

Franklin might be a traitor. Addressing the show's moderator, Tim Russert, Buchanan was direct and accusatory, but without definitive proof: "Now, the FBI has been asking questions. There are no conclusions. No one should assume guilt on anyone's part. But if this has been going on, Tim, we are getting dangerously close to the T-word."[26]

Critics from the Left were equally vocal, not wanting to miss a clear opportunity to advance "Anybody But Bush" conspiracy thinking. Juan Cole, a University of Michigan professor who runs an anti-Bush Web site that focuses on the Middle East, was able to see his own version of the grand conspiracy in the Franklin incident. Cole speculated:

> If [Ariel] Sharon and AIPAC decide that they need the U.S. government to take military action against Iran, it is likely that the U.S. government will do so. They can mobilize the U.S. evangelicals in favor of this step, putting enormous pressure on Congress and the executive. Many Iranian expatriates are extremely wealthy and well connected, and they want such military action. And, firms like Halliburton, which find work-arounds allowing them to make money in Iran (and did so when Dick Cheney was CEO), would love to get rid of the mullas [sic] so they could make the big bucks, and more straightforwardly. So it isn't that AIPAC can snap its fingers and make something happen in Washington. But it can put together powerful coalitions and leverage its influence through policy allies, which does tend to make things happen."[27]

Why Senator Rockefeller Wanted to Investigate Ledeen's "Secret Meetings"

IN DECEMBER 2001 Michael Ledeen, together with Larry Franklin and Harold Rhode of the Pentagon, met in Rome with Middle Eastern sources who had intelligence information regarding Iraq and Iran. Rhode and Franklin both work under Douglas Feith in the Department of Defense; both men are experts on Iran.

The person who arranged the meeting, Manucher Ghorbanifar, had a history with Ledeen that stretched back to when both were involved in the Iran-Contra affair during the Reagan administration. Ledeen was then a consultant to National Security Adviser Robert McFarlane. Ghorbanifar, an expatriate Iranian businessman, had been opposed to any attempt at making a deal to free the U.S. hostages then being held in Iran, concerned that the United States would become "hostage to the hostages." Freeing these hostages was the motive that led various government officials to pursue the intricate swaps of funds, arms, and released hostages that evolved into Iran-Contra. Subsequently, the CIA put out a "burn notice" on Ghorbanifar, prohibiting any CIA personnel from having further contact with him, because the CIA had concluded that Ghorbanifar was a serial liar.

Ledeen, however, insisted that Ghorbanifar's information had been useful: "We met during the run-up to Iran-Contra in Israel. The Israelis had been talking to him for a while and had found him to be basically reliable and on occasion spectacularly well informed." Ghorbanifar was able to provide "a very clear and quite accurate picture of the internal Iranian political situation, and introduced us to some senior ayatollahs who said they wanted to change the nature of the regime." Moreover, Ledeen credits Ghorbanifar as being the first person to explain to him the true nature of the terrorist organization Hezbollah. "At that time, the fall of 1985, our experts believed that Hezbollah was either a home-grown Lebanese group or a Syrian creation. Ghorbanifar insisted that it was an Iranian creation, and so it has been determined. His x-rays of the internal conflicts in Tehran have also stood up very well."[28]

Rhode and Franklin were reluctant to attend the 2001 meeting in Rome. Both were skeptical about Ghorbanifar's reliability until they realized who Ghorbanifar was bringing to the meeting. One of the participants who attended the meeting was so well known to Western counterterrorism officers that his travel to the meeting was problematic in that he had to pass through several international security points.

Moreover, the quality of the intelligence brought forth from the Iranian operatives attending the meeting with Ghorbanifar ultimately justified the meeting as important. According to the official notes of the meeting, the Americans gained tremendous insight into Iran's internal politics as well as the country's involvement in supporting terrorist groups operating outside Iran. According to the meeting notes, several important points emerged:

- President Khatami was trusted by the mullahs and viewed as valuable for his ability to play well in the West, especially with the EU nations.

- Iran's intelligence agencies are a hardcore network of revolutionary zealots capable of causing much trouble. Iran's intelligence agents are reporting that they have successfully penetrated the European embassies in Iran.

- Hard-liners within the regime remain unrelenting in their opposition to normalizing relationships with the United States. Anti-American and anti-Israel sentiments remain strong even among reform-minded leaders such as Khatami. Some practical conservatives within the regime favor limited rapprochement to acquire U.S. oil-drilling technology and investment, as well as to soften U.S. resistance to Iran on the world scene.

- The Shi'a clerics continue to see Iran as surrounded by hostile neighbors, justifying their indoctrination and training of recruits in schools and camps dedicated to terrorism.

- At the start of U.S. military operations in Afghanistan, Iran sent a team of Revolutionary Guards Corps (IRGC), Qods Force ("Jerusalem" Force of special operatives), to Afghanistan to monitor U.S. activities and collect intelligence against possible U.S. targets.

Some specific, actionable intelligence came out of the meeting. The Iranian operatives reported that the mullahs had dispatched a targeting team to Afghanistan to reconnoiter U.S. troops and installations. Rhode and Franklin were given five names and a photo. As a result of these discussions, the American participants became convinced that this was a hunter-killer team with a specific mission to kill U.S. troops in Afghanistan. Government officials passed this information directly to the commander of the Fifth U.S. Special Forces in Afghanistan. Subsequent phone calls convinced him that this information saved American lives and permitted special forces troops to turn the tables on Iranian special forces activities with Afghan warlord Ismail Khan. As Ledeen summarized the importance of the meeting: "The information we obtained in December, 2001, thanks to Ghorbanifar (even though the information did not come from him), saved American lives in Afghanistan."[29]

A second meeting was held in Rome in June 2003. Again, key insights resulted. Here are two highlights:

- The leadership in Iran is now united. There are no remaining divisions between the parliament, Ayatollah Khamenei, or President Khatami. The atmosphere in Tehran is more like Moscow under Stalin. The government has stolen the children of about six hundred parliamentarians to ensure their loyalty. The mullahs are prepared to do whatever they need to do to retain power; the mullahs will not relinquish control over the government, no matter what price they have to pay.

- All the power in the government now derives from Ayatollah Khamenei himself. "Don't worry about who's in what government position in Iran. Trying to analyze this is a waste of time. They are all working together to keep the regime in power."

The Iranians outlined a Five Pillars Policy as determining their future direction. The key tenet is that "decisions are already made," the policies of the five pillars have been set in stone, determined and agreed upon by the Iranian government as directed by Ayatollah Khamenei. The pillars are:

1. *Rule with an iron fist.* Commit any crime necessary, steal children or whatever; do anything required to retain power.

2. *Buy Time.* The Iranian government is winning as long as the world is kept off balance. Some 161 contracts to do business with France have been signed. The contracts are all secret; none have been given to the Iranian Parliament, so none are valid. For instance, France sold Airbus a $41 billion contract guaranteed by the Saudis in Dubai. With the Russians, the mullahs are moving to make a pact with Tajikistan and Uzbekistan. The United States will be "on hold" until after the 2004 presidential elections. Buy time and keep moving.

3. *Do everything possible to destabilize the United States in Iraq.* Destabilize Afghanistan, Pakistan, and Uzbekistan. The United States can never manage Iran; it will be worse that Vietnam. Iran will work with any and all terrorists to accomplish the goal of destabilizing Iraq and Afghanistan. The sky is the limit; whatever money is needed to defeat the United States in Iraq and Afghanistan is available and will be spent to fund terrorism and insurgency.

4. *Develop nuclear weapons in Iran.* Iran will stay on track to develop nuclear weapons as fast as possible. Until then, sign any agreement, say anything, cheat—do whatever is necessary to throw the world off track.

When Iran has atomic weapons, everything changes. Then the United States will not be able to resist the will of Iran. Iran will use whatever it has at that point to defeat the United States, including nuclear weapons. Iran will live in the world exactly the way Iran wants to live. The foreign contractors in Iran helping to build atomic bombs—from China, Russia, North Korea, Slovaks, Bulgarians, Rumanians—let them live well on up to forty thousand dollars a month in salary. The center of the operation is Isfahan, where the nuclear technology is centered; uranium enrichment at Natanz; heavy water at Arak. Today the most important area where the nuclear technologists live is the secret area in Parchin, about one hour south of Tehran.

5. **With nuclear weapons in hand, Iran will assert its power and will upon the world.** Iran will tell the United States, "You're in trouble in Iraq, Afghanistan, Turkey, Azerbiajan, and Uzbekistan. We can help you out of this. What is your counteroffer?" The United States will not interfere in Iran just as the United States does not interfere in Saudi Arabia today.

The Iranians at the meeting said the mullahs had set aside more than four billion dollars to fund insurgency and to press forward with the rapid development of nuclear weapons. If that was not enough, more would be made available. The mullahs are willing to do whatever it takes to achieve their ends. The whole program could be summarized in a single directive: "Do whatever is necessary to buy time to get nuclear weapons. In the meantime, cause trouble, create insurgencies, and promote terrorism." The entire base of the mullahs must be seen as cheating to buy time. While buying time, the mullahs are willing to make whatever concessions they have to make, but they are resolved to never lose sight of their ultimate purposes—to get nuclear weapons, to defeat the United States and to wipe Israel from the face of the earth. The Iranian government will not hesitate to use nuclear weapons to destroy America or Israel, even if two billion people have to die in the process.

Although Ledeen did not attend the 2003 meeting in Rome, his comments on the 2001 meeting are important characterizations of the discussions:

> Extensive conversations were held, ranging from the history of Iranian terrorism to current Iranian operations in Europe and the Middle East. One of the

two Iranians had been the intermediary with [Yasser] Arafat in the1970s, when the PLO trained the men who later became the Iranian Revolutionary Guards. The information was good, and, according to American military personnel in Afghanistan, it saved American lives.

All present at the meetings expressed the desire to continue the contacts. It seemed likely that these contacts could lead to extensive, up-to-date information on the foreign operations of the Iranian Intelligence Ministry (MOIS) and the Revolutionary Guards. This information would include copies of passports, and perhaps even training records of the terrorists.[30]

When the CIA and the State Department learned of the meetings, both organizations demanded an end to them. When efforts were made to revive the meetings in the summer of 2004, Secretary of State Colin Powell intervened to prevent the meetings from taking place. Even though Ledeen had established a reliable source of information, the CIA and the State Department were not interested. Intelligence gathering was their turf and no "back channel," no matter how valuable, would be tolerated outside established protocols.

The Left interpreted Washington's decision to shut down meetings such as those that occurred in Rome, meetings that had been fully approved by the government (including the National Security Council, the CIA, the State Department, and the Department of Defense), as a clear indication that "a rogue regime at the Pentagon was trying to work outside normal US foreign policy channels to advance a 'regime change' agenda not approved by the president's foreign policy principals or even the president himself."[31] If government officials were working outside normal channels, Senator Rockefeller's intelligence committee was ready to investigate, expose, ruin careers, even file criminal charges—whatever had to be done to embarrass the Bush administration and put intelligence-gathering efforts back into the bottle. Ledeen demanded to appear before Rockefeller's committee, but the senator was not interested. As a last resort, Ledeen finally had a formal meeting with the committee's staff, but the committee report did not reflect what Ledeen had told them about the meetings in Rome.

The Democrats had long ago decided what they would tolerate as results from intelligence gathering: first, anything that showed the president had lied in the run-up to the war against Iraq was good, including proof that intelligence was distorted to claim Saddam Hussein had WMDs or was an imminent threat;

second, anything that suggested a need for regime change in Iran or that Iran's drive to obtain nuclear weapons could only be stopped by war was bad and had to be stopped. The Democrats might argue that they were concerned about legality and process, in other words, that intelligence gathering outside the narrowly defined rules was wrong or dangerous. Yet what the Democrats were really after was controlling the message that resulted from intelligence gathering. The Democrats would probably have encouraged even a rogue intelligence-gathering process if the message ended up being the one they wanted to hear.

What was learned from the exercise was even more frightening. Many analysts within both the State Department and the CIA fundamentally agreed with the Democrats' interpretation of events. Seasoned professionals at both State and the CIA were Clinton administration holdovers, a lot of them were "gray hairs," senior analysts whose average ages were in the late fifties and early sixties. Many career analysts at State and CIA were also liberals, whether they openly admitted it or not. They, too, had matured in the 1960s, with a mind-set that admired the antiwar movement, and some even had what approached an anti-militarist, almost anti-American view of the world that John Kerry, the radical activist and anti-imperialist, would easily understand.

A good number in State and the CIA would probably even agree with the Far Left that America's war on terror was just another permutation of U.S. colonial ambitions whether the administration admitted it or not. When President Bush spoke of an "Axis of Evil" or the need to establish democracies in the Middle East, many of these experienced hands at State and within the CIA scoffed, agreeing privately with the Far Left that Bush was naïve and inexperienced, if not simply downright stupid. A lot of top staffers at both State and the CIA were Democrats and proud to be so. Yes, they were serving a Republican administration, but it was just another first-term Bush administration, one they expected would soon be a passing phenomenon. Bush's father lost reelection; the son would likely follow suit.

Many of these left-thinkers in State and the CIA in 2004 could have found a good number of like-thinking comrades within the ranks of the Pentagon, especially among the civilian employees and staffers of all three departments and agencies. Only the percentage of military personnel within the Pentagon changed the odds there.

In 2003 and 2004 Michael Ledeen had intelligence he desperately wanted to pass on to the intelligence community within State and the CIA, but no one was interested. Repeatedly, Ledeen offered to introduce the CIA to sources who could give them firsthand information on the location of Osama bin Laden, but the CIA was not interested. Or again, as Ledeen explained: "More than two months before the onset of the battle for Iraq, Treasury and [the] CIA were informed there were more than a thousand pages of firsthand documents dealing with Saddam's financial operations in Dubai, including weapons purchases and money laundering. These documents were available in Geneva, Switzerland, in the offices of a private person friendly to the United States. He offered to make them all available to any official of the U.S. Government. It was not until mid-June that CIA requested the contact information."[32]

Why Curt Weldon Wrote the White House a Letter

CONGRESSMAN CURT WELDON (R-PA), a member of the House Armed Services Committee, has been equally frustrated at his inability to get intelligence officials to listen to him. In 2003 Congressman Weldon held a series of private meetings in Paris with a former high official in Iran under the Shah. Weldon's source had been working for the past twenty years to help develop a counterrevolutionary movement within Iran. According to Weldon, his source had two informants highly placed in the Iranian government, with access to the most sensitive information regarding Iran's support of international terrorism and programs for developing missiles and WMDs. In April and May 2003 Weldon's source made a number of alarming allegations that were at variance with the intelligence estimates and the views of most experts.

Frustrated and unable to get the attention of the intelligence community within the government, Weldon decided in November 2003 to write a letter directly to the White House.[33] He addressed it to Scooter Libby, chief of staff and national security adviser to Vice President Cheney, and listed the following alarming allegations made by Weldon's source, code-named "Ali":

- On April 25, 2003, "Ali" alleged that Iran was negotiating the purchase of an atomic bomb from North Korea. One day later, on April 26, 2003, the world press first reported that North Korea might sell atomic weapons.

- On April 25, 2003, "Ali" alleged that Iran was greatly accelerating its atomic bomb program. Thirteen days later, on May 8, 2003, the world press first reported that Iran had initiated a crash program to build an atomic bomb, including revised estimates to that effect by the U.S. intelligence community.

- On April 25, 2003, "Ali" alleged that Iranian delegations had recently visited North Korea several times to negotiate the purchase of an atomic bomb. Forty-seven days later, on June 11, 2003, the world press first reported testimony from a North Korean defector that the Iranians had recently visited North Korea several times to explore nuclear cooperation, including possibly the purchase of a North Korean bomb.

- On May 4, 2003, "Ali" alleged an imminent terrorist threat to the United States. Sixteen days later, on May 20, 2003, the world press first reported that U.S. Homeland Security elevated the threat level to orange, based partly on intercepted communications indicating an imminent terrorist threat to the United States.

- On May 17, 2003, "Ali" alleged the existence of a terrorist plot to hijack an airliner in Canada to use in a suicide attack against a nuclear reactor in the United States. Ninety-seven days later, on August 22, 2003, the world press first reported the arrest in Canada of a terrorist cell engaged in pilot training, apparently for the purpose of crashing an airplane into a nuclear reactor.

In December 2004 Congressman Weldon went public with his warning that terrorists were planning to hijack an airliner in Canada and crash it into the Seabrook nuclear reactor in New Hampshire, about forty miles north of Boston.[34] Weldon told the press that his informant indicated the attack was first planned for between November 23 and December 3, 2003, but was postponed to take place after the 2004 presidential election. Frustrated that the CIA had not taken his reports seriously, Weldon decided to take the information directly to the American public. He also indicated that he was writing a book in which he also planned to detail an Iranian plot to conduct an attack on America more lethal than the 9/11 attack.

Congressman Weldon's source needed funding to continue his efforts. Weldon took the case to George Tenet, then the director of the CIA, and got nowhere. He also pressed the issue with the Senate Intelligence Committee, again getting nowhere. Like Michael Ledeen, Congressman Weldon was utilizing an intelligence back channel, something that was certain to draw fire from Democratic critics.

Moreover, Weldon was carrying the same unwelcome message the intelligence community did not want to hear: Iran was developing nuclear weapons, and Iran was a continuing terror threat to the United States and to Israel.

Why Liberals Hate Intelligence Activities

AMERICA'S LEFT has hated U.S. intelligence-gathering activities since the Vietnam War. When the Watergate investigations revealed that America's intelligence-gathering agencies had been conducting surveillance on anti-war organizations such as John Kerry's Vietnam Veterans Against the War (VVAW), the Left decided to shut down domestic intelligence-gathering efforts. Beginning with the Church Committee in 1974, the Democrats have pushed for a series of restrictions hoping to forbid the FBI, the CIA, the National Security Agency, and a multitude of military intelligence agencies from even suspecting that a political organization operating within the United States might be subversive, working in the interests of a foreign government, or an international group whose interests were adverse to the United States.[35]

We saw a recent example of the Democrats' war against intelligence gathering during the 9/11 Commission hearings. Jamie Gorelick, a Democratic member of the commission who had served as a deputy attorney general in the Clinton administration, wrote a 1995 memo that served to create a "wall" between Justice Department officials pursuing suspected terrorists and FBI criminal investigators who might be pursuing the same suspected terrorists. Gorelick's concern was that information gathered under Foreign Intelligence Surveillance Act (FISA) search warrants did not require probable cause, so information gathered there could not be passed over to criminal investigators who had to operate under a probable cause standard to obtain a search warrant.

Putting aside the legal technicalities, the concern was that if the "wall" had not existed, then the FBI might have gotten a search warrant to examine the computer of Zacarias Moussaoui, whose interest in learning to fly aircraft without learning how to land them had attracted FBI attention. If the FBI had pursued Moussaoui, so the argument goes, the 9/11 hijackers might have been found out and the tragedy averted.[36] By all rights, Gorelick should have been a subject of the commission's investigation, not a member of the investigating panel. Yet Gorelick successfully resisted repeated public requests for her resignation. The commission was political, out to blame President Bush for not anticipating and preventing the 9/11 hijacking. So Gorelick, a Democrat, got to stay and play her predetermined partisan role.

Yet the incident remains important because it reveals yet again how paranoid left-wing Democrats have become that strong intelligence efforts would end up investigating them and their ties to extreme leftist groups such as the VVAW, which had openly sided with the Vietnamese communists during the war. Had too many liberal Democrats supported radical Islamic organizations over the years? Was that the real concern?

If the Democrats on the Left are predisposed to see value in the positions taken by enemies of the United States, including Iran, then clearly intelligence that documents the national security threats represented by a rogue regime like Iran runs the risk of being politically embarrassing to these same Democrats. Maybe it's better not to collect the intelligence in the first place. Or perhaps even better, it's best to look like you're collecting intelligence while you're putting up barriers to protect yourself. Thus any investigators getting too close to the truth can be sanctioned with the loss of their job or with criminal charges because they didn't respect the "walls" erected by the Democrats and the Left to protect themselves.

Why Democrats Loathe Neocons

LEFTIST WRITER Seymour Hersh in his attack on Douglas Feith and the Pentagon was careful to target political philosopher Leo Strauss as the intellectual patriarch of the neocons. He noted that several key officials in the Pentagon's top planning ranks—individuals as high as Deputy Secretary Paul Wolfowitz—had studied under Professor Strauss at the University of Chicago.[37] Why all the fuss about an obscure political philosopher?

Strauss was a Jew and a refugee from Nazi Germany. The anti-Jewish sentiments of many neocon critics have already been noted above. Yet there is more here. Strauss advocated a return to the classical political philosophy of Plato and Aristotle. He believed that the ancient philosophers understood true principles of right, whereas the modern philosophers tended to be more relativistic about their values. Beginning with strongly liberal philosophers such as Thomas Hobbes and John Locke, Strauss believed political philosophy made a left turn, and questions of right and wrong merely depended upon who set the rules. To Strauss, modern philosophy was dominated by thinkers such as Friedrich Nietzsche, who believed that the winners wrote the history and that the "supermen" could rise above false notions of right and wrong that earlier victors had created to imprison others. We should not forget for a minute that Hitler too liked Nietzsche, believing that the world would evolve a "super race" by waging a genocide of the Jews. Still, the Far Left embraces value relativism as much as it disdains the traditional moral certainty of the Straussians.

I have known this debate for some thirty-five years. As a graduate student at Harvard I studied political philosophy in the late 1960s and early 1970s, during the turmoil of the Vietnam War when these questions were being hotly debated. One of my teachers was Harvey Mansfield Jr., a strong Straussian. I benefited greatly from Professor Mansfield's insights. My thesis was on a First Amendment question, whether prior restraint or prior punishments could ever be imposed on someone who wanted to speak out politically in a way that would be unpopular.[38]

At a time when the government sought to suppress the publication of the Pentagon Papers, this was an important topic. Among my thesis advisers, I had the excellent good fortune to have Professor Michael Walzer, a brilliant thinker on the Left who soon thereafter left Harvard for a position at Princeton University's Institute for Advanced Studies, the same center where Albert Einstein spent his last years. As for a conservative adviser, I was accepted by Professor Arthur Sutherland of the law school to be the last doctoral student he counseled. As a result, I absorbed the debate from both sides of the political spectrum. The debate was important, especially when applied to the question of the war on terrorism. The liberals were right to seize on the neocons as mortal enemies of their cause, for that's what in truth they are.

How does Leo Strauss apply? What Strauss objected to was the proposition that one set of moral values was as good as any other. "That's just a value choice," was a common rebuttal at the time in arguments about morality. In today's terms, an argument from the Left might be that gay marriage was just as morally acceptable as a marriage between a man and a woman; it all depended on your "point of view," your moral framework for judging. Strauss would object. To Strauss, values were "natural" and "right" because they served to advance humans onto a higher moral and intellectual plane. To Strauss, the argument for gay marriage was a historical accident, one we should be careful not to set in cement, because tomorrow's viewpoints can be expected to favor yet another *en vogue* idea about marriage, just as tomorrow we are likely to have new fashions for our clothes.

In the debate over the war against terrorism, the neocons have argued that freedom is at the heart of every human being and that radical Islamic theocracies are repressive governmental systems in which human beings cannot be free. The Left tends to see Islamic theocracies as just another political choice, perhaps not the one we would choose to live under, but then who are we to say for them? That is the core of the argument. The Left wants to be value relative even when it comes to Islamic terrorists. Aren't they just another brand of "freedom fighter," maybe not our hero, but a hero to Muslims? That's the difficulty that eats at the heart of the Far Left.

The neocons reject this hypothesis, believing that America is perhaps the greatest political experiment ever in human freedom. Yes, perhaps the president speaks too narrowly when he champions "democracy" in the Middle East; after all, the United States itself may well be argued to be a constitutional republic, not a democracy in the purist terms. Still, the core belief on the Right is that America has a core moral purpose, and that purpose is to advance freedom around the world, challenging despotic forms of government (including radical Islamic theocracies) when they get so aggressive as to threaten our national security.

Yes, conservatives on the extreme Right also take exception with neocons, but on different grounds. The neocons see 9/11 as changing the world in that we were attacked on our own soil. Also, the neocons firmly believe that we cannot appease radical Islamic terrorists because history has shown that appeasement only emboldens tyrants. The paleo-conservatives, of whom Pat Buchanan is a brilliant and praiseworthy example, fear that we should not exaggerate our own military ability. Strict conservatives of this view adhere strongly to George Washington's admonition in his Farewell Address that America should avoid foreign entanglements. Still, Pat Buchanan would accept that radical Islamic theocracies are an unfortunate form of government, with the proviso that the United States has no constitutional requirement or duty to go around the world to ensure all existing governments are pure or correct.

The election of 2004 showed the Far Left in America that there is reason for them to hate the neocons. The majority of "red state" Americans, like the neocons themselves, believe in basic American values such as religious and political freedom, and they are willing to accept propositions that we are better off without Saddam Hussein, maybe even that the mad mullahs would do the world a horrible service developing nuclear weapons, even if they only used the bombs to eradicate Israel. The majority of "red state" Americans read the Bible and still believe in God. They also are much more inclined to agree with Plato and Aristotle than they are ready to believe that Nietzsche is anything but out of his mind.

In the presidential election of 2004 the moral majority of America spoke. The "Silent Majority," as Richard Nixon liked to say, rose up and rejected the candidacy of John Kerry. I believe that Leo Strauss, had he still been alive, would have understood what middle America had to say.

PART 2

THE TERRORIST REGIME

6

Iran Exports Terror

IRAN EXPORTS TERRORISM AS well as oil. For more than twenty-five years, Iran has built a terrorist network around the world. With some $150 million a day in oil revenue, the country has ample cash to achieve the regime's two main goals: build nuclear weapons and create a truly international terrorist network. The terrorist organizations Iran has funded have different names—Hezbollah, Hamas, and Islamic Jihad, to name just three—and all three are working together.

Everywhere we look in the world of radical Islamic terrorism, we find the hands of the mullahs involved directly, even if covertly. No government in the world comes even close to competing with Iran as the world's leading state sponsor of terrorism. The radical Islamic terror masters are at war with Israel and America. And the Islamic Republic of Iran intends to prevail regardless of the cost.

The Radical Islamic Terror Masters[1]

TERRORISTS AROUND the world are fully aware of one another; there are terrorist styles and terrorist heroes. Different terrorist organizations are like gangs, each with its own particular credos, its own recognizable uniforms and colors, its own history and heroes. A particular gang may lay claim to a particular turf, but all the gangs know one another, learn to respect one another, and figure out how to work together. Likewise, the terror masters work with one another across territorial boundaries, regardless of organizational affiliation.

Radical Islamic terror groups act like an Islamic Mafia. Yes, the Al Capone gang during Prohibition may have operated principally in Chicago, and the Lucky Luciano gang may have headquartered in New York, but both shared a common purpose in selling illegal liquor. The Meyer Lansky gang may have been composed primarily of Jews, while the J. B. Elkins gang in the West was mostly made up of Protestants, but both gangs wanted Vegas and Reno opened up for casinos. So, too, Hezbollah may be headquartered in Lebanon, and Hamas may operate primarily among the Palestinians, but both terrorist organizations work together and both depend upon Iran for financial support.

Like the famous Mafiosi in America's organized crime history, the radical Islamic terror masters in the Middle East today are well known to one another. Islamic terrorists advance within their particular crime hierarchies based on how efficiently they create terror in their common enemies, specifically in Israel and America. Lessons learned in one struggle are applied to the next.

The United States is truly involved in a world war against radical Islamic terrorism, whether we realize it or not. At the center of this new, emerging world war are the Iranian mullahs.

Hezbollah: Iran's Terrorist "Party of God"

HEZBOLLAH (translated as "Party of God") traces its roots to Najaf in Iraq. Najaf is an important Shi'ite center of theology with an important position in Islamic history. Here is buried the Imam Ali, whom Shi'ites consider the first convert of Mohammad and the rightful successor to the Prophet. Ayatollah Muhammad Hussein Fadlallah, the spiritual leader of Hezbollah, studied in Najaf when he was in exile from Lebanon; there he met and studied under Ayatollah Khomeini, who himself was in exile from Iran. Hezbollah as an organization arose in 1982 from the disorder in the Lebanese Shi'ite community caused by the civil war.[2]

Since its inception, Hezbollah has embraced terrorism as its principal methodology to achieve its major jihadist goals: (1) to conduct a relentless struggle against the State of Israel with a view to "liberate" Jerusalem and annihilate the Jewish state, and (2) to force the United States out of the Middle East as the first step in defeating America worldwide. From the beginning, Hezbollah has held out the dream of a worldwide conquest of Shi'ite ideology, with the aim of establishing the hegemony of a Shi'ite theocracy around the globe.

Suicide is Hezbollah's signature weapon. Weak organizations, such as terrorist gangs, must rely on "asymmetric warfare," techniques designed to leverage minor tactical advantages to major strategic impact. One suicide bomber willing to sacrifice his life can produce headlines around the world, an impact truly out of proportion to the few lives actually lost. The goal is to shock and cause massive psychological damage.

Hezbollah embeds its youth with a sufficiently zealous religious ideology to induce a person to sacrifice his life, to strap on a belt of bombs, to board a bus in Jerusalem or to walk into a crowded Tel Aviv restaurant, and to blow himself up, killing as many people as possible in the process. This requires years of indoctrination, beginning with young children. A social structure must be created to teach young minds the glory of dying for Islam with the prospect of going to heaven as a well-rewarded martyr. That the reward is often expressed in material terms—for instance, the often-repeated seventy-two dark-eyed virgins awaiting the martyr in heaven—is a contradiction generally overlooked by "spiritual" teachers charged with implanting inducements to suicide in the minds of young radicals.

Hezbollah has mobilized powerful forces of social control. The organization comes with all the appropriate symbols one would expect of a radical gang. Hezbollah's famous yellow flag is an emblem so distinctive that one can look across Beirut and see the yellow flags and banners flying as a sign of Hezbollah's strength. The flag displays an upraised green hand brandishing a green AK-47 assault rifle against the background of a green globe—a powerful symbol of worldwide revolutionary intent.

Lest anyone miss the point, a slogan is stolen from the Koran and pasted in Arabic script across the top of the assault rifle, roughly translated as "Only the Party of God [Hezbollah] shall be victorious." A holy verse is thus given a belligerent meaning, perverting the Koran (sura 5, verse 56) from its original purpose, which was to praise the Prophet and his followers for establishing a holy religion for the growth and benefit of human beings, not the indiscriminate murder of innocent civilians, including women and children. Hezbollah thus gives a holy verse a murderous meaning, and a new yellow-and-green symbol of terror is born to the world.

When adherents of Hezbollah march in the streets, they wear yellow masks or headbands marked with green Arabic lettering, proclaiming their allegiance to Hezbollah. The display is similar to particular types of traditional full-body tattoos that distinguish Yakuza gangs from one another in Japan. Yellow and green have become trademarks that distinguish someone as a member of this suicide sect.

Hezbollah can also claim to have innovated the means of implementing their suicidal intentions. Thus Hezbollah is credited by the terror masters around the world with having led the way in developing the explosives and explosive delivery systems that are needed for someone to commit holy suicide. Creative bomb factories and genius bomb makers are part of Hezbollah's legacy. Working for more than two decades, the mad genius engineers of Hezbollah have devised dozens of innovative ways to pack explosives surreptitiously into virtually anything that moves: cars, trucks, boats, even strapping them beneath the clothes of their suicide deliverers. And the bombs cannot easily be discovered until they are exploded.

When Timothy McVeigh packed a rental truck with a fertilizer bomb and parked it next to a major government building in Oklahoma City, terrorism experts saw the signature of Hezbollah even if McVeigh never made the link himself. All human beings, including terrorists, are great imitators. Whenever a suicide bombing occurs anywhere in the world, we have Hezbollah to thank.

Hezbollah also refined techniques of terror kidnapping. Yes, kidnapping is an old crime, made famous in the United States during the 1930s with the kidnapping of Charles Lindbergh's baby. For old-style criminals, ransom money was the expected motive for kidnapping. For terrorists, however, the objective is political. Hezbollah kidnaps people of political significance to ransom them for political concessions—freedom for political prisoners, an end to a military engagement, or a military pullout from an area altogether.

Hezbollah quickly grafted its particular style of kidnapping onto already established terrorist methodologies, such as skyjacking. So when TWA Flight 847 was hijacked between Athens and Rome, the Hezbollah hijackers demanded that Israel release all the Shi'ite prisoners captured in Lebanon. Today when we see the insurgents in Iraq using Hezbollah's techniques of car bombings and politically motivated kidnappings, experts immediately suspect the involvement of Iran.

Hezbollah Attacks America

OVER THE last two decades Hezbollah violence has attacked the United States, typically with significant impact. Consider the following examples:

- *October 23, 1983.* A suicide truck driven by Hezbollah suicide bombers attacked the U.S. Marine Corps barracks in Beirut, killing 241 American troops. The truck carried a cargo of 5,450 kilograms of TNT, making the explosion one of the largest conventional bombing attacks ever investigated to that date. The Result: President Reagan decided to withdraw all U.S. troops from Lebanon. Hezbollah looked upon the result as a clear strategic victory and a confirmation of its suicide bombing techniques.

- *January 18, 1984.* The Islamic Jihad murdered American University of Beirut president Malcolm Kerr. This began a series of kidnappings of American citizens in Lebanon, often with the complicity of Tehran. On March 16, 1984, William Buckley, the CIA agency station chief in Beirut was kidnapped and murdered; his remains were finally returned to the United States in 1991. In March 1985 Hezbollah kidnapped Terry Anderson, a U.S. citizen and an Associated Press journalist in Beirut; Anderson was not released until December 1991. The Result: Within the Reagan administration an unauthorized group began what became known as the Iran-Contra affair, an attempt to secure cash with which to pay Iran to persuade Hezbollah to release the U.S. hostages being held in Lebanon. The resulting political scandal severely damaged President Reagan's second term in office. Hezbollah again celebrated a victory, concluding that a few hostages could bring a great nation such as the United States to its knees.

- *June 25, 1996.* A truck bomb exploded outside the perimeter of the U.S. portion of the Khobar Towers housing complex in Dhahran, Saudi Arabia, killing nineteen U.S. military service personnel and wounding hundreds more. Saudi members of Hezbollah, acting under instructions from Tehran, carried out the suicide bombing attack.[3] The Result: President Clinton hesitated to retaliate, fearing that he lacked proof of criminal responsibility and worrying that sending a cruise missile to the wrong target or causing too much collateral damage could be politically damaging to him domestically. Hezbollah again celebrated a victory with additional confirmation that America was weak and could easily be defeated.

Hezbollah gained enormous prestige with these successful attacks against the United States, proving the effectiveness of their suicide methodology and gaining new adherents throughout the Islamic world.

Hezbollah Attacks Israel

IN THE 1990s Israel launched a series of military incursions into Southern Lebanon to attack Hezbollah bases and retaliate for strikes against Israel. In April 1996 Hezbollah launched hundreds of Katyusha rockets into the security zone and northern Israel, prompting the IDF, Israel's military forces, to launch Operation Grapes of Wrath: massive artillery and bombing strikes against Hezbollah positions in Southern Lebanon. In August 1996 the new Israeli prime minister, Benjamin Netanyahu, offered to withdraw from Southern Lebanon if the Lebanese government would secure the border; the Lebanese government refused. In February 1997 two Israeli helicopters collided while ferrying troops to Southern Lebanon, resulting in the deaths of seventy-three soldiers. As Israeli casualties mounted, all major candidates in Israel's 1999 elections promised to withdraw Israeli military forces from Lebanon.[4]

When the last Israeli soldier left Lebanon on May 24, 2000, Hezbollah celebrated a huge victory. As Aaron Mannes, the former director of the Middle East Media Research Institute, noted: "Israel's withdrawal was greeted with jubilation throughout the Arab world, and Hezbollah was lauded for reversing decades of Arab defeats by Israel. The Lebanese-Israeli border, particularly the Fatma Gate, became a tourist attraction where Lebanese and other Arabs could go and throw stones at Israel. The Israeli withdrawal particularly inspired the Palestinians to believe that Israel could be defeated. Less than four months later, the Palestinians launched the al-Asqa Intifada."[5] Clearly the Palestinian organizations were taking encouragement and learning from the lessons and successes of Hezbollah in Lebanon.

Hezbollah's Worldwide Reach

NOTHING BETTER demonstrates Hezbollah's international reach than the attacks the organization successfully launched against Jews in Argentina. In the Tri-border area of South America where Argentina, Paraguay, and Brazil meet, there are approximately thirty thousand Muslims living, many of them

Shi'ites from Lebanon. The frontier nature of this tri-border territory makes it a natural hideout for criminal activity and for terrorists. The Paraguayan city of Ciudad del Este is known as a fund-raising and money-laundering center for Hezbollah.[6]

In March 1992 a Hezbollah bomb leveled the Israeli Embassy in Buenos Aires. In July 1994 a Hezbollah car carrying an estimated 400 kilograms of explosives blew up outside the AMIA Building in Buenos Aries, destroying much of the building that housed the offices of Argentina's Jewish communal organizations, killing eighty-five and wounding an additional four hundred people. Both attacks were in retaliation for the incursions into Lebanon that the Israeli Defense Force was undertaking at the time.

In January 2003 the Secretariat of State Intelligence (SIDE), Argentina's intelligence service, issued a 150-page report summarizing its findings that the responsibility for the 1994 bombing of the Jewish communal services building was the responsibility of Hezbollah and Iran. The report named Imad Mughniyah, the head of Hezbollah's military wing, as authorizing the attack by Hezbollah agents in the Tri-Border region. As evidence, the SIDE report cited intercepted telephone conversations among Hezbollah operatives. The report also placed the blame for the 1992 bombing of the Israeli embassy on Hezbollah and Iran.[7]

Mughniyah was born in South Lebanon in 1962. For a short time he studied at the American University in Beirut, then he joined the Force 17 elite commando unit of Yasser Arafat's Palestinian Liberation Organization's Fatah unit. After the PLO was expelled from Lebanon, Mughniyah was recruited by the Iranian Islamic Jihad organization, the military arm of Hezbollah. Mughniyah was for a time responsible for the personal security of Hezbollah's spiritual leader, Ayatollah Fadlallah. He planned the bomb attacks on the U.S. Marine base in Lebanon that killed 241 American troops on October 23, 1983. He was personally involved in the hijacking of TWA 847, and he masterminded the attacks on the Khobar Towers and coordinated the plans with Hezbollah in South America to conduct the bombings in Argentina.

U.S. intelligence also believes Mughniyah was involved in the Christmas Eve 1999 hijacking of an Air India aircraft, which was taken over by Islamic terrorists armed with knives and scissors. This hijacking is believed to have been a kind of dress rehearsal for the 9/11 hijackers. Mughniyah coordinated with the Sunni Palestinians to get them trained in the Shi'ite Hezbollah training camps in Lebanon. U.S. intelligence suspects that Mughniyah has been in contact with Osama bin Laden, for whom his terrorist innovations are believed to have been an inspiration. Currently Mughniyah is at large and on the FBI list of most wanted terrorists.[8]

Western intelligence sources estimate that Hezbollah operates on an annual budget of approximately one hundred million dollars, most of which comes from Iran. These funds go toward funding terrorist activities as well as paying for the operation of Hezbollah communal organizations such as schools and hospitals.[9]

On its own, Hezbollah probably raises another fifty million dollars per year over and above the one hundred million dollars provided by Iran. Hezbollah raises considerable funds through Islamic "charities" worldwide, front organizations that appear to serve legitimate community needs but whose real purpose is to act as a subterfuge for funneling money to Hezbollah terrorists. Hezbollah also engages in the typical activities expected of an organized crime syndicate: trafficking in illegal drugs and money counterfeiting (especially U.S. one-hundred-dollar bills). Other forms of criminal activity include cigarette smuggling, car thefts, and credit card forgery. As noted by Israeli intelligence sources: "It is often difficult to pinpoint whether a Hezbollah operative who engages in criminal activity does so on behalf of Hezbollah or for his or her own benefit; usually the two are combined."[10]

Hezbollah maintains a substantial arsenal in Lebanon, including ten thousand Iranian-manufactured mobile long-range land-to-land missiles: the Fajr-3, with a range of approximately twenty-five miles, and the more powerful Fajr-5, with a range of about fifty-five miles—both capable of inflicting significant damage in northern Israel. In addition, Hezbollah's large quantities of arms include antitank missiles, Katyusha rockets, and antiaircraft cannons and missiles. No other terrorist organization in the world is considered as well organized or as well armed as Hezbollah.[11]

Hezbollah is also active both in Canada and the United States. Under instructions from Imad Mughniyah, another important operative, Mohammad Dbouk, was sent from Lebanon to run the Hezbollah cell in Vancouver, Canada. The Vancouver cell was reportedly receiving the proceeds from a Hezbollah cigarette-smuggling ring in North Carolina. Even though Canada has refused to consider Hezbollah a terrorist organization, Hezbollah has been using Canada since the 1990s as a base to recruit, raise funds through charities, forge documents, and launder money. Mohammed Hussein Al-Husseini, a Hezbollah member, told Canadian authorities that Hezbollah was working hard to recruit in Canada: "Hezbollah has members in Montreal, Ottawa, Toronto—all of Canada."[12]

In January 2004 Mahmoud Youssef Kourani was indicted by the U.S. Attorney's office in Detroit, Michigan, for conspiring with his brother, the Hezbollah chief of military security for Southern Lebanon, "to provide military support for the group, which led a guerrilla war against Israel's 18-year occupation of a border zone in southern Lebanon." Kourani was charged with being a "member, fighter, recruiter, and fund-raiser for Hezbollah who operated in Lebanon and later within the United States."[13]

According to the indictment, Kourani entered the United States illegally through Mexico in February 2001 and took up residence in Detroit. He hid his Muslim identity by not attending mosques and by shaving his head to alter his appearance.

This arrest followed a sentencing two weeks earlier of Elias Mohamad Akhdar, who pleaded guilty in July 2003 to a conspiracy of violating the RICO Act by trying to transfer hundreds of thousands of dollars to Hezbollah in Lebanon. In addition to Detroit, the FBI has been investigating Hezbollah ties in the large Muslim communities of New York, Boston, and Los Angeles.

On February 24, 2004, then CIA Director George Tenet was reported to have testified to the Senate Select Intelligence Committee that Hezbollah has cultivated an extensive network of operatives on American soil and has "an ongoing capability to launch terrorist attacks within the United States."[14]

One more profile is important. Hassan Nasrallah, still in his forties, born in 1960 in a South Lebanese village, is the secretary-general, the political leader, of Hezbollah. He, too, was trained in a Shi'ite seminary in Najaf, Iraq. He has achieved great repute in the world of radical Islam for his successful use of suicide bombings against Israel. In January 2004 tens of thousands lined the road leading to Beirut International Airport to celebrate the return of twenty-three Lebanese militants from Israeli prisons. "Fireworks lit the sky above the predominantly Shi'ite southern suburbs of Beirut and street celebrations continued late into the night. Equally exuberant, if less flashy, festivities took place in the West bank and Gaza as over 400 Palestinian prisoners returned home."[15]

Why were the prisoners released? Israel had just suffered one of the bloodiest suicide bombings in months, and in exchange for the prisoners released, all the Jewish state received in return was the release by Hezbollah of a kidnapped Israeli and the remains of three others.

For this victory, Hassan Nasrallah received the praise of none less than Ayatollah Ali Khamenei, the religious leader of Iran's theocracy, and Ahmed Yassin, the spiritual leader and founder of the Palestinian terrorist group Hamas. The warm praise flowing in to Nasrallah acknowledged that he had shown the way and that more kidnappings of Israelis were certain to follow.[16]

Nasrallah is a hard-liner who in 1989 and 1990 had actively opposed the invasion of Syrian military forces into Lebanon. For this opposition, Iran called Nasrallah back to Tehran for "more religious instruction." At that time, Abbas al-Musawi, was elected secretary-general of Hezbollah. Musawi was more willing to accept Syria's hegemony over Lebanon. Only in February 1992, when Musawi was assassinated by an Israeli helicopter assault, did Nasrallah return to Lebanon to be elected to the leadership of Hezbollah. This time, Nasrallah acquiesced and accepted that Damascus would make decisions for Beirut.[17]

A key point here is that today Lebanon must be considered a client state of Syria. In return, Syria defers to Iran on matters of critical regional political importance. The terrorist states are working together to the point where they control the internal workings of key terrorist organizations such as Hezbollah. Note also that the March 1992 car bombing of the Israeli embassy in Buenos Aries was considered a retaliation by Hezbollah for the Israeli attack that killed Musawi. Hezbollah let Israel know that even Israelis living outside Israel were not safe from assassination if Israel continued to kill Hezbollah leaders in Lebanon. Hezbollah always thinks globally.

Syrian President Bashar Assad has a warm relationship with Nasrallah and Hezbollah. In 2000 Nasrallah was received for the first time at the presidential palace by Lebanese President Emile Lahoud. No leader of Hezbollah had ever before been so publicly honored by the Lebanese government. Later, in the summer of 2000, when U.N. Secretary-General Kofi Annan visited Beirut, Lebanese officials arranged a private meeting with Nasrallah so he and Annan could be photographed as they were shaking hands.[18] Israelis were shocked to see the secretary-general of the U.N. so warmly embrace an enemy whose suicide bombing attacks and missiles had killed so many Israeli citizens.

Today Hezbollah operates as an autonomous government in Southern Lebanon. A sometimes uneasy truce remains in effect with the Lebanese government. If Lebanon were to move in the direction of having a theocracy such as Iran, the catalyst for change would most likely be Hezbollah, either through the gradual evolution of increased successes in parliamentary elections or through more dramatic means, including the possibility of a military action against the government. And the sometimes dormant Lebanese civil war would enter yet another bloody stage.

Most European nations still refuse to identify Hezbollah as a terrorist organization, preferring to pretend that its principal purpose is to provide community social services in Southern Lebanon.

In December 2004 senior Shi'ite cleric Ayatollah Fadlallah, the spiritual leader of Hezbollah, called upon the Vatican to join with him in opposing President Bush's war on terrorism, which Fadlallah maintained unfairly harms Muslims. In Fadlallah's view, the 9/11 attacks were planned by the Jews to incite Americans to hate and attack Muslims. This obvious form of anti-Jewish hate and fantasy recreation of history was being seriously reported by the world press. Fadlallah claimed, "This campaign against Islam is part of a prefabricated plan to create an enemy for Westerners, following the collapse of the Soviet Union." The ayatollah did not miss the chance to suggest that all the United States wanted in the Middle East was oil, as he condemned countries supporting the United States as those who "look the other way and thus indirectly encourage practices against Muslims, especially in third-world countries or countries rich in natural resources."

Fadlallah, however, did express his usual admiration for Kofi Annan's stance in support of Hezbollah. "We urge the UN secretary-general to implement the law and adopt the necessary measures to halt this crime against Islam and Muslim Arabs in many countries so that action is not restricted to verbal condemnation." Where are the U.N. resolutions condemning Hezbollah for the suicide attacks launched against Israeli citizens? We will be setting ourselves up for a severe disappointment if we expect the United Nations to have a standard of justice that would care when Jews (or Americans) are murdered by terrorists. If Osama bin Laden could find a state that would appoint him its ambassador to the United Nations, the U.N. no doubt would have a seat for him in the General Assembly.

The mullahs consider Hezbollah a good investment and a fine success story. Hezbollah has managed to expel from Lebanon the two countries the mullahs consider the greatest enemies of Islam—the United States and Israel. Moreover, Hezbollah has secured a political position of strength within Lebanon, effectively reaching across to Syria after Syria reduced the Lebanese government to a subservient position. Hezbollah's success with Syria has translated for the mullahs into a greater closeness between Syria and Iran. And the two rogue states realize that working together further strengthens both themselves within the region and Hezbollah as a powerful weapon that can now be turned directly to attack Israel.

The common goal of Israel and Syria is to push the Jews out of the Holy Land. To achieve this dream, Hezbollah has reached out to Hamas, a sister terrorist organization that has the added advantage of already being present among the Jews in the Holy Land.

Regardless of whether Americans or Europeans understand what is happening, the terrorist masters in the Middle East are thinking strategically. This is not a problem that can be understood if we only look at the mullahs in Iran or if we look at Hezbollah as somehow distinct from Hamas. Syria is part of the equation, working in partnership with the mullahs to advance the successful techniques developed by Hezbollah so they can be applied in conjunction with Hamas to gain final control over a reclaimed Palestine that has no place whatsoever for Jews.

Hamas: A Brotherhood for Killing Jews

THE NAME Hamas is an acronym formed from the organization's formal name in Arabic: Harakat Al-Muqawama Al-Islamia ("The Islamic Resistance Movement"). The group was formed officially on December 8, 1987, coinciding with the outbreak of the first *intifada* against Israel. Hamas takes its roots from the Muslim Brotherhood, a group formed in Egypt in the 1920s whose primary purpose was the establishment of a "pure" Islamic state, though the group was also known for charitable good works, including religious, social, and educational endeavors.[19]

Hamas, however, is an Islamic jihadist organization that operates primarily in the Gaza Strip and other Palestinian-controlled territories. The organization is openly committed to the destruction of Israel, "the Zionist state," through the process of holy war. The most extreme of all Palestinian organizations, Hamas tolerates no compromise on the question that the land occupied by Israel rightfully belongs to the Palestinians and must be recovered by the Palestinians without compromise. Hamas has strongly opposed all Mideast peace processes that involve allowing Israel to remain a nation in any form on any land the Palestinians intend to reclaim. This position has drawn Hamas to the Far Left rhetorically, arguing, as do many socialists worldwide, that Israel is a neocolonial usurper that has stolen the land of Palestine from its rightful owners, namely the Palestinians. The polemical output of Hamas is rabidly anti-Jewish.

This "gang" is recognized by its distinctive green flag. In street demonstrations, Hamas radicals carry weapons and wear green masks to hide their faces. Green banners and green headbands with black Arabic writing are the Hamas trademark recognized by all who live in the region as a symbol designating membership in the group. The Hamas emblem displayed on the flag is a picture of the mosque of the Dome of the Rock in Jerusalem. On the right is the phrase in Arabic, "There is no God but Allah." On the left is written, "Mohammed is the messenger of Allah."

Two curved swords rest under the dome, symbolizing courage and nobility in battle. Above the dome is a map of Palestine that points down like a dagger. The symbolism conveys the group's determination to recover their holy land by force. Along the sides of the dome are green, white, and black stripes like lightning streaks, each with a red triangle at the top. With green the group's dominant color, the red, white, and black are available for stylistic combinations on shirts, headbands, and banners.

Hamas has largely adopted the terrorist techniques of Hezbollah, relying on suicide bombers and car bombs to attack Israeli civilians. Hezbollah leaders have trained the Hamas operatives, and the Hamas style indicates acceptance of Hezbollah's principles of waging asymmetric warfare against Israel, with the confidence that Israel cannot win a war of attrition against a determined and persistent enemy. Hamas has refined Hezbollah's suicide bombing methodology by adding when possible the touches of drive-by grenade tossing and occasionally running cars into crowds of Israeli citizens.

Whenever a bombing occurs in an Israeli restaurant or market, or a suicide bomber boards an Israeli bus, the perpetrators are suspected immediately to be members of Hamas. A signature Hamas bombing was the March 27, 2002, bombing of a Passover Seder in Netanya that killed 29 and injured 140. The holiness of the day and the sacrilege of the attack added horror to the suicide bombing. Favorite Hamas targets include Israeli soldiers at checkpoints along the West Bank and Gaza boundaries. The Israeli "wall" that delineates Palestinian territory was largely designed to counter Hamas terror tactics.

Hamas continues to run social, medical, and educational programs in Palestinian areas, frequently in conjunction with mosques. Terrorist criminals see this type of communal activity as an excellent cover, and the mosques provide an excellent recruiting ground, including an excellent place to contact newly migrated Palestinians. Hamas relies upon Islamic charity to fund much of its activities, including providing the resources needed to put terrorist operatives into the field. The Hamas annual budget is estimated at around fifty million dollars, with as much as ten million to twenty million dollars per year coming directly from Iran. Even though the Iranian mullahs are Shi'ites and Hamas is a Sunni organization, both work together to advance their common goal to destroy Israel.[20]

The intensity of Hamas attacks picked up once the al-Aqsa intifada began in the wake of Bill Clinton's attempt in the final days of his presidency to force a Camp David agreement between Yasser Arafat and Ehud Barak. The precipitating cause of the violent outbreak was supposedly a visit by the Likud chief and later prime minister, Ariel Sharon, to the Temple Mount. On September 29, 2000, violence began in Gaza and the West Bank. Reportedly, Hamas leaders began holding daily meetings with their counterparts in Fatah (the armed wing of the Palestinian Liberation Organization) and Yasser Arafat's Palestinian Authority. Hezbollah also stepped up its level of support to Hamas.[21]

Hamas engineered a wave of suicide bombings throughout Israel, including the June 1, 2001, bombing at Tel Aviv's Dolphinatium disco (twenty-one teenagers killed, more than one hundred injured) and the August 9, 2001, bombing of a Sbarro restaurant in Jerusalem (fifteen people killed, more than ninety injured). Many of the suicide bombers came from the West Bank, since it is closest to Israeli population centers and has many more available access points. In Gaza, where the terrain is less favorable to suicide bombers who want to slip into Israeli population centers unnoticed, the suicide attacks involved combined assaults on military targets, resulting from joint Hamas-Fatah operations with guidance from Hezbollah operatives.

The pressure on Israel was building as day after day the world's televisions were flooded with images of suicide bombing after suicide bombing. The al-Aqsa intifada, fueled as it was by Hamas in the foreground and Hezbollah in the background, was threatening to get out of control. Israel had no choice but to retaliate with Operation Defensive Shield, a strategy that involved incursions into Hamas-controlled areas, such as the West Bank town of Nablus. The goal was to hunt down the Hamas terrorists where they lived and to destroy their infrastructure.

So, too, Israel began building a wall to deprive Hamas terrorists of easy entry, especially from the West Bank. Though controversial, the wall has been effective. During the first half of 2004 Israel Defense Forces (IDF) "successfully foiled every suicide bomb attack originating from the northern West Bank,

Above: The nuclear power plant at Bushehr, 750 miles (1,200 km) southwest of Tehran.

Below: An interior view of the Bushehr facility.

Above: Technicians measure part of the Bushehr nuclear plant reactor.

Below: The Iranian Shahab-3 missile is capable of reaching Israel.

Above and below: Satellite views of the heavy water facility at Arak.

Satellite view of the gas centrifuge uranium enrichment plant at Natanz showing:
  1. the centrifuge assembly area
  2. a building housing a centrifuge pilot plant of more than two hundred machines
  3. ongoing construction of underground structures intended to house gas centrifuge cascades
  4. construction of an underground structure intended as a support building for the two main enrichment halls

This detail of an earlier satellite view of Natanz shows:

1. ongoing construction of an underground support building for two cascade buildings
2. ongoing construction of underground structures meant to house gas centrifuge cascades
3. centrifuge assembly area
4. underground truck route
5. tunnel entrance
6. administration building

Above and below: Iranian lawmakers chant slogans such as "Death to America!" and "Death to Israel!" as they stand up to show their "yes" vote to approve the outline of a bill requiring the government to resume uranium enrichment.

Above: Public hangings conducted with construction cranes are a routine form of execution in Iran.

Below: This March 2001 image captures a woman as she is being prepared for her execution.

Above: At a June 11, 1997, dinner in Washington, President Bill Clinton accepts the applause of donors and Democratic National Committee members. Stan Chesley and Bernard Schwartz stand to the president's right; Hassan Nemazee stands to Clinton's left. Below: On July 12, 1999, Ahmed Batebi holds up a bloody T-shirt in Tehran. The shirt belonged to a friend who had been injured during clashes between police and student demonstrators.

specifically those from the cities of Nablus and Jenin, areas that have become infamous for exporting suicide bombers." In comparison, there were 35 successful suicide attacks murdering 156 Israeli citizens in the time period between October 2000 and completion of the wall along Israel's northern rim.[22]

Ultimately, Israel resorted to a series of assassination attacks aimed at killing key Hamas leaders. On Monday, March 22, 2004, an Israeli helicopter missile strike killed Hamas founder Ahmed Yassin outside a Gaza City mosque. This assassination sent shock waves around the world. Yassin was a recognizable figure in a wheelchair; he had been crippled as a teenager when a soccer accident paralyzed him. In May 1989 an Israeli military court had sentenced Yassin to lifetime imprisonment for the crimes of incitement, kidnapping, and murder, all offenses Yassin had been judged to direct as the leader of Hamas. He was released in 1997 as part of a prisoner swap deal Israel made with Jordan.

Yassin's assassination was sensational. Reports from the scene indicated that he was being pushed in his wheelchair from a mosque after morning prayers when he was hit directly by the missile. Grotesquely, Yassin's body was vaporized but his intact head was recovered among the remaining twisted metal of his wheelchair. More than two hundred thousand Palestinians, many carrying billowing green Hamas flags, flooded the streets in Gaza City for Yassin's funeral. At the cemetery, Yassin's body was carried between rows of militants armed with antitank missiles and machine guns.[23]

Yassin was not only the founder of Hamas, he was also the most prominent Muslim cleric in Gaza since the 1970s. He had established in Gaza Al-Mujama Al-Islami ("The Islamic Center"), a charitable network of religious, educational, and social welfare institutions funded by wealthy Gulf state donors. This center was the "civic nucleus of Hamas," embodying the principles of charity and good works so central to Islam.[24] The charity also served as a front for raising terrorist money and for recruiting terrorist operatives and suicide candidates from among the Palestinians who were part of the center's communal activities.

On April 17, 2004, Israeli helicopters fired two missiles into a white sedan in the Gaza Strip, killing Abdel Aziz Rantisi less than a block from his home. Rantisi was often credited as the cofounder of Hamas. In December 1992 he was deported along with four hundred Hamas and Islamic Jihad activists to South Lebanon. When he returned to Gaza in 1993, he was arrested and remained under administration detention until mid-1997. In June 2004 Rantisi barely escaped an Israeli attack that fired some seven missiles toward his car.

After Yassin's killing, Rantisi had become the new leader of Hamas. At that time, Rantisi was defiant, swearing to a cheering crowd of Palestinians in Gaza that Ariel Sharon and the other leaders of Israel would "never feel security or safety." Rantisi was considered a hardcore enemy of Israel who had sworn that he would never accept any peace that allowed Israel to exist.[25]

With both Yassin and Rantisi hunted down and killed from the air by Israeli military forces, the point was clear: Israel was prepared to kill anyone who replaced these leaders. Whatever it took, Israel was determined to break the back of Hamas and put an end to the violence of this second intifada. Israel had no choice. Unchecked, Hamas and Hezbollah would create the same type of chaos that had chased the Israelis from Lebanon. The Israelis had to stand and fight on their own soil, and that is exactly what they did— through military incursions directly into Hamas strongholds, through walling themselves in with a protective barrier, through implementing a strategy of systematically killing every leader of Hamas and every replacement leader, as well as through a series of well-executed and ruthless assassinations.

Israel, expectedly, received worldwide condemnation for eliminating by assassination the Hamas leadership. After Rantisi was murdered, British Foreign Secretary Jack Straw announced: "The British government has made it repeatedly clear that so-called targeted assassinations of this kind are unlawful, unjustified and counterproductive."[26] Israel's instinct for self-defense kept the targeted assassination program going throughout 2004, with a series of spectacular hits that made clear to Hamas that anyone who assumed leadership within the organization would be considered by Israel a "marked man."

On September 26, 2004, Israeli security officials operating in Damascus, Syria, killed Hamas operative Izzideen al-Shiekh Khalil when his car exploded outside his home in a residential area heavily populated by Palestinian refugees. Ahmad Haj Ali, an adviser to the Syrian information minister, called Khalil's killing a "terrorist and cowardly action." He went on to say that the killing "was meant to deliver a message that says: 'We (the Israelis) are capable of striking anywhere in accordance with the Israeli agenda.'"[27] Israel had reached across boundaries to get Khalil in Damascus; moreover, in killing him with a car bomb, the Israelis communicated that they too were willing to give Hamas and Hezbollah some of their own medicine. If car bombs worked for the terrorists, maybe they would work as well for the Israelis.

This assassination in Damascus made even clearer that a regional conflict was at play here—one that was being funded out of Tehran, orchestrated with

Syria, and implemented through Hamas and Hezbollah as key partners who could coordinate with other terrorist groups, including the Fatah of Arafat's own Palestinian Liberation Organization.

The United Nations Puts Hamas on the Payroll

ON OCTOBER 3, 2004, Israel released a satellite photograph of a U.N. vehicle being used to move rockets for Palestinian terrorists. Israel claimed that the U.N. Relief and Works Agency (UNRWA) for Palestine Refugees in the Near East supported Hamas and demanded the U.N. conduct an investigation.

In response, Peter Hansen, head of UNRWA, told the Canadian Broadcasting Corporation: "I am sure that there are Hamas members on the UNRWA payroll and I don't see that as a crime. Hamas as a political organization does not mean that every member is a militant and we do not do political vetting and exclude people from one persuasion as against another." Israel's U.N. ambassador, Dan Gillerman, immediately objected, telling Israel Radio that Hansen "for years has expressed anti-Israel, biased, unrestrained positions and statements." The U.N. claimed the satellite photo showed a stretcher being taken from the truck, not a missile.[28]

UNRWA is not the only relief agency Hamas seeks to exploit. In March 2002 a Palestinian Red Crescent ambulance was stopped at a checkpoint south of Ramallah. The ambulance was transporting a sick Palestinian child and his relatives, but a suicide explosives belt was found under the child's stretcher. During the subsequent interrogation, the ambulance driver, Islam Jibril, a wanted Fatah Tanzim terrorist, admitted that he used the ambulance to carry explosives to terrorist associates in Ramallah.[29]

Hamas Operatives in the United States

ON JULY 27, 2004, the U.S. Department of Justice unsealed an indictment against the Holy Land Foundation (HLF), the largest Muslim charity in the United States, charging that the HLF had funneled $12.4 million over a six-year period to individuals and groups associated with Hamas. The $12.4 million was transferred to Hamas, according to the indictment, between 1995 (when President Clinton named Hamas a terrorist organization) and 2001 (when federal agents raided the HLF offices in Richardson, Texas, and closed down the organization).[30]

Then, on August 20, 2004, the U.S. Department of Justice unsealed a second indictment, naming a senior political leader of Hamas and two others who operated in the United States over a fifteen-year period to launder millions of dollars to the terrorist organization to finance murders, assaults, kidnappings, and passport fraud.[31]

An individual common to both indictments was Mousa Abu Marzook. Marzook was born in the Gaza Strip in 1951. He studied in the United States in the 1980s, where he pursued a Ph.D. in industrial engineering. For fifteen years, he lived in Louisiana and Virginia. In the United States, Marzook founded both the HLF and a parent organization, the Council on American-Islamic Relations (CAIR). Both organizations appeared innocent enough. HLF was billed as an Islamic charity set up to implement "zakat," or charitable giving, one of the five pillars of Islam. The CAIR was touted as a "civil rights" organization designed to promote Muslims living and working in America. The FBI and the Department of Justice believe the whole point was to create an elaborate scheme for Hamas operatives in the United States to collect dollars here and pass them to Hamas overseas to fund acts of terrorism against Israel.[32]

Marzook at the time of the indictments was living in Damascus, Syria. In 1991 Marzook had moved to Jordan, where he served as chairman of the Hamas political bureau. In Jordan he was suspected of planning terrorist attacks with other Hamas operatives. In 1995 he was arrested in the United States at JFK Airport in New York as he was returning from a trip to the Middle East. The United States deported Marzook to Jordan. In 1999 Jordan deported Marzook to Syria.

Syria charged that the August 2004 indictments were a prelude to a U.S. decision to impose sanctions against it. Ahmad Haj Ali, an adviser to Syria's information minister, had a second excuse ready for the Associated Press: "America is in the middle of presidential election campaigns, with the dilemma of its economic policies and wanting to shift the focus away from Iraq and Palestine, (Washington is) increasing the heat against Syria."[33] Ali sounded like he had listened to too many John Kerry attacks against President Bush.

None of the charges have yet been proved. Still, the charges give credence to comments made by Ken Piernick, a retired FBI agent who was the head of the unit inside the FBI's counterterrorism bureau that handled Hamas and Hezbollah. In April 2004 Piernick told the *New York Sun* that Hamas and Hezbollah logistical cells in the United States were ready to be activated into operational terrorist cells within our borders: "Where there are cells of supporters, with not too much additional energy applied by motivated recruiters or leaders, they can shift them into a more operational posture. In the United States up until recently we have not seen that shift from either Hamas or Hezbollah. But that doesn't mean they are not able to do that. They are very able to do this. And second, they are not going to do it in a way that we are likely to see it. It will be subtle and secretive."[34]

Hezbollah Hate Television Shut Down in the United States

AT THE end of December 2004 the U.S. State Department added al-Manar, the official television station of Hezbollah, to the Terrorism Exclusion List. This decision effectively barred al-Manar from broadcasting in the United States. Up until that decision, al-Manar was available in the United States through Intelsat, a Barbados-owned satellite company with offices in Washington DC, and through GlobeCast, a satellite provider owned by the French. IntelSat and GlobeCast immediately removed al-Manar once they received the State Department's notification.[35]

Around the globe an estimated ten million to fifteen million people watch al-Manar daily. One critic has appropriately called al-Manar "The Suicide Channel."[36] The whole purpose of the channel is to indoctrinate potential suicide victims and their families to accept the glorious mission of killing yourself for Allah. The programming includes preparing the families for the inevitable psychological impact of sacrificing their children to the cause.

Consider this segment below, taken from an al-Manar broadcast that portrays how a mother on Mother's Day deals with the suicide of her son:

Interviewer: "In addition to your being the mother of a martyr, it so happened that your son was martyred on this very day—'Mother's Day.' Let's begin with a few words from you to all our viewers today. What are the feelings and emotions of a martyr's mother every year on this day?"

Umm Said: "In the name of Allah the Compassionate and Merciful, Allah be praised for granting my son to me, on this blessed day. I cannot begin to explain what this day means to me, how great and significant it is for me and all the martyrs' mothers. I am talking about the martyrs' mothers and all mothers in Lebanon. Whatever I could say about them would not be enough, especially since they paid the price in blood, liberated southern Lebanon, and brought us closer to victory. They granted us a great reward.

"It is enough that they granted us paradise, the greatest thing in this world. I wish a good year to all the martyrs' mothers and our children, may Allah honor them. Allah be praised for having granted us our sons. Allah be praised."

Interviewer: "Do you feel that as a martyr's mother you have a special status that is different from that of mothers who don't have martyred sons?"

Umm Said: "Definitely, definitely . . ."

Interviewer: "How do you cope with this?"

Umm Said: "If I am in the company of others, I can sense the respect and the pride. They say, 'She's a martyr's mother.' What does this name mean? For me, it's very meaningful. I walk with my head high. Allah be praised, Allah be praised, every hour and every minute."[37]

Hour after hour of the station's programming presents all aspects of hate and religion that make the decision to commit "holy suicide" compelling to Hezbollah and its followers. Hezbollah's General Secretary Hassan Nasrallah frequently appears in person to make sure the messages of "Death to Israel" and "Death to America" come through loud and clear.

Expert Avi Jorisch has studied al-Manar intensively. Here is his graphic summary of the station's message:

Al-Manar defines its public enemy as the United States (the Great Satan) and Israel (the little Satan). Its programming themes are anti-Americanism, anti-Zionism, and revolution. U.S. foreign policy is presented as hegemonic and oppressive. The visual interpretation of this perspective is shown by a graphic video depicting the Statue of Liberty with a skull face, holding a blade instead of a torch as cascades of blood drip down her gown. As this horrifying image is being shown, names of nations in which the United States is said to have intervened—such as Iran, Panama, Somalia, Afghanistan, and Laos—pop out on the screen, and with a grand finale message that "America owes blood to all of humanity." Indeed, al-Manar equates U.S. leadership with that of the fascists of World War II; for example, photographs of President George W. Bush and Adolf Hitler are displayed side by side with the caption "History Repeats Itself."

The United States is depicted as an evil entity because it supports institutional-
ized state terrorism—that is, Israel.[38]

The Hezbollah reality is an *Alice in Wonderland* world where "up" is
"down" and "left" is "right." This probably is required for what amounts to a
religious cult willing to indoctrinate youths into thinking that suicide is not
death but glorious martyrdom that results in life everlasting in a heavenly
paradise. Have we learned nothing from the twentieth century? How many
twisted philosophies—the "isms" of Nazism, communism, etc.—do we have
to hear preach this reverse logic of hatred in which "good" is "evil" and vice
versa before we get the point?

Unfortunately, Hezbollah and the mad mullahs in Iran who serve as the
wizards behind this particular screen of Oz understand the powerful psychological impact of their inverted message. "Preach enough hate in as big a lie as you
can imagine" is a formula demagogues have used for centuries. That many will
believe the lie has been the calculation of propagandists throughout history.
Whenever we see hatred of the Jews, we should sound an alarm. Those preaching hatred of the Jews inevitably want to kill us as well. Most typically, Jew-
haters end up wanting to kill everyone but themselves. Yet to stop Jew-haters
when their evil power reaches levels of world importance may take a world
war, such as the one we are currently fighting, whether we realize it or not.

On December 14, 2004, the French Council of State ordered the French
satellite company Eutelsat to end broadcasts in France and Europe from the
Hezbollah-owned Lebanese television station al-Manar. The highest administra-
trative court made this ruling after determining that al-Manar violated a ban
on hate speech. A spokesperson for al-Manar claimed the French Council of
State had been pressured by Israeli and other Jewish lobbies to make this adverse decision.[39]

But even this decision would not stop Europeans from watching al-
Manar. Four different satellites carry al-Manar to Europe; seven satellites
broadcast al-Manar around the world.[40]

On December 24, 2004, Iranian Foreign Minister Kamal Kharrazi was in
Beirut to meet with Hezbollah leader Hassan Nasrallah and Lebanese President Emile Lahoud. Kharrazi objected strongly to the U.S. decision to ban al-
Manar: "How can a media organization be considered terrorist? Where is the
freedom of expression? In other words, anyone in the future who speaks out
against the Americans will be accused of terrorism. This is their philosophy."

Kharrazi's response utilized a typical tactic of the mullahs—throw the blame back on the United States and Israel. After all, in the mad mullahs' peculiar mind-set, the United States and Israel are the Satans of this drama, not the mullahs.

The Karine-A

ON JANUARY 3, 2002, the Israel Defense Force seized in the Red Sea, some three hundred miles south of Israel, a freighter owned by the Palestinian Authority. The four-thousand-ton freighter, named the *Karine-A*, was loaded with fifty tons of rocket launchers, antitank missiles, mortars, AK-47 assault rifles, sniper rifles, shotguns, short- and long-range Katyusha rockets, and powerful C-4 explosives.[41] Some of the antitank missiles had been manufactured in Iran. The weapons were packed in special waterproof containers that were designed to be dropped in the Mediterranean Sea where they could be picked up by smaller craft and brought to shore. Israeli Defense Minister Binyamin Ben-Eliezer estimated that the Palestinian Authority had spent more than one hundred million dollars on the arms shipment.

The captain of the ship, Omar Akawi, told reporters that he had been a member of Yasser Arafat's Fatah movement since 1976 and that he undertook the risky operation to help the outgunned Palestinians defend themselves. Akawi added that he picked up the ammunition shipment off the Iranian coast in the Persian Gulf, and the arms were headed for Palestinian-controlled Gaza. Akawi believed that Hezbollah was involved because he recognized a Hezbollah man when the weapons were loaded.[42]

The Palestinians would have gained tactical advantages had these weapons been successfully delivered. The Katyusha rockets would have permitted militant terrorists to hit populated sections of Jerusalem and Tel Aviv. The antitank munitions could have limited Israel's ability to enter Palestinian-controlled territory.

Israel immediately charged that Yasser Arafat was involved in the arms shipment. Arafat's reaction was less than convincing. First, he charged that Israel had "made up" the story of the *Karine-A;* then, in view of the evidence that was presented, Arafat objected that the operation was too sophisticated to have been planned by the Palestinian Authority. Still, Akawi held to his story that he was on a mission for the Palestinian Authority.[43]

On October 18, 2004, an Israeli court sentenced Akawi to twenty-five years in prison for weapons smuggling.

The *Karine A* incident again demonstrates that terrorists are operating together in attacking Israel, overlooking divisive factors to cooperate in the pursuit of the common enemy. As Michael Ledeen has pointed out, "The CIA soon had dramatic evidence of Sunni-Shi'ite cooperation in the celebrated case of the *Karine-A*, the ship loaded with tons of explosives and Iranian weapons intercepted in early 2002 by the Israel Defense Forces en route from Dubai—a major Iranian operational base—to the Palestinian Authority. Iran is the operational definition of Shi'ism, and the Palestinians are Sunnis. The weapons were Iranian and the ship and its captain were Sunni. If that didn't cause our experts to reconsider the theory of unbridgeable Sunni/Shi'ite hostility, what would?"[44]

Moreover, the reach of the terror masters is more than regional; ultimately it's global—first Israel, then America. To accomplish their goals, the terror masters will make whatever deals they have to make to bring together different terrorist organizations and the many rogue states supporting them. Al-Qaeda is but one of the many names under which the enemy operates.

We should expect to see different terror heroes at different moments and various terror organizations that are at the top today or tomorrow. Still, the enemy in all its various forms remains the same—radical Islamic extremism. Among the radical Islamic extremists there are no terror masters more determined or more ruthless than the mad mullahs ruling Iran.

Iran Sends Insurgents into Iraq

ON DECEMBER 15, 2004, Iraqi Defense Minister Hazem Al-Shaalan accused Iran of sending insurgents into Iraq and of supporting the al-Qaeda group operating in Iraq led by Abu Musab al-Zarqawi, the Jordanian-born al-Qaeda terrorist. Al-Zarqawi's group was charged by Shaalan with running a brutal campaign of hostage-taking, beheadings, and bombings, all aimed at victimizing Americans and Iraqis who are determined to build a democracy movement within Iraq.[45]

Shaalan also pointed to the arrest of Moayad Ahmed Yasseen, also known as Abu Ahmed, the leader of the Jaish Mohammed (Mohammed's Army) terrorist group in November 2004 during the coalition-led operations to uproot insurgents in Fallujah. "When we arrested the commander of Jaish Mohammed, we discovered that the key to terrorism is in Iran, which is the number one enemy for Iraq," said Shaalan, leaving no doubt about the role Iran was playing in fueling the insurgency. Shaalan further charged that Jaish Mohammed was cooperating with al-Zarqawi and al-Qaeda in the killing and beheading of several Iraqis, Arabs, and foreigners in Iraq. "They are fighting us because we want to build freedom and democracy and they want to build an Islamic dictatorship and have turbaned clerics to rule in Iraq."[46]

In January 2005 Iraqi Defense Minister Shaalan made two very sharp statements objecting to Iranian interference in Iraq. On Wednesday, January 5, 2005, Shaalan accused Iran of sending insurgents across the border: "We have a strong belief that Iran is the main [party] accused in the deterioration of the security situation in Iraq, such as illegal entry, smuggling of arms and means of sabotage. The proof which we have bears witness to Iran's responsibility in many operations that have shaken Iraq's stability."[47]

The next day Shaalan expressed concern that Iran had sent more than a million Iranians into Iraq to pose as Iraqis in the upcoming elections. He was concerned that Iran was trying to engineer an Iranian-backed Iraqi government. "It is estimated that the minimum that Iran wants is to dominate southern Iraq. If we go to Basra, we will not hear an Arabic accent, rather we will hear a Farsi accent, and this is also true of Najaf and Al-Kut provinces." The defense minister called this influx of Iranians "a sign of significant meddling." Shaalan was forceful that Iraq had proof: "We have intelligence indicating that Iran is sending fake families to Iraq, many of whom are based in Karbala, Najaf, Baghdad, Al-Amara, and Al-Kut; the documents are in our hands."[48]

The number of a million Iranians slipping across the border into Iraq was the same figure cited by Jordan's King Abdullah II, who charged in December 2004 that the mullahs wanted to create a "Shi'ite Crescent from Iran to Syria and Lebanon."[49]

Figuring out the mullahs' intentions in Iran is not easy, except to calculate that they are up to no good. The only clear objective the mullahs have is to beat the United States. The clerics who currently rule Iran want the United States swept out of the Middle East. Should democracy take hold in Iraq, the principle of theocratic rule that is central to the mullahs' view of the world would be challenged. This the mullahs cannot tolerate.

Yes, Iranians are predominately Shi'ites, and as such, they want to reach out to the Shi'ites in southern Iraq. There are, however, complications. Just because both are Shi'ites does not mean they are the same people. Remember, Iranians are by nationality Persians and their language is Farsi. The Iraqi Shi'ites speak Arabic and are not Persians. Still, Iranian Shi'ites have strong ties to Iran. Traditionally, "the most promising Iranian students and clerics have studied at the seminaries of Najaf and Karbala to perfect their knowledge of Arabic and their exegesis of religious texts. Clerical Iraqi and Iranian families have often intermarried—though there is much less intermarriage now than there was in the early 20th century before highly nationalistic dictatorships in both countries started forming contemporary identities."[50]

Do not forget the eight-year war Iran fought with Iraq from 1980 through 1988. Shi'ites on both sides fought bitterly against one another. Today Iran wants a Shi'ite crescent stretching from Tehran to Damascus and Beirut, but only if the crescent is governed by an Islamic theocracy with the Iranian mullahs at the top. The mullahs are religious, but once their religion hijacked the government, the religion transformed into a theocracy that acts like a nationalistic tyranny surging ahead in an expansionist mode.

A London-based Arabic newspaper carried an interview with Iranian defector Haj Sa'idi, a former intelligence officer who was in charge of activities in Iraq. Sa'idi claimed that Iran had infiltrated agents from the Iranian Revolutionary Guards into Iraq from Zakho in the north to Umm al-Qasr in the south, an infiltration not limited to Shi'ite cities.

He reported that Iran also brought the radical cleric Muqtada al-Sadr to Tehran and allegedly spent up to eighty million dollars a month to train, equip, pay, and clothe Al-Sadr's dissident militia. Former intelligence officer Haj Sa'idi asserted that Iran had rented some twenty-seven hundred apartments and rooms in Karbala and Najaf for infiltrated agents from the Iranian National Guard who were sent to Iran to assist al-Sadr.[51]

The Iranian Revolutionary Guard is also reported to have trained some eight hundred to twelve hundred of Al-Sadr's "Mahdi army" at three camps along the southern Iraqi border. Hezbollah, one of the mullah's surrogate terrorist arms, also did its best to organize extremist Islamic "charities" to shuffle funds to al-Sadr's terrorist purposes instead of their own. Still, for all the attention he has drawn to himself, al-Sadr is by no means accepted by the other Shi'ite clerics in Iraq.[52]

There is good evidence al-Sadr and his minions tried to kill the Grand Ayatollah Ali al-Sistani (who is an Iranian by birth), perhaps with dreams that al-Sadr could replace al-Sistani as a leader of the Iraqi Shi'ites. There was little likelihood that would ever happen, except maybe in al-Sadr's dreams. Al-Sistani is revered for his wisdom and scholarly mastery of Islam; to most Iraqi Shi'ites (and to most observing Americans), al-Sadr is a hotheaded wannabe, not a legitimate heir to a serious Shi'ite imam like al-Sistani.[53]

The vast majority of Shi'ites in Iraq could rightly consider Muqtada al-Sadr to be a questionable religious leader at best and the Mahdi army of his followers a bunch of thugs at worst. Al-Sadr is popular with the mullahs, not because he is a Shi'ite, but because he is willing to submit to their authority and to do their bidding in Iraq.

Unfortunately for al-Sadr and for the mullahs, there has been no popular outpouring of support for the thirty-year-old rabble-rouser or his Mahdi army in Najaf or anywhere else in Iraq. Honest Iraqi Shi'ites are appalled that al-Sadr would desecrate mosques with sandbags and machine guns just to protect himself while he hid like a coward.[54]

Iran is trying to have the situation in Iraq both ways. By moving in Iranian Shi'ites to vote in the Iraqi election, the mullahs are playing along with the democracy movement, trying to stack the deck in their favor. By supporting vocal extremists like al-Sadr, the mullahs are playing the anti-American card, trying to create a scene the liberal anti-American press will portray worldwide to argue that the insurgency in Iraq has created for the United States another "Vietnam quagmire."

Either way, the mullahs have done what they do best—they caused trouble in the hope that no matter what happens, they will come out the winners. Nor were the mullahs particularly concerned whether they had to work with Shi'ites or against Shi'ites. So, too, forming an alliance with al-Qaeda seemed perfectly in order as well. The mullahs are determined to oppose America and to do their utmost to break the democracy movement in Iraq. How they accomplish those goals is simply a matter of tactics. The mullahs are more than willing to be expedient in their goal to unsettle any movement forward in Iraq. What the mullahs did not compromise was their determination to advance themselves and their cause of exporting their radical Islamic theocracy at any and all costs.

In the final analysis, the mullahs are opportunistic. They also think nationalistically. Like all tyrants, the mullahs want to impose their own vision of themselves on the rest of the world, whether the world wants to accept them or not. The mullahs are also insane with hate, and suicidal. No matter how bizarre the thought is, the mullahs would accept a nuclear attack on themselves in retaliation for a nuclear strike on Israel. Why? The mullahs would calculate they would wipe out a huge percentage of the Jews in the world by dropping nuclear bombs on Israel, while an Israeli nuclear retaliation on Iran would only kill a small percentage of the world's Muslims.

7

Sleeper Cells and Nuclear Bombs

The Threat to American Homeland Security

Until the moment American Airlines Flight 11 slammed into the north tower of the World Trade Center at 8:46:40 a.m. on Tuesday, September 11, 2001, few people in the United States worried that there might be lethal terrorist sleeper cells living among them. By 9:03:11 a.m., when United Airlines Flight 175 slammed into the south tower of the World Trade Center, most people who watched the tragedy unfold on television realized that they were witnessing a terrorist attack, not an airplane accident.

The horrifying sights of the building exploding in fireballs, the smoke billowing miles into the air, people jumping to their deaths from the high floors are images that were burned that morning into the American consciousness like virtually no other image in the country's history.

At 9:37:46 a.m., when American Airlines Flight 77 crashed into the Pentagon, few had any doubt that terrorists had attacked us on our own soil. Then United Airlines Flight 93 went down in a rural field in Somerset County, Pennsylvania, at 10:15 a.m., and the country knew to say a prayer that the Capitol or the White House had not been hit.

A major point of this book is that the tragedy of 9/11 might well be small in light of what the terrorists have planned for America. If the mad mullahs can pull it off, the sight of a nuclear cloud roiling over New York or Washington DC would dwarf the glee they derived from our misery over the 9/11 attacks.

Most likely a nuclear terrorist attack in a major U.S. city would come just as 9/11 came—unannounced and unanticipated. A sleeper cell like the nineteen terrorists who destroyed the World Trade Center and hit the Pentagon may be living with us right now, unseen, below the surface, ready to strike when the order is given. It is frightening to think that people who are living among us now as apparently ordinary citizens are secretly planning when, where, and how to explode a nuclear weapon in one of our major cities.

Why Sleeper Cell Terrorists Are Hard to Find

AMERICA HAS porous borders. One problem is that those borders are so large. Our northern border with Canada stretches more than four thousand miles; our southern border with Mexico runs about half that length, some two thousand miles. The second problem is that long stretches of both borders are unpopulated and not regularly patrolled, except possibly by aircraft from above.

Every year, nearly three hundred thousand immigrants are admitted from Canada, a country that typically does not detain those claiming refuge. Every year some ten thousand immigrants with questionable backgrounds disappear into Canada's ethnic communities. Government authorities estimate that there are somewhere between nine million and twelve million illegal aliens living today in the continental United States. In reality, there is no way of knowing the precise number. Most illegal immigrants pass quiet lives in ethnic communities where no one knows exactly how they got into the country.[1]

U.S. authorities have no doubt there are terrorist sleeper cells in our midst. In 2002 the FBI concluded in an internal review that somewhere between fifty and one hundred Hamas and Hezbollah operatives had infiltrated into America. The FBI believed these operatives "were in America working on fund-raising and logistics, and they had received terrorist and military training from Lebanon and other countries in the Middle East, giving Hamas and Hezbollah the capability of launching terrorist strikes."[2]

In 2004 the FBI suggested that al-Qaeda sleeper cells were believed to be operating in forty states, awaiting orders and funding for new attacks on U.S. soil. The bureau believed that these agents were being funded "by millions of dollars solicited by an extensive network of bogus charities and foundations," with the cells using "Muslim communities as cover and places to raise cash and recruit sympathizers."[3] U.S. law-enforcement authorities claimed to have satellite photos and communications intercepts that documented between sixty and seventy camps in Pakistan-occupied Kashmir and in Pakistan.[4] Still, finding sleeper-cell terrorists is very difficult, especially with the presumption of innocence and extensive legal rights and civil liberties granted suspects under U.S. law.

Scott Wheeler, an investigative reporter writing on the Internet, demonstrated the problems inherent in uncovering terrorist sleeper cells. Wheeler became interested in the United Association for Studies and Research (UASR), a group identified as a Muslim think tank based in Springfield, Virginia. He quoted a George Mason University professor who claimed that the UASR was a "front organization for a terrorist group," a "phony organization" that was part of a "shell game of international terrorism."[5] Wheeler noted that many meetings at the UASR started at midnight, with participants emerging to use their cell phones in the parking lot, as if to avoid government counterterrorism units that may have hidden listening devices inside the building.

As Wheeler probed, he found that the UASR had questionable connections. The group was founded by Mousa Abu Marzook, a Hamas operative discussed in the previous chapter, a Palestinian by birth who is now a fugitive living in Syria under federal indictment for his involvement in the Holy Land Foundation Islamic charity scandal. According to a report in the *Washington Post*, Marzook participated in a real-estate scheme designed to defraud affluent Muslims into buying development homes in Prince George County, just ten miles from the White House, with the result that the development company partly owned by Marzook went bankrupt while all proceeds were siphoned off to fund Hamas terrorist activities overseas.[6]

Wheeler was also suspicious that the UASR's current head, Ahmed Yousef, had ties to Hamas. Yousef gave an interview to a Middle Eastern magazine in which he claimed that 9/11 was a Jewish plot: "No one could have captured the pictures [of the 9/11 attacks] so perfectly except for the cameras in the hands of several Mossad agents, who were near the scene of events and succeeded in filming the scene so that it will always serve Zionism to remind the world of the Arabs' and Muslims' crimes against America." Why would Mossad do this? As Yousef explained, Mossad had "a grand scheme—and right-wing forces may have participated in it, and Evangelical

Christians agreed to it. All of them agreed that this scheme should be carried out in this way to push America into war."

Yet inevitably those suspected of being sleeper-cell terrorists hire attorneys who claim that their clients are being discriminated against simply because they are Muslims. Wheeler had uncovered interesting circumstantial evidence, but he did not have enough proof to support the claim that the UASR was a terrorist front organization.

Even with the extensive tools allowed law-enforcement officials under legislation passed since 9/11, legal barriers still impede law-enforcement efforts to find sleeper cell terrorists. Consider the case of Dhiren Barot, a suspected al-Qaeda operative who spent time in New Jersey in 2000 and 2001. The FBI was trying to track whether any of Barot's associates remained in the area when a federal court ruled that a key investigative tool of the FBI was no longer available. Specifically, the court decided that the use of a special subpoena known as a national security letter (NSL) was unconstitutional. When the FBI tracked companies that Barot had been involved with through e-mails, the court ruling prohibited the agents from getting key customer information without judicial review.[7]

Nor do the Patriot Act powers solve the problem. Federal terrorist investigators still must play by rules, and the rules as interpreted by the courts still typically specify that the suspect's rights are paramount. Our system of criminal laws is designed to err on the side of presumed innocence.

In a society as open as ours, there are hundreds of mosques in which zealous preaching could convey a message intended to convert or recruit terrorist prospects, as well as hundreds of Muslim charities whose fund-raising purposes may be questioned as illegitimate. Then there are religious and ethnic support organizations whose purposes might be suspect. But after decades of liberal court rulings dealing with civil rights, any attempt at religious or ethnic profiling is an unacceptable practice for law-enforcement officers. Profiling is even frowned upon even when marginally suggested by editorialists or pundits.[8]

During the 2004 presidential campaign Vice President Dick Cheney made comments that suggested the administration was taking the threat of nuclear terrorism seriously: "The biggest threat we face now as a nation is the possibility of terrorists ending up in the middle of one of our cities with deadlier weapons than have ever been used against us—biological agents or a nuclear weapon or a chemical weapon of some kind—to be able to threaten the lives of hundreds of thousands of Americans."[9]

From a terrorist's point of view, it may still be relatively easy to slip into America unnoticed. Who among us doubts that if the 9/11 terrorists had possessed a nuclear weapon, they would have used it?

Do Terrorists Have Suitcase Nuclear Bombs?

ON SEPTEMBER 7, 1997, former Russian National Security Adviser Alexander Lebed created a worldwide sensation when he was interviewed on CBS's 60 Minutes. He claimed that 100 of 250 suitcase-sized nuclear bombs were missing and no longer in the control of the Russian military.[10] The suitcase bombs described by Lebed are small but powerful. Said to measure twenty-four-by-sixteen-by-eight inches, each suitcase bomb was capable of killing up to one hundred thousand people if detonated in a major U.S. city during business hours. The Russians predictably denied that the suitcase nukes existed. But if the suitcase nukes hypothetically existed, the Russians insisted they were all accounted for.[11]

Then, on January 24, 2000, Representative Dan Burton (R-IN) brought a mock-up of a suitcase nuclear bomb to a congressional hearing on Russian espionage. Burton displayed the suitcase bomb to the congressional committee and to the press. The startling photos of the prototype suitcase bomb made headlines around the globe.[12] At the hearing, Representative Curt Weldon (R-PA) elicited testimony from Stanislav Lunev, an ex-Soviet colonel who defected to the United States in 1992 after he had worked for more than ten years in the United States as an intelligence operative. Lunev claimed he had collected information on the U.S. president and senior U.S. political and military leaders so they could be targeted for assassination in the event of war. As part of this mission, Lunev claimed to have obtained from the Soviet Union several suitcase nuclear bombs that were prepositioned in the United States and stored in hiding places where they could be concealed until needed.[13]

Subsequent research verified that the Soviet Union did produce suitcase nuclear bombs, just as the United States had developed small tactical nuclear weapons of the Davy Crockett type and what were known as "backpack" nuclear weapons. Typically, these weapons have a relatively small yield, in the range of one kiloton; additionally, the suitcase nuclear bombs had a relatively short life span, with key components required to be replaced approximately every six months.[14]

By 2002 international experts studying suitcase nuclear bombs had examined Soviet records comprehensively. Their conclusion doubted that any of these munitions had been lost: "Thus, the hypothesis that a number of portable nuclear devices remained outside Russia or were stolen during the transfer to Russia does not appear convincing. Both the circumstances of that transfer and the likelihood that reasonably complete records exist (even though they might be divided among several holders) lead to a conclusion that former republics of the Soviet Union are an unlikely source of unaccounted for suitcase nukes."[15]

Still, reports that terrorists have acquired suitcase nukes persist. On March 22, 2004, Osama bin Laden's authorized biographer, Pakistani journalist Hamid Mir, reasserted to the Australian Broadcasting Corporation that al-Qaeda had purchased suitcase nuclear bombs.[16] Mir said the claim was made by bin Laden's deputy, Ayman al-Zawahri, in a November 2001 interview: "Dr. Ayman al-Zawahri laughed and he said 'Mr. Mir, if you have $30 million, go to the black market in central Asia, contact any disgruntled Soviet scientist, and a lot of . . . smart briefcase bombs are available. They have contacted us, we sent our people to Moscow, to Tashkent, to other central Asian states and they negotiated, and we purchased some suitcase bombs."[17]

The Russians would like us to believe that all suitcase nukes have been found and are safely accounted for. Probably too there are some in our government who want us to think that suitcase nukes were always low yield and difficult to maintain at operational levels, so there was no need for worry. Yet, thinking cynically, but perhaps realistically, where there is a lot of cash available and where criminals are involved, weapons that exist can usually be purchased, even if they are supposedly safely hidden away.

Moreover, if al-Qaeda, or any other terrorist organization for that matter, has a suitcase nuke and is waiting for a good opportunity to use it, the likelihood is that the terrorists could also buy the nuclear talent needed to keep the weapon operational. Since 1997 there has been constant speculation by credible authorities that suitcase nukes exist and that terrorists like al-Qaeda are in the market for them. Unfortunately, the only definitive proof we could get that would end the debate would be the same type of catastrophic proof we got on 9/11. As we have noted before, terrorists pursue weapons, and they like to use them when they get them.

How do the mullahs fit into this particular equation? In July 2004 a report surfaced on the Internet that government terrorism officials were privately admitting concerns that Hamas was merging with elements of al-Qaeda to carry out military strikes against the United States.[18] While certain philosophical differences may divide Hamas and al-Qaeda, the two groups have begun cooperating tactically in the global holy war, operating under the banner "International Islamic Front for Jihad Against Jews and Crusaders," according to the government officials who warned about more attacks on U.S. soil.

Dirty Bombs

A DIRTY bomb is not really a nuclear bomb. Instead, a dirty bomb uses a conventional explosion to disperse deadly radiation. Technically, dirty bombs are considered "radiological dispersion devices." Some designs call for devices that simply emit radiation without requiring an explosion to produce the deadly result. This variation is known as a "radiation emission device." For this discussion, we are going to focus on devices that involve explosions, and we will code-name the device a radiation explosive device (RED).

On December 21, 2004, just four days before Christmas, the United States elevated the terror threat level to orange, and Department of Energy scientists were dispatched to Washington, New York, Las Vegas, Los Angeles, and Baltimore in response to credible intelligence reports that al-Qaeda was planning to launch a dirty-bomb attack in one of those cities. On the same day, the Department of Homeland Security sent out large fixed radiation detectors and hundreds of paper-size radiation detectors to police departments across the nation, including the cities of Washington, New York, Los Angeles, Las Vegas, Chicago, Houston, San Diego, San Francisco, Seattle, and Detroit.[19]

Many sources are available to obtain the radioactive material needed to construct a dirty bomb. One good candidate is cesium-137, a highly radioactive substance that is commonly used in heavy industry. While uranium is at the top of the list of radioactive materials available in illicit trafficking, "cesium-137 is the second-most common with 53 seizures between 1993 and 1998, which contributed to 22.6 percent of all radioactive material seizures."[20] Authorities estimate that there are more than eighteen thousand sources of industrial radiation available today in America, involving a wide range of different chemicals and an equally wide range of applications from medical technology to food irradiation.[21]

An analysis of half-life and radioactivity, as well as a realistic evaluation of how portable and dispersible a radioactive substance really is, leads to a conclusion that "only a small fraction of the existing millions of sources pose a high security risk."[22] Still, the challenge of protecting radioactive materials is huge, simply because there are tens of thousands of sites worldwide from which terrorists could steal or buy the radioactive materials they would need to make a dirty bomb.

Detonating radioactive material would cause fallout and contamination that would cause radiation sickness in many of those exposed. Serious illness, even death, could result, depending upon the amount and intensity of the radioactive material released and the health or susceptibility to radiation poisoning of those persons exposed to the hazard. Physical areas impacted by the dirty bomb would need to be quarantined and detoxified before they could be used again. The cleanup process could be long and expensive; some structures might be so toxic that destroying them might be the only solution.

A terrorist attack using a RED would produce chaos and fear; however, the number of actual casualties might be relatively small. We can imagine a coordinated attack where a group of terrorists planned simultaneous or near-simultaneous dirty-bomb explosions within one city, with the aim of shutting down the city, at least temporarily, and intensifying the shock-and-fear value of the attack by successfully pulling off multiple coordinated attacks.

Combine the RED with the suicide car-bomb methodology. Five terrorists driving automobiles with a RED in the trunk could effectively shut down a city as large as Manhattan, produce a number of deaths, and induce fear that would be felt around the nation for weeks, if not months, simply as a result of the media "feeding frenzy" coverage that would be certain to result. One terrorist could be assigned to explode the RED at a specified time in the Lincoln Tunnel. The second terrorist car bomb could stop on the George Washington Bridge, detonating the RED at or near the center of the bridge. Either of these bombs, if sufficiently large, might also cause significant structural damage to the tunnel or the bridge, causing enough debris to clog the tunnel and enough impact to collapse either the whole bridge or a major section of it.

A third car could explode in the heart of Midtown, at one of the busiest intersections, such as Fifth Avenue and Fifty-seventh Street. A fourth car-bomb explosion could be targeted for the Wall Street area, perhaps designating the intersection of Broadway and Wall Street as ground zero. The fifth car could be assigned a destination of Times Square, at Forty-second Street. Having five car bombs explode like this on any given day in New York City would bring the town to a sudden halt, kill hundreds of people, contaminate parts of the city for months if not years, and cause massive fear that other attacks could be scheduled to follow either in New York City again or in any other major U.S. metropolis: Cleveland, Detroit, Boston, Chicago, Los Angeles, or San Francisco.

While these scenarios appeal to the terrorist mind, there are practical difficulties. Not only is stealing the required radioactive material difficult, the terrorists handling the substances might become seriously poisoned in the process. Assembling the RED would require technical skills and a safe laboratory environment to prevent further radiation contamination. Last, while the impact of the RED might be psychologically great, the true amount of death and destruction the explosion would produce is relatively small to terrorists who are dreaming of detonating nuclear weapons within our major cities.

For these reasons, the threat of dirty bombs is real, though we should not assume that a dirty bomb would be the weapon of choice, especially not for a group of skilled terrorists who would have the backing of a nuclear-armed rogue state such as Iran. The mad mullahs and their terrorist associates would, if possible, opt for a much more deadly scenario, one that could truly bring the civilized world to its knees in the space of one day. If serious terrorists are going to spend their time devising attacks, the terror masters directing them will move to the most feasible attack that can cause the maximum amount of damage. Why bother with anything less? That's how the terror masters can be expected to think.

The Improvised Nuclear Device: The Preferred Choice of Serious Terrorists

SUITCASE NUKES made great television when Congressmen Dan Burton and Curt Weldon held up the mock suitcase nuke. The device looked lethal, but also shiny and professional. The whole deal was a neat package, even if most of us had no idea how the silver-looking apparatus inside really operated. The mechanics of the device were not the point. The packaging was the image. That a terrorist might carry a suitcase bomb that looked like a photographer's equipment case and simply leave it in a public location (New York's Grand Central Station or Washington DC's Union Station) was a frightening idea. The terrorist could simply walk away, maybe even escape, and the device would explode before any bomb squad could decide what to do first. Even at one kiloton of yield, the image created was that the suitcase bomb could leave at least a minor mushroom cloud in the center of New York or Washington and vaporize a building or two, maybe even a few blocks, spraying the after-effects of subsequent radioactive death for miles.

The problem was that as serious researchers looked into the question, suitcase nukes were problematic. Maybe the former USSR had let a few get away. Still, their yield was low, and the devices required constant maintenance to remain operational.

What has emerged as a more serious threat, especially with the mad mullahs going nuclear, is what is known as the improvised nuclear device (IND). The IND has become the preferred choice of serious terrorists.

Why? The answer is a simple one. An IND requires the terrorists to get their hands on a quantity of fissile nuclear material for the purpose of fabricating a crude nuclear bomb. The IND does not have to be small enough to fit in a suitcase. The size can be considerably larger, maybe even large enough to fill the back of a truck, to take a page from Timothy McVeigh's Oklahoma City bombing. A larger mass of fissile material can cause a larger explosion, producing more serious damage. That is important, because terrorists are theatrical and they crave massive destruction for its image value and its shock quotient.

Also important is that the IND can be detonated with a crude mechanism, especially if the bomb relies on enriched uranium, which is much easier to detonate than plutonium. An IND produced on this model can be driven into a major city and parked. If the terrorists are smart enough not to use a rental truck, they might even drive it through the Lincoln Tunnel or over the George Washington Bridge without getting stopped by the police for an inspection.

How realistic is it to assume that terrorists could produce an IND? This is the critical question.

First, there are huge quantities of fissile nuclear material available all over the world, frequently without adequate inventory control or protection safeguards in place. The threat is real simply because "the amount of fissile material that might theoretically be accessible to terrorists is staggering."[23] The International Atomic Energy Agency (IAEA) defines the quantities of fissile material needed to be weapons significant as the amount of highly enriched uranium (HEU) or plutonium needed to make a nuclear weapon roughly equivalent to the explosive power of the Hiroshima and Nagasaki bombs. This translates into the requirement to have available about twenty-five kilograms of weapons-grade HEU and a much smaller quantity of plutonium, only eight kilograms.[24]

There is "substantial and credible evidence that both terrorist groups and hostile states are actively seeking to acquire stolen fissile material for nuclear weapons."[25] The U.S. military has uncovered in post-Taliban Afghanistan a significant quantity of al-Qaeda writings and drawings illustrating how to construct crude nuclear devices. U.S. analysts believe that al-Qaeda's alleged WMD commander, Abu Khabbab, was focused on efforts to obtain nuclear weapons capability.[26] On September 11, 2002, the first anniversary of 9/11, ABC News smuggled a fifteen-pound (6.8-kilogram) cylinder of depleted uranium, on loan from the National Resources Defense Council, into the United States and televised the story. On September 11, 2003, ABC News successfully repeated the experiment to smuggle the same cylinder of depleted uranium into the United States; again, the test was nationally televised. ABC News came to a frightening conclusion: "Security procedures at U.S. borders cannot detect highly enriched uranium."[27]

How hard is it to make an IND? Again, the simplest mechanism involves uranium. The Hiroshima bomb was basically a "gun-type" bomb, a design that "involves slamming masses of highly-enriched uranium together in a gun barrel-like tube."[28] Manhattan Project physicist Luis Alvarez affirms that making such a bomb is not complicated: "With modern weapons-grade uranium . . . terrorists, if they had such material, would have a good chance of setting off a high-yield explosion simply by dropping one half of the material onto the other half. . . . Even a high school kid could make a bomb in short order."[29]

A successful IND would need to have yields in the ten- to twenty-kiloton range, which would be equivalent to ten thousand to twenty thousand tons of TNT. A twenty-kiloton yield would be roughly the size of the bomb that destroyed Nagasaki. A bomb of this size would devastate the heart of any major U.S. city and would cause fire and radiation damage over a much wider area. By comparison, the conventional explosive that Timothy McVeigh used to destroy the federal building in Oklahoma City in 1995 involved five thousand pounds of fertilizer. The truck bomb used in the 1993 attempt to destroy the World Trade Center used about fifteen hundred pounds of fertilizer. Their TNT equivalent yields were 1.8 tons and 0.5 tons, respectively. "Thus even a nuclear yield of a few tons could, under certain circumstances, cause the destruction of a number of skyscrapers potentially resulting in many thousands of casualties, as well as widespread contamination."[30]

Critics on the political left have been making a case that the obstacles to successfully creating and detonating an IND make the likelihood pretty remote that a terrorist group could pull off a nuclear explosion in a major U.S. city. The easiest way for terrorists to get their hands on a nuclear weapon would be to steal or buy an existing bomb from the arsenal of some nuclear country, such as Pakistan or Russia. Consider this objection voiced in December 2004 in the pages of the *Washington Post*:

> It is unclear how quickly either country (Russia or Pakistan) could detect a theft, but experts said it would be very difficult for terrorists to figure out on their own how to work a Russian or Pakistani bomb.
>
> Newer Russian weapons, for example, are equipped with heat- and time-sensitive locking systems, known as permissive action links, that experts say would be extremely difficult to defeat without help from insiders.
>
> "You'd have to run it through a specific sequence of events, including changes in temperature, pressure and environmental conditions before the weapon would allow itself to be armed, for the fuses to fall into place and then for it to allow itself to be fired," said Charles D. Ferguson, science and technology fellow at the Council on Foreign Relations. "You don't get it off the shelf, enter a code and have it go off."[31]

The argument from the political left continues to examine how difficult it would be for terrorists to get their hands on enough HEU and how technically difficult it would be to create an IND from scratch. For the sake of argument, the critics assume that the terrorists would want at least fifty kilograms of bomb-grade uranium. That would mean buying and smuggling into the United States about 150 pounds of HEU. Reviewing the history of what we know about black market transactions to date, the successful transactions have been for much smaller quantities; besides, most often the terrorists simply get scammed by con artists who see an easy opportunity to make a quick buck. Assembling the IND would require a complex team of chemists and engineers experienced with nuclear technology. Then the assembly team would have to have a secure location where it could work covertly to put the device together.[32]

Even if the IND were preassembled, shipping it into the United States represents problems. Conceivably, an IND with about fifty kilograms of bomb-grade uranium could be made small enough to fit into a corner of a shipping container. The device could be transported on an oil supertanker; the thickness of steel used in a supertanker's hull and the use of double hulls would make detection more difficult. Still, to get through customs, the device would probably have to be packed in a lead-shield container. So getting a prefabricated IND into the United States represents additional problems.[33]

Then critics point to the Japanese cult Aum Shinrikyo, a group that was "intent on world destruction when it began its 1993 quest for a nuclear weapon, [and] had all the means to pull it off, on paper at least: money, expertise, a remote haven in which to work, and most important, a private uranium mine."[34] Yet the group made so many mistakes in judgment and planning that the plan to develop an IND was abandoned. Instead the group attempted the technically easier task of a chemical attack, which was executed in 1995 when members released the deadly poison sarin on the Tokyo subway.

Yet, given all these obstacles, the same critics acknowledge that a "primitive device could be assembled in a small garage using machine tools readily available at an auto shop and concealed in a lead-plated delivery truck about the size of a delivery van."[35] The technical problems are, according to the critics, the reason we have not yet seen a terrorist-delivered nuclear explosion in one of our major cities.

As comforting as the critics' analysis is, one major factor has come upon the scene that fundamentally alters the equation: *the atomic mullahs have now come upon the world.*

Operation IND: How the Mullahs Could Detonate a Nuclear Bomb in New York City

A GOOD reason that the mullahs and al-Qaeda might decide to work together is that the mullahs are about to have plenty of enriched uranium and al-Qaeda has the operational network to deliver a bomb. Moreover, as we have seen, there is good reason to believe that both Hezbollah and Hamas have operatives in place today within the United States. This gives Iran some operational resources on the ground to assist the al-Qaeda terrorists who may be in charge of actually driving the bomb into the city and detonating it. The Hezbollah- and Hamas-linked individuals indicted to date suggest that both organizations have managed to plant some highly educated individuals who might be able to recruit associates from within the ranks of American companies working right now on nuclear technology.

Studying how the 9/11 plan was executed gives us a blueprint for how the terror masters would put together an operational IND to deliver a nuclear attack on a U.S. city. The *9/11 Commission Report* presents a reasonably complete step-by-step summary of how al-Qaeda proceeded.[36]

For discussion purposes, we will code-name the plot Operation IND. The mastermind behind 9/11 was Khalid Sheikh Mohammad (KSM), whose nephew was Ramzi Yousef, the planner of the 1993 attack on the World Trade Center (WTC). KSM had spent time getting an education in the United States. He was also well traveled, with ties to terrorists in areas of the world ranging from Afghanistan and Pakistan to India, Indonesia, and Malaysia. He also had experience with a large selection of different terrorist schemes, including "conventional car bombing, political assassination, aircraft bombing, hijacking, reservoir poisoning, and, ultimately, the use of aircraft as missiles guided by suicide operators."[37]

The 9/11 plot also evolved as KSM studied the 1993 bombing of the WTC and decided he did not want to use a bomb to attack his target. He worked on the "Bojinka" plot to bomb twelve U.S. commercial jets over the Pacific during a two-day span, which triggered his thinking about coordinating multiple simultaneous attacks involving commercial airplanes. KSM considered himself a "terrorist entrepreneur," and he applied the "one idea leads to another" model as he evolved the 9/11 plot.[38]

A terrorist mastermind planning Operation IND would clearly study the Oklahoma City bombing, the first bombing of the WTC, and the bombing of the USS *Cole* in Yemen. Assume the target city would be New York. The detonation of a nuclear weapon as a follow-up to the 9/11 WTC attack would be sufficiently spectacular. And the economic damage done to the United States by taking out a large part of Manhattan would have a strong appeal to the terrorists. The second-most logical target would be Washington DC. The opportunity to destroy major segments of the U.S. government with one bomb blast would compete for top billing in the terrorists' imaginations.

A weapons team could be assembled in Iran, and a group of operational terrorists could be pulled together from around the world to be dropped in New York. Having access to Iran's many nuclear facilities already in place eliminates several major problems. The work to create an IND could be carried out clandestinely, almost as part of the daily operations of the sites where the work building the IND needed to be done. No one need know exactly what anyone else was working on; the Operation IND team could blend in with the hundreds of other nuclear scientists and technologists already working at Iranian nuclear facilities.

The weapon would most likely use HEU as fuel, with the design built along the gun-type design. Iran has sufficient uranium enrichment capabilities in place. Any permission granted by the IAEA to keep some enrichment centrifuges running for "research and development" purposes would make a perfect cover for some clandestine uranium enrichment to fuel the IND. When the reactor at Bushehr goes on-line, Iran would have fuel by-products that could be devoted to plutonium production. Still the delivery and detonation of a plutonium device is so much more complicated that it decreases the likelihood of a successful weapons-delivery effort in New York. The principle of "keep it simple" would probably dictate making the first IND a uranium device.

A nuclear Iran could keep in-house every part of the IND fabrication, from fuel enrichment to the weapon's design and manufacture. Probably the uranium would be produced in a metallic form for maximum power and minimum size and for ease of transportation. The device itself might be designed in a modular structure, so component pieces could be shipped separately and assembled after they arrive on the East Coast. This way the team on-site in the United States would have no fuel-enrichment or manufacturing requirements—just the need to assemble the parts as they arrived.

Mohamed Atta was the team leader of the operational terrorist group that implemented the 9/11 plan. Similarly, Operation IND would need to select an equally competent team leader. Like Atta, the team leader for Operation IND would have to speak English and have reasonable familiarity with the United States and American customs. Additional requirements would be for the person to be skilled at people management. Keeping a team of terrorists motivated and on purpose, yet comfortable enough to blend in, takes considerable talent not commonly found.

The 9/11 team members had different skill sets and command responsibilities. Some were selected to pilot the planes, others were selected to be the "muscle terrorists" who would subdue passengers and overpower the crews in the cockpits. Operation IND would need terrorists who knew New York and were comfortable presenting themselves as drivers and crew of the types of commercial trucks found every day on the streets of Manhattan. Depending on where the IND was to be delivered and how it was to be made "live," the operational team might need a member with some technical or engineering skills.

The weapon could be shipped to the United States via commercial carrier. Given the embargo currently blocking trade between the United States and Iran, components of the IND would have to be transported from Iran to countries where the pieces could be included in ship cargoes sailing to ports in

New York or Newark. Given the Hezbollah and Hamas ties already established in the United States, operatives who could be used in Operation IND might already be working at the ports or in banks where commercial shipping financial records could be created to finance and cover the component shipment. If bribes needed to be paid, the mullahs would wire funds through intermediaries in other nations to fraudulent bank accounts in the United States that had been set up to fund Operation IND, using fake personal identification or "front companies" equipped with business registration papers that made them appear legitimate.

The New York field team would have to be in place some months ahead of H-hour. Providing a sufficient window for arrival time would give terrorist operatives enough time to make one or more attempts at entry into the United States. Operatives would probably be assigned different methods of entry and their attempts staggered so that discovery of one might not tip off U.S. authorities to anticipate the arrival of a team or the beginning of a plot. Team members might not even be told in advance what they were doing or who else was on the team. Lists of arrival locations or Hezbollah-Hamas contact operatives to contact once in the United States might be all the information required prior to transit.

Operation IND would have some go, no-go decision points. These would key on whether all the components arrived on time and were delivered to the assembly point as predetermined. The plan might even involve some redundancy where more than one set of components might be scheduled for shipment, limited only by not wanting to send more redundant parts than absolutely necessary. There would be a trade-off between wanting to send the minimum number of shipments to reduce the odds of detection and wanting to send enough parts so the IND could be assembled even if everything did not arrive on time as anticipated.

Several days or weeks before H-hour, the truck planned to deliver the weapon would begin making scheduled runs into New York to establish a pattern of being seen and known. More than one truck could be used, so even the terrorist operatives would not themselves be sure who was "live," just to reduce nervousness or overreaction during the operation. Also, using more than one truck would always permit an advance truck to go over the delivery route so the mission could be called off if security were especially tight on the day planned for H-hour. Logistics could be made more secure by having components delivered to a location within Manhattan, so the fully assembled

IND would not have to be driven through a bridge or across a tunnel for placement as planned at H-hour.

The mullahs may be the driving force behind Operation IND, but the action itself would combine skills sets from across different terrorist organizations. Al-Qaeda may be best equipped to provide the delivery team on-site in New York. Hezbollah and Hamas would have responsibility of selecting and coordinating the activities of operatives already on-site in the United States. The nuclear scientists and engineers working at the nuclear facilities in Iran may come from nuclear operations in Iraq or Pakistan, possibly even North Korea.

Iran's involvement as a state-sponsor removes key barriers that critics have identified with IND operations as previously imagined or possibly even attempted. A rogue terrorist group no longer has to go on the black market to purchase HEU or to buy a weapon from an existing arsenal. Instead, the required HEU and the manufacture of the weapon itself would be undertaken as another task to be completed by Iran's state-operated ongoing nuclear operation. Nor would a complex team need to be positioned within the United States. At most, one or two operatives with scientific or engineering skills would need to be included on the U.S. operative team. The U.S. field team for Operation IND would have responsibilities limited to final weapon assembly, weapon delivery, and weapon detonation.

New York City Devastated by Operation IND: The Minute-by-Minute, Hour-by-Hour Horror of a Nuclear Explosion in the Heart of Manhattan

THE TERRORISTS' operational team would calculate the timing of the attack to permit them to enter the city with the least chance of detection and to arrive at the maximum opportunity to kill people. Entering New York City just as morning rush hour is tapering off would allow the terrorists to seek the cover of many vehicles crowding the highways. The police might spot check, but the urgency in most rush hours in New York is to keep traffic moving. Detonating the IND as the lunch hour is beginning gives the greatest chance to have people in the streets. Also, late morning arrivers would be at work by now, so the maximum expected population density for the day should have been achieved.

Detonating the IND in Midtown positions the bomb where the largest number of people would be located, in the many skyscrapers that house the city's offices. Assume the IND is detonated outside the Empire State Building at 11:45 a.m. Assume that the weapon is a 150-kiloton HEU gun-type bomb. Damage estimates can be scaled down to approximate damage and casualties should the bomb be a lower-yield weapon. Assume the day is the beautiful day that 9/11 was—clear and cool, few clouds in the sky, with a light wind from the east. Assume the population density is uniform, with an average of 125,000 people per square mile. Assume the bomb's shock wave spreads out evenly, not affected by the structures.[39]

For the terrorists, the mission is a suicide mission. Those driving the truck will remain in place, acting normal, so those inside the truck can trigger the device before anyone becomes suspicious. Remote detonation of the IND, or timed detonation, would be too risky. The way to make sure the device explodes is to stay in place and trigger the detonation locally. All terrorists on the weapons delivery mission are vaporized as the weapon detonates.

One Second After Detonation

WITHIN THE first second, a shock wave with an overpressure of 20 psi (pounds per square inch) extends four-tenths of a mile from ground zero. This destroys the Empire State Building and all other buildings within that radius, including Madison Square Garden, Penn Station, and the New York Public Library. The reinforced steel in the skyscrapers does nothing to support them. Everything within the first four-tenths of a mile from ground zero is reduced to a pile of debris hundreds of feet deep in places. No one in this area survives or even knows what happened to them. The blast kills somewhere between 75,000 and 100,000 people instantly. Those outside in direct line with the blast are vaporized from the heat. Those inside the buildings who survive the blast are killed as the buildings collapse.

A mushroom cloud and fireball expand upward. Instantly, all communications that depend on this area for broadcast stop. National television stations and hundreds of radio channels are instantly off the air. Cell phones throughout the region malfunction. New York City drops off the world communication map. It is not like 9/11, where the rest of the world could switch on their televisions and watch live what was happening.

Four Seconds After Detonation

THE SHOCK wave extends for at least a mile with an overpressure of 10 psi at the periphery of this radius. Out to the edge of this ring, all concrete and steel-reinforced commercial buildings are destroyed or so severely damaged that they begin to collapse. The few buildings at the edge of this ring that remain standing have their interiors destroyed. Many of those within still-standing buildings are protected enough to survive the initial blast but are killed by flying debris. As the shock wave spreads out, an additional 300,000 people are killed and 100,000 more are injured. Almost no one in this ring escapes injury. Those below ground in the subways will escape this first blast with few injuries, though the loss of electricity may shock the cars to a stop. Blocked exits may trap all subway passengers underground indefinitely.

All power in New York City goes out or experiences difficulty. Telephone service stops. There is no radio or television from New York City and no information passing to the outside world about the damage or casualties.

Six Seconds After Detonation

THE SHOCK wave expands to 1.5 miles from ground zero. The pressure at the edge of this ring has dropped to an overpressure of 5 psi, enough force to severely damage steel-reinforced commercial buildings. The damage spreads to Carnegie Hall, the Lincoln Center, and the Queensboro Bridge. Gone are Grand Central Station and the Met Life Building. They Chrysler Building is gone, as are virtually all the name-recognized buildings along Park Avenue and Fifth Avenue that surround what only six seconds ago was the Waldorf Hotel. The thermal pulse kills another 30,000 people who were in direct sight of the blast, including virtually everyone on the street at the time of the blast. Some 500,000 people in this ring are dead. Another 190,000 within buildings are killed by flying debris or are crushed when the buildings collapse. Of those buildings left standing, about 5 percent burst into flames instantly; within twenty-four hours virtually all buildings that remain standing catch fire. A conflagration begins at city center.

The outside world has virtually no contact with New York City. Panic begins to spread around the country as people watching television or listening to radio begin to realize there is no television or radio available. The first six seconds is too short an interval for government officials in Washington DC to have any real idea what has happened to New York.

Ten Seconds After Detonation

THE SHOCK wave expands to a radius of 2.5 miles, but it still carries an impact with an overpressure of 2 psi at the periphery, enough to cause varying amounts of damage to steel-reinforced buildings. An estimated 235,000 additional people die instantly as this ring expands, with an additional 500,000 casualties as the casualty ratio begins to exceed the kill ratio. Those wearing darker clothes are more severely burned from the thermal pulse. Combustible materials instantly burst into flame. Within twenty-four hours all buildings that remain standing in this radius will begin to burn out of control as all water service has ceased to function.

Sixteen Seconds After Detonation

THE SHOCK wave expands to a radius of four miles with an overpressure force of 1 psi at the edge. Steel-reinforced buildings at the periphery suffer relatively little damage, but as far south as Battery Park and the Statue of Liberty the damage is still significant. The impact is being felt across the East River into Queens and across the Hudson River into New Jersey. Buildings north of Central Park are hit by enough force to cause flying debris and severe structural damage. Now the deaths and casualties are spread across 30 square miles. There are many fewer deaths in the ring that stretches from 2.5 miles (the 10-second impact periphery) and 5 miles (the 16-second periphery). An additional 30,000 in this further extension of the blast are severely injured.

Radioactive fallout reaching across into New Jersey will begin within twenty-four hours to produce mild sickness for virtually everyone who was outside when the IND was detonated and many inside. The initial symptoms will be vomiting, diarrhea, and fatigue. Over the next few days as many as 30 percent of the population with a 10-mile range of the blast will begin to die from a combination of burns, infection, and radiation damage to tissue, bone, and blood cells. The radiation effects will sweep across New Jersey for dozens of miles, with some seriously affected by radiation sickness as far away as 100 miles from ground zero.

One Hour After Detonation

BY NOW word has spread throughout the nation and the world, though the news blackout and the effect on television and radio transmission has led to panic and confusion. The president has called out the military, but there is no way to enter New York City. All tunnels and bridges connecting to New York are either gone or so seriously damaged that they are unusable.

New York City has no power, no water, no police, no fire department. No roads in Manhattan within a five-mile radius of the blast are usable. Roads from the southern tip of Manhattan to above Central Park are filled with debris. Fires are burning out of control. Many injured are trapped in buildings and unable to escape.

Very few find exits from the subways, and when they do exit they emerge into a destroyed city of chaos. There is no telephone service in New York and cell phones will not connect for service.

Pandemonium and fear spread rapidly among survivors. Military helicopters hover overhead, trying to ascertain what has happened.

LaGuardia, JFK, and Newark Airports all shut down. All aircraft heading to the New York area would be redirected to land at other destinations. The president would order all aircraft to land as quickly as possible, as the nation's commercial air traffic system is brought to an orderly and quick halt.

Thousands of families and businesses around the country who are aware of the tragedy will begin scrambling to find information about loved ones and business associates who were scheduled to be in New York City that day.

By the End of the Day

MORE THAN 1.5 million people are dead in New York City and another 1.5 million severely injured. Fewer than 25 percent of the injured will survive longer than a week. The old will die first, along with the very young. Those survivors who can move around will not know what to do. Looting will break out, as will random acts of violence. Thousands will be trapped in elevators, sealed in what are about to become their tombs. Those not at home will be unable to communicate with loved ones, to find out what has happened to husbands, wives, and children. For all but a few there will be no words said of "Good-bye" or "I love you."

Soon those who can emerge above the rubble will realize they are on an island with no escape. The Hudson and the East rivers are too strong to swim across. Who will come for rescue when the radiation will kill all who enter the devastation without protective clothes? The survivors will be homeless, mostly without food or water. There are no hospitals for the injured, and even if there were, there is no way to transport the injured to medical treatment. Darkness and the cold of night will descend with no apparent answers available to anyone.

Disaster recovery will be nonexistent in the first twenty-four hours as officials in the state government in Albany and the federal government in Washington realize they cannot get relief and rescue resources into Manhattan as the city begins to burn out of control.

Across America, the nation will come to a stunned standstill of shock and disbelief. Public officials all over the land will call for all police and fire departments to report for duty. Pleas will go out nationwide for National Guard and military assistance to maintain calm and prevent rioting or looting. No one knows for sure what needs to be done, or if there will be another attack.

In the span of less than one hour, the nation's largest city will have been virtually wiped off the map. Removal of debris will take several years, and recovery may never fully happen. The damage to the nation's economy will be measured in the trillions of dollars, and the loss of the country's major financial and business center may reduce America immediately to a second-class status. The resulting psychological impact will bring paralysis throughout the land for an indefinite period of time. The president may not be able to communicate with the nation for days, even weeks, as television and radio systems struggle to come back on line.

No natural or man-made disaster in history will compare with the magnitude of damage that has been done to New York City in this one horrible day.

The United States Retaliates: "End of the World" Scenarios

THE COMBINATION of horror and outrage that will surge upon the nation will demand that the president retaliate for the incomprehensible damage done by the attack. The problem will be that the president will not immediately know how to respond or against whom.

The perpetrators will have been incinerated by the explosion that destroyed New York City. Unlike 9/11, there will have been no interval during the attack when those hijacked could make phone calls to loved ones telling them before they died that the hijackers were radical Islamic extremists. There will be no such phone calls when the attack will not have been anticipated until the instant the terrorists detonate their improvised nuclear device inside the truck parked on a curb at the Empire State Building. Nor will there be any possibility of finding any clues, which either were vaporized instantly or are now lying physically inaccessible under tons of radioactive rubble.

Still, the president, members of Congress, the military, and the public at large will suspect another attack by our known enemy—Islamic terrorists. The first impulse will be to launch a nuclear strike on Mecca, to destroy the whole religion of Islam. Medina could possibly be added to the target list just to make the point with crystal clarity. Yet what would we gain? The moment Mecca and Medina were wiped off the map, the Islamic world—more than one billion human beings in countless different nations—would feel attacked. Nothing would emerge intact after a war between the United States and Islam. The apocalypse would be upon us.

Then, too, we would face an immediate threat from our long-term enemy, the former Soviet Union. Many in the Kremlin would see this as an opportunity to grasp the victory that had been snatched from them by Ronald Reagan, when the Berlin Wall came down. A missile strike by the Russians on a score of American cities could possibly be preemptive. Would the U.S. strategic defense system be so in shock that immediate retaliation would not be possible? Hard-liners in Moscow might argue that there was never a better opportunity to destroy America.

In China, our newer Communist enemies might not care if we could retaliate. With a population already over 1.3 billion people and with their population not concentrated in a few major cities, the Chinese might calculate to initiate a nuclear blow on the United States. What if the United States retaliated with a nuclear counterattack upon China? The Chinese might be able to absorb the blow and recover.

The North Koreans might calculate even more recklessly. Why not launch upon America the few missiles they have that could reach our soil? More confusion and chaos might only advance their position. If Russia, China, and the United States could be drawn into attacking one another, North Korea might emerge stronger just because it was overlooked while the great nations focus on attacking one another.

So, too, our supposed allies in Europe might relish the immediate reduction in power suddenly inflicted upon America. Many of the great egos in Europe have never fully recovered from the disgrace of World War II, when in the last century the Americans a second time in just over two decades had been forced to come to their rescue. If the French did not start launching nuclear weapons themselves, they might be happy to fan the diplomatic fire beginning to burn under the Russians and the Chinese.

Or the president might decide simply to launch a limited nuclear strike on Tehran itself. This might be the most rational option in the attempt to retaliate but still communicate restraint. The problem is that a strike on Tehran would add more nuclear devastation to the world calculation. Muslims around the world would still see the retaliation as an attack on Islam, especially when the United States had no positive proof that the destruction of New York City had been triggered by radical Islamic extremists with assistance from Iran.

But for the president not to retaliate might be unacceptable to the American people. So weakened by the loss of New York, Americans would feel vulnerable in every city in the nation. "Who is going to be next?" would be the question on everyone's mind. For this there would be no effective answer. That the president might think politically at this instant seems almost petty, yet every president is by nature a politician. The political party in power at the time of the attack would be destroyed unless the president retaliated with a nuclear strike against somebody. The American people would feel a price had to be paid while the country was still capable of exacting revenge.

None of these scenarios bodes anything but more disaster. The point is simple: America cannot tolerate the risk that some insane group of radical Islamic terrorists might want to buy their way into heaven by exploding a nuclear device in the heart of New York City. The consequences are too devastating to imagine, let alone experience. As a nation we must realize that this type of attack *can* happen. It may only be a matter of time, unless we act right now. We must not permit the mad mullahs to have a nuclear capability they can turn clandestinely into a nuclear weapon to use in attacking America. That we might believe we can solve the problem diplomatically is exactly the conclusion the mullahs are praying we will come to.

8

Oil Extortion

How High the Price of Oil?

THE MULLAHS VIEW OIL as a weapon. Realizing that they are sitting on one of the great easy-to-access pools of available oil in the world, the mullahs believe they have power. The prestige of having a corner on a commodity as important to the world economy as oil is only equaled in the eyes of the mullahs with the prestige they imagine they will have once they possess nuclear weapons. The prospect of possessing two weapons so powerful—oil plus nuclear weapons—is a terrorist's dream.

With oil prices at or above forty dollars a barrel, the mullahs have the opportunity to enter a world of profits they have never experienced before. What do the mullahs plan to do with their oil weapon? They plan to use it just like they will use nuclear weapons once they have them. Terrorists use weapons once they get their hands on them, because terrorists never know when somebody might take the weapons away from them. "Use it or lose it" is how a terrorist calculates weapons.

Iran's Oil Profile

IN 2004 successful efforts at oil exploration increased dramatically the estimates of Iran's proven oil reserves. The figure had been running at a reserve of about 90 billion barrels through 2003, which placed Iran at the fifth-largest oil-producing country worldwide in terms of proven oil reserves. In 2004 the estimate of Iran's proven reserves jumped to around 130 billion barrels, an increase of almost 45 percent, which would have placed Iran at number two in terms of worldwide oil reserves.[1]

Saudi Arabia has by far the largest oil reserves of any country in the world, estimated currently at somewhere around 260 billion barrels. Experts estimate that Saudi Arabia could well contain up to 1 trillion barrels of ultimately recoverable oil, with expectations that the country's proven reserves will be officially pegged at around 460 billion barrels within a few years. Iran is at a much earlier stage of exhaustive oil exploration activities, so estimates of Iran's total available pool of recoverable oil reserves are not yet considered reliable.

Iran's oil production is hovering around 3.9 million barrels per day (bbl/d). The peak production for Iran was 6 million bbl/d in 1974 when the world was in the throes of the OPEC oil embargo. Most experts believe that Iran will need considerable investment in developing the country's oil technology infrastructure if the country is to exceed current production numbers. With oil surging in price in 2004, Iran's gross revenue from oil can be estimated to be somewhere in the range of $150 million per day.

U.S. Department of Energy evaluations emphasize that Iran has not passed oil revenues very deeply into the country's economy. Consider this Energy Information Administration (EIA) analysis:

> Despite relatively high oil export revenues, Iran continues to face budgetary pressures: a rapidly growing, young population with limited job prospects and high levels of unemployment; heavy dependence on oil revenues; significant (but declining) external debt; high levels of unemployment; expensive state subsidies (billions of dollars per year) on many basic goods; a large, inefficient public sector and state monopolies (bonyads, which control at least a quarter of the economy and constitutionally are answerable only to supreme leader Ayatollah Ali Khamenei); international isolation and sanctions.[2]

Iran relies heavily on oil export revenues, which constitute about 80 percent of its total export earnings, 40–50 percent of the government budget, and some 10–20 percent of gross domestic product.

With the governmental control in the hands of the mullahs and with little of the oil wealth passed down to benefit Iran's citizens, the theocracy can allocate huge resources to the development of nuclear weapons and the exportation of terrorism, while reserving a substantial margin for themselves.

The Mullahs Make Oil Deals with India and China

IN OCTOBER 2004 the Chinese state-owned oil giant Sinopec Group signed a $70 billion oil field development and liquefied natural gas agreement with the National Iranian Oil Company, Iran's government-owned oil conglomerate. Under the agreement, Sinopec will buy 250 million tons of liquefied natural gas from Iran over thirty years while agreeing to help develop the huge Yadavaran oil field near the Iraqi border. China agreed to buy 150,000 barrels per day of crude oil at market places from the Yadavaran oil fields for the next twenty-five years. China's demand for oil is huge and growing. In 2004 China overtook Japan as the world's second largest oil importer, with the United States still ranked number one.[3]

On January 7, 2005, Iran and India announced they had signed a deal calling for India to buy from Iran 7.5 million tons a year of liquid natural gas and to participate in the development of a number of different Iranian oil fields, including the Yadavaran oil field, alongside the Chinese.[4] When the Indian deal was announced, the press releases began to make clearer that both the Chinese and the Indians expected to have equity stakes in these newly developed oil fields and in any processing plants that went along with the deal. Iran had signed twenty-five-year deals with each country, receiving from China and India unspecified commitments of capital and technical expertise in the development of these newly discovered oil resources.

The deals with China and India were negotiated in direct contradiction of the U.S. Iran-Libya Sanctions Act that threatens substantial penalties for countries and firms making energy investments in Iran. With China being a permanent member of the U.N. Security Council, this disregard for the U.S. position gives notice that China cannot be relied upon to support tough U.N. sanctions designed to put off Iran's plans to develop nuclear weapons.

Moreover, the deals signal that the mullahs are positioning their primary economic resources—oil and natural gas—to leverage increased international political power for themselves. Pakistan undoubtedly feels threatened to see its neighbors—India and Iran—getting together economically. Thinking nationalistically, the Shi'ites in Iran and the Sunnis in Pakistan have reasons to vie for regional power, with Pakistan of necessity being concerned whenever a regional force like Iran sides with one of its traditional enemies, such as India.

With their enormous and growing populations, China and India are clearly moving to claim Iranian oil, not worrying that U.S. sanctions are being violated and U.S. oil companies are excluded from the action. So, too, both China and India are nuclear powers with national interests that cannot be assumed to be consistent with long-term U.S. interests.

Is the World Running out of Oil?

FOR THE past fifty years pundits have consistently predicted that the world will run out of oil. Yet today there seems to be more proven oil reserves than ever before. A huge oil reserve seems to lie under Iran, Iraq, Kuwait, and Saudi Arabia. Just exactly how large the remaining oil reserves are has not yet been fully determined.

There are indications that the underground pool of oil reserves extends to a full range of countries around the Caspian Sea, including several nations that were part of the former USSR, such as Azerbaijan, Turkmenistan, Uzbekistan, and Kazakhstan. Oil exploration in these countries is in many ways just beginning. For most of the twentieth century the world had little understanding that Afghanistan was not the only country ending in -stan, but that the designation stood for a lot of countries that were dominated by tribal communities living in mountainous and remote terrains. Islam is a major force all through these countries, which sets up a complex equation when non-Muslim Russia is taken into consideration.

Kazakhstan alone may emerge to change the world's oil calculation. A country bordering both Russia and China, Kazakhstan has a population of a little more than fifteen million and a religious heritage that is split between Islam and Russian Orthodox. In 2000 the Kashagan oil field was discovered off Kazakhstan's coast in the Caspian Sea. This reserve is estimated to be the second-largest oil field in the world, twice the size of all the North Sea oil fields combined. The estimated thirteen billion barrels of recoverable oil in the Kashagan oil field is expected to come on-line in 2008 after an investment of some twenty-nine billion dollars to develop the field being made by an international consortium of companies including Shell, Total of France, ConocoPhillips, and ExxonMobil. A second Kazakhstan oil field at Tengiz is estimated to hold another twenty-five billion barrels of recoverable crude oil.[5]

China has already begun importing oil from Kazakhstan. In 1997 the Chinese National Petroleum Corporation bought 60 percent of Kazakhstan's third-largest field, Aktyubinsk, at what was then considered above-market prices. Construction began in September 2003 on an oil pipeline connecting Kazakhstan and China. In addition to oil, Kazakhstan is also rich in uranium, currently producing 8 percent of the world's supply.[6]

Meanwhile, oil company researchers have been paying greater attention to the work of Thomas Gold, who has long argued that crude oil forms as a natural organic process occurring between the crust and the mantle of the earth, somewhere between five and twenty miles deep. Gold's theories suggest that oil is constantly being produced by the earth and is not the long-decaying byproduct of prehistoric forests and ancient animals. If oil turns out to be a renewable resource, not a "fossil fuel" with limited availability, the entire horizon for projecting the world's available crude oil energy supply will undergo a paradigm shift in terms of human comprehension and subsequent intellectual structures for comprehending and projecting in the various energy sciences.[7]

Still, two trends seem to dominate current thinking on energy questions. Experts expect that the percentage of oil exports originating from the OPEC countries will increase from the current market share of around 28 percent to a projected 40 percent share by 2010.[8] Second, the United States has begun importing more oil than it produces domestically. By 2010 58 percent of the oil used in the United States will be imported, and by 2025, the country will import more than 70 percent of its oil needs. While oil production from Mexico, South America, and Africa is increasing, for its oil supply in the foreseeable future, America may well be dependent on states that are less stable or politically favorable.[9]

For the mullahs, the developing world oil opens up several major possibilities. Clearly, having abundant oil reserves positions Iran to be a world player of strategic importance. For the mullahs, oil is an important chip to get into the geopolitical game. What strategy the mullahs will decide to play remains open to several different possibilities. The first objective is to secure the needed investment capital to develop Iran's oil reserves into actual production. Countries like India and China, together with the Europeans, can probably provide all the capital that is required.

Once the oil fields are producing, the mullahs can enter into the world of bargaining and extortion. Friends can be provided cheap oil in return for continued investment. The United States already views China as a potential adversary; a close alliance with Iran may provide China an additional degree of freedom when it comes to negotiating with or challenging the United States. Taiwan, if nothing else, will continue to remain a bone of contention between

the United States and China, with no particularly favorable prospect of resolution unless or until Taiwan is ready to relinquish its sovereignty to the Communists controlling the mainland—something not likely to happen without
military intervention.

The mullahs, if fully accepted as respected partners in the world arena,
will continue to demand that the Holy Land that is now Israel be returned to
the Palestinians, whom the Iranians consider to have the legitimate title on
the land. The 1973 OPEC oil embargo showed the world the dramatic impact
of decisions made by Middle Eastern countries willing to combine in purpose
and to use oil to extort demands that U.S. support for Israel be diminished, if
not ended. As a result of the 1973 embargo, the price of oil escalated, nearly
quadrupling from a low of twelve dollars per barrel when the embargo began
to a high of approximately forty-two dollars per barrel in 1974.[10]

The Politics of Oil Extortion

JUST BECAUSE the mullahs have a substantial amount of oil does not mean
they can easily pull off oil extortion. The oil market is complex, and market
forces will create more supply when prices increase. Clearly, the mullahs
would like to see oil increase 400 percent again. If oil were to hit two hundred
dollars a barrel, the mullahs would be in line to receive one of the greatest
windfall profits ever recorded. The mullahs will study the 1973 oil embargo
and see what they can learn from it. We should do the same here as we lay out
a methodology for how the mullahs might calculate their best advantage.
Make no mistake—the mullahs are more than willing to use oil to extort the
world markets, they simply have to figure out a strategy that has a reasonable
chance of succeeding.

The reasons for the 1973 Arab oil embargo are complex. Certainly, President Nixon's decision to release the dollar from the gold standard that had
been in effect since the Bretton Woods pact at the end of World War II was a
factor. When the United States suspended the convertibility of the dollar into
gold on August 15, 1971, allowing the dollar to fall in price on world markets,
a fundamental economic readjustment followed around the globe. The dollar
was devalued 8 percent in relation to gold in December 1971, followed by a
second devaluation in 1973. Arab nations began to feel that a major change
in the price of crude oil was needed to reestablish their relative economic position and to make sure that oil, their most precious natural resource, was not
simply stolen from them.

Also, the Arab world was in the throes of great anger following Israel's victory in the 1973 Yom Kippur War. Even Egypt and Syria, not major oil producers themselves, felt humiliated. A dramatic increase in the price of oil was seen as a way of punishing the United States for its support of Israel, a small country that the Arabs believed they could eliminate easily, except for the economic and military support of the United States.

What the Middle East oil-producing countries learned from the 1973 Arab oil embargo was the power of oil extortion. Long lines for gasoline could be produced in virtually every American city, the economy of the United States virtually brought to its knees, simply by a unified and determined decision of the oil-producing states to raise their prices dramatically and to hold at the new level.

Today Iran is well on the way to establishing a solid number-two position behind Saudi Arabia as the leading oil producer in the Middle East. This is being done without a single oil contract in place between Iran and any U.S.-based oil company. The Iranians have achieved their position by selling oil to China, India, and Japan. And the Europeans are lining up for their position on the Iranian oil pipeline. This pushes the United States closer to Saudi Arabia as the principal supplier of Middle Eastern oil to America. The resulting configuration presents multiple opportunities for the mullahs to renew the politics of oil extortion, especially for an Iran armed with nuclear weapons.

The first ploy is simple. At any time the Iranians could simply decide to restrict supply or do the equivalent by dramatically raising the price. The mullahs could make this decision as a means of forcing the world to do something or concede something the mullahs consider politically important at the moment. With China, India, and Japan forced to go to other sources to obtain their supplies, the upward pressure on world oil prices would be felt by everyone. That the Chinese, Indians, and Japanese have equity stakes in the management of Iranian oil fields might not be decisive to the Iranians. The mullahs could simply make a unilateral decision without taking into consideration the views of their partners.

What alternatives would the Chinese, Indians, and Japanese have? With recalcitrant business partners, one can go to court, but what court would be appropriate in this instance? No world court would have any enforcement powers. If the Chinese, Indians, and Japanese decided to use military threats to recover their oil rights, the mullahs could stand ready to launch nuclear retaliations against even the smallest military incursions.

The mullahs acting unilaterally in their narrow self-interest to achieve some particular point of political or religious significance to them could bring the world to its knees by a strong-arm use of oil blackmail techniques. That is the problem with a nuclear-armed Iran once the mullahs get to command a substantial market share in world oil production.

War with Saudi Arabia?

BUT JUST because Middle Eastern states are Islamic does not mean they see everything eye to eye. There are important nationalistic differences that dictate, for instance, that Iran and Saudi Arabia will not always agree on matters of international political importance. Besides, by nationality, the Saudis are Arabs and the Iranians are Persian. This leads to important and complex differences in culture and historical development. Moreover, the Iranians are predominately Shi'ites, while the Saudis are predominately Sunnis. This religious difference does not doom the two nations to conflict, but the two hold views of Islam that they believe should take precedence over, if not replace, the other as the correct version of Islam.

A key complication has arisen as radical Islamic terrorism has gained in strength and vehemence. Osama bin Laden is Saudi Arabian by birth. Yet he opposes the ruling family of Saudi Arabia, believing the House of Saud has sold out to the Americans. Reading bin Laden's twisted rhetoric, we can discern that his principal enemy is Saudi Arabia, at least when his principal enemy is not presented as Israel or the United States. The Saudis have funded a streak of radical Islam known as Wahhabism. This Saudi tactic, to fund the extremists in their midst in order to appease them, has come back to bite the Saudis in the person of bin Laden and the radical extremists to whom he appeals.

Iran, as we have seen, has extensive ties throughout the world of international terrorism. Postulate that Hezbollah and Hamas in their mad reasoning decide in conjunction with al-Qaeda that all-out war against the Saudis makes sense to them in their war to erase Israel from the face of the earth and to cripple America, the Great Satan. With nuclear weapons, Iran would have the tools in hand to threaten a Saudi Arabia that is only conventionally armed. Would the United States protect Saudi Arabia by threatening nuclear retaliation against Tehran if the mullahs were to launch nuclear missiles toward Riyadh? The terror masters working in collusion might risk threatening Saudi Arabia as a means of forcing the United States to back off in its support for Israel. This type of calculation prompted the decision to launch the 1973 oil embargo.

A nuclear strike against Saudi oil fields would also achieve the goal of punishing the Saudi ruling family, a family the extreme radical Islamic terrorists feel deserves to be punished. After all, by allowing the United States to have military bases in Saudi Arabia, the Muslim extremists believe the presence of Americans has defiled the holy sites of Mecca and Medina. Even the threat to attack Saudi Arabian oil fields would send the price of oil skyrocketing on world oil markets.

Attacking the economy of the United States is a key goal of the terror masters. The most obvious impacts of the 9/11 attack were the deaths inflicted and physical destruction done when the World Trade Center and the Pentagon were hit. Perhaps even more important was the subsequent hit the U.S. economy took as a result of the attack. The city of New York estimated that some three billion dollars in tax revenues alone were lost due to the attack.[11] The U.S. stock market lost approximately seven trillion dollars in wealth as prices on the exchanges headed south. More than 1.2 million jobs were lost, with industries such as airlines and tourism being hit the hardest.[12] Some three years later, the economy is still struggling to recover completely.

Any crisis the Iranians could engineer that would result in higher oil prices would produce a major negative impact on the U.S. economy. If oil were to hit two hundred dollars a barrel, gasoline for automobiles in the United States might cost as much as five dollars a gallon.

Today there is probably enough excess capacity in the world's market of proven oil reserves that higher prices would stimulate greater production, making it unlikely that oil could sustain a level as high as two hundred dollars a barrel. The models for predicting oil prices, however, would most likely have to be recalibrated to take into consideration a war between oil-producing Middle Eastern states where a tactical objective of one or more of the combatants would be to attack the oil fields of the other country or to attack the ports and pipelines essential to the transportation of oil.

Thirty-five years ago, prior to the Arab oil embargo, the price of oil was about three dollars a barrel. Today the price of oil has reached above forty-five dollars a barrel, a 1,500 percent increase. For oil to increase 400 percent now and hit two hundred dollars a barrel, we would have to experience dramatic economic shifts. With a freely floating dollar and with our growing dependence on foreign oil, price shifts this dramatic could cause massive shifts downward in the value of the dollar, perhaps several major devaluations of the dollar, and most likely a crisis in managing payments on the national debt. The economic world structure resulting from such an upward shift in the price of oil would most certainly be adverse to the United States.

This is exactly what a terrorist state would be tempted to calculate, even if causing an upward shift of that magnitude took decades to effect. Radical Islamists have been fighting the State of Israel since 1948. In their time frame of eternity, what difference would another ten or twenty years mean, especially if the strategy employed also crippled the economic strength of the United States in the process? Besides, how long would the United States continue to support Israel if the price of that support was even a doubling of the cost of oil above its current price?

A Tanker War in the Persian Gulf

IRAN'S MILITARY is no match for the United States. According to a 2004 comprehensive study of Iran's military capabilities conducted by Anthony Cordesman, a former senior Defense Department official, "Iran is a far less modern military power in comparative terms than it was during the time of the Shah, or during the Iran-Iraq war."[13] This report, conducted for the Center for Strategic and International Studies (CSIS) in Washington DC presented strong evidence that Iran has not been able to acquire strong numbers of modern aircraft nor has the country been able to reconfigure and rebuild its major surface ships. By Gulf power standards, Iran has a substantial conventional military force, though it now has "a largely conscript force with limited military training and little combat training."[14]

Still, the CSIS report warned that Iran "has significant capabilities of asymmetric warfare," given the long-range missiles the country has acquired from China and North Korea. Moreover, Iran "poses the additional threat of proliferation," given the country's determination to develop nuclear weapons.[15]

During the 1980s war with Iraq, when Iran's conventional military forces were stronger than today, Iran still was not able to defeat Iraq. The military outcome was almost humiliating in that Iran was reduced to launching human-wave attacks against entrenched Iraqi tank and artillery positions, a suicidal approach in the face of a superior military adversary. When one considers how easily U.S. forces defeated this exact same Iraqi military, one could reasonably conclude that defeating Iran's conventional military forces would be even easier for the United States to achieve.

Yet the CSIS report was concerned that Iran could conduct asymmetric attacks on shipping in the Gulf region. In other words, utilizing missile attacks, Iran could have a much more seriously damaging strategic impact here than one would otherwise predict from evaluating the relative weakness of Iran's conventional military forces overall.

The importance of the Persian Gulf for oil shipping cannot be overemphasized. Iran is a threat to Gulf shipping as well as to shipping in the Gulf of Oman. The U.S. Energy Information Agency (EIA) makes clear how important the Gulf is to the world's oil supply:

> The Persian Gulf contains 715 billion barrels of proven oil reserves, representing over half (57%) of the world's oil reserves, and 2,464 Tcf of natural gas reserves (45% of the world total). Also, at the end of 2003, Persian Gulf countries maintained about 22.9 bbl/d of oil production capacity, or 32% of the world total. Perhaps even more significantly, the Persian Gulf countries normally maintain almost all of the world's excess oil production capacity. As of early September 2004, world *excess* oil production capacity was only about 0.5–1.0 million bbl/d, all of which was located in Saudi Arabia.[16]

Iran maintains a key geographical position on the northern coast of the Strait of Hormuz, positioning Iran to easily attack oil shipments passing through the Gulf. As the EIA stresses:

> In 2003, the vast majority (about 90%) of oil exported from the Persian Gulf transited by tanker through the Strait of Hormuz, located between Oman and Iran. The Strait consists of 2-mile-wide channels for inbound and outbound tanker traffic, as well as a 2-mile-wide buffer zone. Oil flows through the Strait of Hormuz account for roughly two-fifths of all world traded oil, and closure of the Strait of Hormuz would require use of longer alternative routes (if available) at increased transportation costs.[17]

The 15 to 15.5 million barrels per day of oil that passes through the Strait of Hormuz goes east to Asia (for Japan, China, and India) and west to Western Europe and the United States, via the Suez Canal or around the Cape of Good Hope. Iran could cripple oil flow worldwide by attacking oil shipping in the Strait of Hormuz. To accomplish this goal, Iran does not need a conventional army, navy, or air force. What Iran needs are cruise missiles.

The CSIS report confirms that "Iran depends heavily on its ability to use antiship missiles to make up for its lack of airpower and modern major surface vessels." Iran currently operates four antiship missile systems acquired from China. One of these, the CS-801K, is a Chinese-supplied, air-launched antiship missile that is sea-skimming with a range in excess of twenty nautical miles. The CS-801K has been test-fired by Iran's F-4E fighter jets, and analysts believe the missile gives Iran a 360-degree attack capability, referencing the ability of aircraft to maneuver rapidly and attack shipping with far more agility than if the missile could only be ship-launched.[18]

Even more frightening reports circulating on the Internet suggest that Iran has purchased eight Sunburn or Sunburst antiship missiles (SS-N-22) from Ukraine and has deployed them for use around the Strait of Hormuz. The Sunburn missile represents a significant increase in the threat level in that it accelerates to a speed of Mach 2.2 (1,520 mph, more than twice the speed of sound) in thirty seconds. The Sunburn missile has a sophisticated guidance system and can carry a 200-kiloton nuclear warhead or a 750-pound conventional warhead.

Even conventionally armed, the Sunburn would be difficult to stop from destroying any ship against which it was launched. The Sunburn cruises toward its target at an altitude of approximately sixty feet. These Russian-built cruise missiles are considered to be a major technological advance. U.S. experts acknowledge that Iran has been on the market to buy Sunburn cruise missiles, but they continue to doubt that Iran as of yet has any operational Sunburn systems.[19]

Iran's cruise missiles also represent a threat to U.S. Navy ships operating in the Gulf. In 1982, during the Falklands War between Argentina and Great Britain, the world was shocked when the Argentineans sank the British destroyer HMS *Sheffield* with a French-made Exocet missile. The *Sheffield* at the time was one of Britain's newer computerized destroyers, specially built to defend against missile attacks.[20]

On March 17, 1987, an Iraqi-piloted Mirage F-1 fighter launched two Exocet AM39 missiles at the USS *Stark*, a frigate on duty in the Gulf. Both missiles hit the *Stark* undetected, one tearing a ten-by-fifteen-foot hole in the ship's steel hull, the second missile plowing into the ship's superstructure. While the ship was not sunk, thirty-seven American seamen lost their lives. The attack on the *Stark* came when Iran and Iraq were attacking each other's oil shipping in a phase of the Iran-Iraq War that came to be called "the Tanker War."[21]

These two incidents froze in the imagination of the world how vulnerable ships were. That war vessels of two of the world's greatest naval powers could be sunk or crippled by cruise-type missiles fired by aircraft from military powers not in the first ranks was frightening. Should a modern U.S. aircraft carrier operating in the Gulf suffer major damage or be sunk by a cruise missile, the incident would have a devastating psychological impact on the American public. The liberal press would be certain to enter into a "feeding-frenzy" on the story.

Cruise-missile attacks on tankers or navy warships are for the terrorist mind a perfect example of "asymmetric warfare." One cruise missile damaging a major U.S. naval vessel; one cruise missile causing fear in the population of the world's greatest military superpower—this is the exact type of out-of-proportion damage terrorists dream of causing. One cruise missile destroying a supertanker could shock the world oil market, causing the price of oil to spark.

Given Iran's strategic position in the Gulf, imagine the mullahs wanting to start up a new "tanker war" or deciding to disrupt or shut down oil shipments by firing cruise missiles at supertankers. We might even imagine the mullahs would decide to be selective, perhaps attacking only ships carrying Saudi oil, for instance. The disruption in the world oil market could be huge, as would the resulting impact on world oil prices.

As oil revenues continue to grow in magnitude, a rationally calculating Iran should become increasingly averse to causing disruptions. Yet to inflict short-term harm, or to cause a crisis that would spike oil prices up suddenly, Iran might try a few selective attacks on certain supertankers, just to make a point. Even a strategy to begin attacks on tankers slowly, gradually escalating the attacks, would make for some very difficult to predict scenarios, especially with Iran having nuclear weapons in waiting. The only sure outcome of any strategy by Iran to attack tankers in the Gulf is that oil would become more expensive.

These Tables Can Be Turned

GULF OIL depends on safe shipping in supertankers and smooth flow through long pipelines. Once we realize this, the vulnerabilities are not only ours. Equally vulnerable is Iran. One strategy to get the attention of the mullahs would be to cut off their oil. While the mullahs have decentralized their nuclear technology to make their production capabilities less vulnerable to air strikes, the Iranian oil delivery system is still dependent upon a few oil fields, a few ports, and a few pipelines—all of which are above ground and in the open.

Bringing Iran's oil-delivery system to a halt could be accomplished by either a U.S. or an Israeli series of air strikes that could be accomplished in a short period of time. Iran's only real defense to this attack strategy is that the price of oil would skyrocket if America or Israel truly inflicted some heavy damage on its oil-delivery system.

Yet the damage done to Iran's oil production and delivery system could be replaced relatively quickly, possibly with even superior equipment and technology. But the mullahs would be severely pressed if their cash flow dried up in a few afternoons. Today China and India are in the first stages of extracting oil from Iran. For some considerable period of time to come, a military strike on Iran's oil flow would be most damaging to the mullahs themselves. Even the Iranian people would suffer relatively less grief than might be expected normally, just because the mullahs have passed so little of their newfound oil windfall profits down to the people.

Ironically, America today is not drawing oil from Iran. A strike on Iran's oil fields, shipping ports, and pipelines would affect the United States by putting pressure on the world oil market. This would cause a price increase for all nations. Still, the economic impact of a short-term jump in oil price might be less dramatic than the impact on oil prices if, for instance, Iran eliminated Israel with a nuclear strike, or if the mullahs decided to disrupt oil flows by starting another tanker war to achieve some particular political or military goal deemed to be vital at the moment.

These attack strategies should be put into the category of "last resort." Still, when some scenarios call for massive air strikes on Iran's nuclear weapons capability, or even a land-and-air military invasion of Iran, a tactical strike on Iran's oil flow merits consideration as an alternative. Certainly, if the situation came to one where Iran's adversaries were contemplating a nuclear strike, the option to take out Iran's oil flow would merit serious consideration.

9

Repression in Iran

The Mullahs' Reign of Terror

LEGITIMATE GOVERNMENTS DO NOT have to resort to violence and repression to maintain control over their own citizens. But Iran's mullahs are at the top of the list of virtually every international authority reporting on human rights violations. For a quarter of a century the mullahs have maintained power by crushing any opposition and restricting their "democracy" to candidates of their choosing.

Torture, imprisonment without rights, arbitrary arrests, families unable to contact members arrested for unspecified crimes—these are regular occurrences in the mullah-controlled Iranian theocracy. Imposing their twisted version of Islamic law, the mullahs condemn their own women to second-class citizenship whereby they are separated from men and denied the advantages allowed men. Moreover, women are reduced to a cruel sexual servitude that often has brutal, even fatal, consequences, and are punished for what in most societies would be considered normal behavior.

While the mullahs have stashed billions of dollars for developing nuclear weapons, the general populace has suffered economically. Drug use is escalating, and young girls and women are sold into the world sex trade. The mullahs rule with an iron hand over a population that is kept economically depressed and politically repressed.

The mullahs have reduced themselves to staying in power by force, dominating a population in which a large majority would like to see them gone. A recent telephone poll indicated that as many as 85 percent of Tehran's residents seek fundamental change.[1] Countless Iranians have lost faith in the Islamic Republic, believing now that the revolution has only produced greater repression under a religious tyranny than they had known previously.

By controlling the press and trying to muzzle the Internet, the mullahs allow the world to see little of what truly goes on inside their reign of terror.

Mullahs Stack the Deck in Parliament

IN JANUARY 2004 the Iranian Council of Guardians rejected some twenty-five hundred of the eight thousand candidates to the legislative election for seats in Parliament. The vast majority of the rejected candidates, including some eighty-seven members of the outgoing parliament, were "reformists," candidates opposed to the mullahs and their regime. The elections held in February had less than a 50 percent turnout of voters, one of the lowest turnouts since the 1979 revolution.

This action by the mullahs was deplored by the international community. In July 2004 the International Federation for Human Rights Leagues (FIDH) "expressed its deep regret and disappointment that large numbers of candidates were prevented from standing in this year's parliamentary elections, including many sitting members of the Majlis, thus making a genuine democratic choice by the Iranian people impossible. This interference was a setback for the democratic process in Iran."[2] This type of harsh language from an international human rights watchdog group is consistent with all the severe criticism the mullahs usually receive.

The Council of Guardians is a supervisory body that approves or disapproves candidates for the parliament, the presidency, and the Assembly of Experts (which chooses the supreme leader). The council has twelve members, six of whom are chosen by the supreme leader, Ayatollah Khamenei, and six are lawyers chosen by the parliament. The council is led by the conservative Ayatollah Ahmad Jannati, who has called for Iran to leave the Nuclear Nonproliferation Treaty (NPT) so Iran would be free to develop nuclear weapons openly. Jannati was publicly critical when the United States gave humanitarian aid to Iran for victims of the December 2003 earthquake, saying that he had given America a "slap in the face."[3]

One issue over which the council and reform candidates to the parliament clashed had to do with the age at which children would be allowed to marry. The reformers wanted to raise the age from nine to thirteen for girls and from fourteen to fifteen for boys. The mullahs opposed this type of reform, arguing that the lower ages should remain unchanged because marriage is a good way to fight "immorality" among teenagers.[4]

In the mullahs' theocracy, one could lose the right to run for parliament by taking exception on a moral issue as fundamental as this. The mullahs evidently have no objection to preteen girls being able to marry. This may be the way to run a theocracy, but it has nothing to do with democracy.

A United Nations special envoy on freedom of opinion and expression visited Iran in November 2003 and warned that "the current practice of the Council of Guardians of screening, mainly on the basis of subjective criteria, the candidates to the election, is an impediment to the effective exercise of the right to take part in the conduct of public affairs and the right to the free expression of voters."[5] The council's action also violated Article 25 of the International Covenant on Civil and Political Rights, an agreement Iran ratified but refused to accept.

The Continuing Crackdown on Free Expression

IRAN'S SUPPRESSION of journalists came to the attention of the world in July 2003 when Iranian-born Canadian photojournalist Zahra Kazemi died in Iranian custody after being arrested for taking pictures of a student protest outside a prison in Tehran.

At first, Iranian authorities claimed Kazemi had died of a stroke. Later, the truth came out. Kazemi had been beaten to death; her skull was fractured, and she died of a brain hemorrhage.

After an Iranian security guard was charged with murder and acquitted in a highly controversial trial, the Iranian government changed its story and said that Kazemi's death had been an accident. A statement issued by Iran's judiciary made a lame attempt to close the case: "With the acquittal of the sole defendant, only one option is left: the death of the late Kazemi was an accident due to a fall in blood pressure resulting from a hunger strike and her fall on the ground while standing."[6] No, there was another much more likely explanation: Iran was covering up for the brutal prison guard who clubbed Zahra

Kazemi over the head and broke her skull. Lying doesn't bother the mullahs, nor does the ridiculous logic that if their rigged court acquits one of the mullahs' thugs, the fault must be the victim's.

The FIDH characterized Iran's judicial process as nothing more than a mockery of justice in their handling of Kazemi's brutal death:

> The first judicial hearing was held on 17 July 2004, almost one year after the death of Mrs. Kazemi. No charges were brought against the Public Prosecutor of Tehran, who is still in place despite the fact that his responsibility in the arrest of Zahra Kazemi has been clearly established. On 18 July 2004, the case was resumed by the Court. The hearing was held in violation of the right to a fair trial since the case was resumed by the Court. The hearing was held in violation of the right to a fair trial since the persons involved in the case according to the reports of the Article 90 Commission and the Commission of enquiry appointed by President Khatami were not heard by the Court, in spite of a specific request by the lawyers of Mrs. Kazemi's family. In addition, foreign journalists and diplomats were not allowed to enter the courtroom on 18 July, which had not been the case the day before.[7]

On July 25 the court's judgment acquitting intelligence agent Mohammad Reza Aghdam Ahmadi was made public. The entire procedure was a transparent travesty engineered to whitewash a murder resulting from the beating Zahra Kazemi received while being interrogated.

The mullahs regularly use arbitrary arrest and prolonged detention to quiet critics. Human Rights Watch, another international watchdog organization, reported on the case of Moshen M., a young doctor and student activist who had spoken out against the regime on a university campus and had written several reformist newspaper articles critical of the mullahs. Human Rights Watch interviewed him on December 8, 2003, by telephone from Ankara, Turkey, where he'd managed to seek refuge. Moshen M. described how he was abducted by the Iranian police:

> I came out of my apartment to go to work, and headed to my car. Suddenly, a group of plainclothes men with guns drove up. One of them had a walkie-talkie. They said, "If you work with us, we will help you. There is a report of drug use in your home." I said, "Do you have a search warrant?" They showed me a piece of paper. "Who sent this?" I asked. "The judge from the Revolu-

tionary Court." . . . They searched my home for hours. I tell you, even if you had gone to your enemies' home, and you had carte blanche, you would not have done what they did to my home that day.[8]

The police confiscated all Moshen M.'s notes, diaries, his family photographs, his personal videotapes, his speeches—everything they could find.

They told me that I had to go to the Intelligence office. . . . When they took me to the office, they said, "Write down everything you have done." I would write something down, and they would tear it up. They would give me a new piece of paper and say, "Write down what you have done." I would write, and they would tear it up. This happened eleven times. Finally, they said, "You write what we tell you to write. You are very smart, you are very educated, and yet you have written the same thing eleven times even though we have torn it apart every time." I said, "Because it is the truth."

The plainclothes police took Moshen M. to detention. His incarceration turned into months of harassment and interrogation. Here is how it started:

They blindfolded me and said, "You are arrested." They took me to a car, told me to lie down in the back seat, and we drove around for 45 minutes. One of the men in the car said, "People this smart will pay a price." Finally we stopped, we went down some steps, and I remember that I fell because of the blindfold. They kept telling me to keep my head down. "Head down, head down, head down." I sat in a room in the basement until the first interrogation began.

Moshen M.'s mistake was simply that he had the courage to speak out. For this crime he had been targeted by the Ministry of Intelligence.

Nor is there any freedom of religion in mullah-controlled Iran. On June 14, 2003, while there were several days of street protests going on in Tehran, Iranian authorities rounded up activists of an opposition group called the Religious National Alliance. Three in this group—Taghi Rahmani, Reza Alidjani, and Hoda Saber—were also accused of taking part in a secret meeting to plot the unrest that had gripped Tehran's university campus for the previous four nights. Rahmani, a prominent critic of the regime, received an eleven-year sentence for trying to overthrow the Iranian government. Reza Alidjani received a six-year term, and Hoda Saber nine years. Altogether, the court sentenced fifteen regime opponents to jail sentences, all charged with attempts to overthrow the Islamic regime, threatening national security, and "belonging to banned movements and spreading anti-regime propaganda."[9]

In December 2004 a group of journalists who had been detained by the government gave public testimony to a presidential commission about being detained without arrest warrants and being tortured during interrogations conducted by secret guards operating under the authority of the judiciary. In response, Saeed Mortazavi, the chief prosecutor of Tehran, threatened each of the former detainees "with lengthy prison sentences and harm to their family members, as punishment for their testimony." Mortazavi continued to issue subpoenas for journalists without specifying charges. He also was reported to be telephoning journalists on a daily basis to harass and threaten them. On January 3, 2005, Mortazavi held a press conference to deny any mistreatments of detainees; he also threatened to prosecute former detainees "for allegations against security forces and prison officials that are politically motivated."[10]

For judicial officers to threaten journalists with death is no way to provide freedom of the press, unless you see the world through the eyes of a theocracy. Then what is free to print is only what the mullahs want printed, and that generally involves praise of their wisdom in running such a right-thinking religious society, whose right thinking is imposed upon the citizens with the full force and power of the government the mullahs also conveniently run. In Iran, the mullahs firmly control the media. In recent years, the Iranian judiciary has closed down at least one hundred opposition publications.[11] Yet, if you are a journalist from a prominent American newspaper who is willing to write favorably about the theocracy, the mullahs might well arrange for you an all-expenses-paid four-star visit to Tehran.

Repression of opposition views is the keystone of the theocracy's determined plan to maintain control over the minds of the regime's citizens. A Human Rights Watch study covering the period from April 2000 to February 2004 concluded that "plainclothes agents wrecked the offices of reformist newspapers, attacked preeminent intellectuals during public lectures, kidnapped student leaders, beat protesters with batons, broken bottles, and wooden clubs during peaceful political gatherings, and delivered many individuals to detention centers and prisons." In carrying out these repressions, the mullahs have used the *Basiji*, reserve groups or militias, generally of young men who do not become full members of the *Pasdaran* (the Islamic Revolutionary Guard Corps; IRGC), and the *Ansar-e Hizbollah* (the "Partisans of the

Party of God"), members of the radical groups who enforce the actions of the *komitehs* (revolutionary "committees") that are constituted around a mosque or a mullah to exercise local control. Human Rights Watch also concluded that the judiciary "is also using plainclothes agents to silence those who criticize the government."[12]

Solitary Confinement, Interrogations, and Mock Trials

EVIN PRISON was built in the hills of northern Tehran in 1971. The prison grew to international infamy for the severe mistreatment of political prisoners conducted there under the Shah by SAVAK, the secret police. The mullahs have made sure that the reputation of Evin Prison for cruel and inhuman treatment of political dissidents has not been diminished.

One of the prison's darkest hours occurred in 1988 when uncounted thousands of political prisoners were executed after cursory trials.[13] There has also sprung up a network of unofficial illegal detention centers not under the control of the National Prisons Office. Iranians use the term *nahad-e movazi* (literally, "parallel institutions") to describe this underground network where unofficial prisons "are not officially registered as prisons, do not record the names of their prisoners, and information about their budgets, administration, and management is not known even by relevant government authorities."[14] The number of such unofficial prisons is unknown, but reports indicate that there are many in Tehran, and their number is growing. As one former prisoner commented: "You need to understand that Prison 59 is not just a place, it is a concept. One begins to think that there are underground prisons everywhere. And even for those of us who are free, we feel constantly as though we are walking on the screams of our colleagues."[15]

According to Human Rights Watch, Prison 59, one of the more notorious underground prisons, is controlled by the Iranian Revolutionary Guard Corps (the IRGC, or *Pasdaran*) and is in the IRGC compound in Vali-e Asr, Tehran. Human Rights Watch concluded after interviewing several writers, journalists, and students who had been released from Prison 59 that "those prisoners who do not confess after being subjected to solitary confinement in Evin are taken to Prison 59 in order to cut them off from information and break them psychologically. Several prisoners, returned to Evin after spending some time in Prison 59, were threatened with being sent back there if they did not cooperate."[16] Despite reports that Prison 59 had been closed, Human Rights Watch interviewed individuals who had been held there as late as July 2003.

Iranian detainees use the term "white torture" to describe Iran's common use of incommunicado solitary confinement as a technique to break the resolve of prisoners. Prisoners are "held in solitary cell blocks, many in secret detention centers, often underground, with twenty-four-hour artificial light. They are denied communication with other prisoners and access to attorneys, family members, and medical health professionals."[17] One writer described his solitary confinement in the mullah-run prison:

> In the first few hours, it is very hard. You have never been this close to walls in your life. You don't want to sit, because it is chalk, and you are not used to sitting on chalk. You stand. You pace. You start to get dizzy. After you get dizzy, you lean on a wall. After three or four hours, your legs get tired, and you sit. And then you scream and no one hears you.
>
> And you feel like they are holding you, like they are physically holding on to you. Your hair and nails grow faster. A lot of prisoners say that solitary is like being like "the dead in their coffins" because we had heard that the dead's nails grow even in their coffins.[18]

Interrogations are brutal. Initial questions are irrelevant: "Why do you drink?" "Why did you leave your first wife?" Prisoners were commonly subjected to these "initial rounds of softening-up interrogations focusing on moral or sexual 'crimes.'" Then detainees are questioned by "intellectual" interrogators who focus on their writings or their political beliefs. "Interrogators often used threats against prisoners' families or the promise of release in order to obtain confessions or disavowal of their stated political opinions on video camera."[19]

Trials in the Islamic Republic of Iran are not required to be public. Frequently there is no legal representation and no jury. Punishment is arbitrary and often brutal. Consider the trial and punishment of Moshen M., the activist dissident discussed earlier:

> My next trial was not public. The people in the room were a Ministry of Intelligence official, the judge, and myself. The judge said, "We will tell you what you did, and what your sentence is." My sentence was five years imprisonment *tazire*,[20] fifty lashes, and 500 *tomans* fine.[21] I said that I wanted to appeal, the judge told me that I had ten days to file my appeal. I told the judge that I needed a lawyer in order to be able to understand how to file an appeal. He said, "You will not have a lawyer."[22]

Moshen M. received a suspended sentence after he received the notice of the international press. When he pressed to have his "crime" removed from his record, the reaction of the authorities was severe:

> They told me, "You will have your [50] lashings now." I asked for a minute to prepare myself, and they refused. They said that my crime was insulting the Leader. They took off my coat, stood me up against a wall, and whipped me until I was purple. After the lashings, I was taken to the emergency room. When I put my coat on, I tell you, I do not know how I walked out. As I left, the man said, "You are a counterrevolutionary, and you will pay for everything."[23]

Moshen M. was one of the fortunate ones; he fled Iran successfully. Many other regime opponents who are pulled into the regime's prison web never emerge. In 1988, over a two-month period, the mullahs executed some thirty thousand political prisoners whose families never learned what happened to them.[24]

Abuse of Women

WOMEN UNDER the mullah's rule are routinely abused and terrorized. "In Iran for 25 years, the ruling Islamists have enforced humiliating rules and punishments on women and girls, enslaving them in a gender apartheid system of segregation, forced veiling, second-class status, lashing and stoning to death."[25]

While the segregation of women is a fairly common practice in Islamic societies, the Iranian theocracy takes the custom to a new level of severity. The explicit examples include: "there is no co-ed elementary or secondary education in Iran, and the mixing of girls and boys in universities has always been controversial and a subject of commotion (some branches of the Islamic Free University even introduced separate classes for men and women); there are different sections for men and women on the buses; most seriously, being in the company of a person of opposite sex, other than an immediate family member or the spouse, is a crime punishable with lashes (in the recent past in public places) and/or jail."[26]

Women are required to wear traditional Islamic garb, which included concealing their hair, wearing a veil over their faces, and not exposing their feet. The theocracy insists that "women who do not comply with the strict rules of *hajib* promote a contemptuous attitude toward themselves becoming mere objects for men's pleasure. Moreover, such conduct causes a drop in the marriage rate. A woman with a pleasant appearance hinders other girls from finding a husband. It also makes the selection difficult for men. They will constantly think of a model who is beyond everybody."[27]

Mehrangiz Kar, a prominent lawyer, writer, and human rights activist, explains the problem: "Any woman who appears unveiled in public—before they would arrest her, insult her, and put her in prison and also they flogged her—now the judge can choose between a jail term and a fine."[28] Members of the *Basij* patrol the streets to arrest any woman who dares violate the dress code.

Domestic violence against women in the Iranian Islamic Republic is a difficult, though commonplace, problem. A woman who is beaten by her husband is unlikely to receive any assistance from the police or judicial system. Under the civil code, a woman has a duty to submit to her husband. Women are economically dependent upon their husbands. Under Islamic law, a man can divorce virtually at will, while a woman seeking a divorce is in for a difficult time. Moreover, when a divorce occurs, the man under Islamic law gets custody of the children.

The testimony of a woman in Iran who was subjected to domestic violence for years is dramatic evidence of the mental cruelty that divorce and separation from children can mean to a mother. Sedigheh, an Iranian woman appearing on Radio Free Europe in November 2003, discussed the abuse she suffered in her marriage: "I remember once he beat me up so hard that for a week I couldn't leave the house. There were bruises all over my face and I had pain all over my body. I couldn't go out. And also violence is not just physical, some forms of behavior and comments bring us more pain than physical beating."[29]

Finally, Sedigheh got the courage to leave home and seek a divorce. After her divorce, she was forced to suffer the loss of her children: "[My husband] didn't even let [my daughter] go to school for some time so that I was not able to go there and meet her, and when he was forced to send the child to school he dropped her off and picked her up himself. He also told the principal not to let me see the child. During our life together, I allowed him to beat me if I knew it would stop him from torturing the child. And being away from my child was the worst torture for me. I still have nightmares about those days and nights."[30]

The life of a woman in the mullahs' theocracy is not nearly worth the life of a man. The mullahs who have hijacked Islam have "expended tremendous amounts of time and efforts controlling, harassing and punishing women and girls in the name of Islam."[31] In Tehran, there are an estimated 84,000 women and girls in prostitution, a figure that doesn't take into account the city's 250 brothels reportedly in operation. The sex slave trade in Iran is considered one of the country's most profitable businesses. Iranian government officials, according to widely published reports, are involved in buying, selling, and sexually abusing women and girls. Iranian women and girls sold into the sex trade from Tehran may end up being passed around the Persian Gulf states, or they may be sold into the sex slavery rings operating in Britain, France, and Germany.[32]

Several factors contribute to the flourishing sex trade in Iran. Many of the girls working in prostitution or sold into the sex trade come from impoverished homes. "High unemployment—28 percent for youths from 15 to 29 years of age, and 43 percent for women from 15 to 20 years of age—is a serious factor in driving restless youth to accept risky offers to work."[33] Sex traders take advantage of opportunities when women and children are vulnerable. After the 2003 earthquake in Bam, "orphaned girls have been kidnapped and taken to a known slave market in Tehran where Iranian and foreign traders meet."[34]

There has been a tremendous increase in the number of runaway teenage girls. In Tehran there are an estimated twenty-five thousand homeless street children, most of them girls. "The girls are rebelling against fundamentalist-imposed restrictions on their freedom, domestic abuse and parental drug addictions. Unfortunately, in their flight to freedom, the girls find more abuse and exploitation."[35] Up to 90 percent of the teenage girls who run away from home will end up in prostitution. Pimps see street children and runaway girls as easy prey. "In one case, a woman was discovered selling Iranian girls to men in Persian Gulf countries; for four years, she hunted down runaway girls and sold them. She even sold her own daughter for $11,000."[36]

Experts estimate that there are more than 2 million drug addicts in the nation's population of approximately 70 million. The majority of those addicted to drugs are young, but 70 percent of Iran's population is under age thirty-five. In 2001 some 193,000 drug addicts were detained in Iran, then freed after they were fined and whipped.[37] The *Basiji* and the *Ansar-e Hizbollah* patrolling the streets for the mullahs now have an expanded list of miscreants they can arrest. In addition to intellectuals and writers who speak out against the regime, the list of targets now includes runaway teenagers, drug addicts, and prostitutes.

Yet having all the power in the hands of the mullahs has certain advantages for the mullahs and their enforcement agents, the police, and the judges. Women who want divorces may have to have sex with the judge. Women who are arrested for prostitution may be forced to have sex with the arresting officer. Women prisoners, especially virgins, who are accused of being runaways or political discontents, face one of the regime's more ugly hazards, namely rape. "To rape women prisoners, especially virgin girls, who are accused of being against the regime, is a normal and daily practice in the Islamic Republic's prisons, and by doing so, the clerics declare that they adhere to the merits of the Islamic principles and laws, preventing a virgin girl to go to heaven. Mullahs believe that these are ungodly creatures and they do not deserve the heaven, therefore they are raped to make sure that they will end up in hell."[38]

One of the great political conundrums is why the American Left, especially the feminist movement, is not up in arms over the rampant abuse of women under the mullahs' regime. Evidently, even the feminists have decided to give the mullahs a pass. Perhaps the explanation is that the mullahs are also blatantly anti-American, and their criticisms of America so closely parallel the Far Left's that the two have too much in common for the Far Left in America to be critical about anything the mullahs do. Sometimes it seems as if the extreme political left in the United States has never found an international enemy of America that it did not like.[39]

The mullahs' perverse interpretation of Islam, combined with their control over the government and the regime's law-enforcement structure, gives them license to run one of the most demeaning and damaging social structures blatantly adverse to women that has ever been devised in the history of human politics or religion. We must remember that this is the world view the mullahs would impose on us if ever they had the opportunity to do so. The freedom our society provides women, that we see women as equals to men, is one of the great sins for which the mullahs condemn us. We are all going to hell, in the religious judgment of the mullahs, in part because we do not abuse women as do they.

Women Are Hanged and Stoned Under the Mullahs' Law

ON SUNDAY, August 15, 2004, sixteen-year-old Ateqeh Rajabi was publicly hanged on a city street in the northern Iranian town of Neka. Her crime was "engaging in acts incompatible with chastity," which translates into her being accused of having sex with a married man. The man was given one hundred lashes for the offense and released after Rajabi was hanged.

The young girl was believed medically incompetent, suffering psychological difficulties that gave her the mental competency of an eight-year-old. She was tried without legal representation. At her trial, she became angry and hurled insults at the local judge, Haji Reza, who also serves as the chief judicial administrator of the city. In her protest to the court, the girl was said to have removed some of her clothes in the courtroom. This act made Reza so furious that he personally put the rope around the girl's neck and gave the signal to the operator of the industrial crane to raise the arm and pull Rajabi to her cruel death.

Her hanging brought forward an internationally expressed protest from Ramin Etabar, an Iranian doctor:

> The murderous mullahs of Iran have executed another minor. The interviews of locals in the city of Neka conducted by Radio Farda revealed that this child was either mentally retarded or was suffering from a psychiatric illness. As a physician and human rights activist I cannot express my outrage enough. The terrorist regime in Iran has been killing children for the past twenty-five years. The virgin girls are raped by these Islamic hooligans the night before their execution in order to "prevent them from going to heaven." We the Iranian people hold the E.U. and corporate sponsors of the terror regime responsible for continuation of tyrannies in Iran. Please do your humanitarian share of responsibility and forward this content to the press, multinational corporations and governmental officials of your country of residence. May god bless the souls of the genocide victims of the Islamic Republic of Iran.[40]

The reaction was equally strong from England's director of Amnesty International, Kate Allen: "The killing of Ateqeh Rajabi reads like a catalogue of the most appalling human rights violations. The public hanging of a child, believed to be mentally incompetent, after a trial in which she reportedly had no lawyer, and all for the crime of 'acts incompatible with chastity.' It totally beggers belief. The death penalty is cruel and inhumane at the best of times. But to hang a child flies in the face of all that is humane, not to mention Iran's obligations under international law."[41]

Another case brought to light involved Leyla Mafi, a nineteen-year-old Iranian woman with a mental age of eight. When she was eight years old,

Mafi was sold by her mother into prostitution. She recalls when her mother "first took me to a man's house" the experience was "a horrible night. I cried a lot . . . but then my mum came the next day and took me home. She brought me chocolate and cheese curls." Mafi was forced by beatings and threats to continue "visiting men" from then on.[42]

Mafi's story is a sordid tale of abuse. She became pregnant and gave birth to her first child when she was nine. For this she was sentenced to one hundred lashes by the Iranian courts for prostitution. At the age of twelve, her family sold her to an Afghan man who made her his "temporary wife." In other words, under Islamic law, the man was committing no crime as long as they were married; when he was tired of Mafi, he could divorce her and look for another more interesting wife.

While married to the Afghan man, Mafi's mother-in-law became her new pimp and she began selling Mafi's body to other men without her consent. At the age of fourteen, she became pregnant again and had twins. For this she received another one hundred lashes. When the temporary marriage was over, Mafi's family sold her a second time, this time to a fifty-five-year-old man who was married with two children. This man again put Mafi into prostitution, having the male customers come to his home.[43]

Mafi was sentenced to death by a court in the city of Arak, in central Iran, on charges of "acts contrary to chastity" for working in a brothel and giving birth to illegitimate children. The court maintained that Mafi was in full mental and physical health and that she had confessed to her crimes. While waiting for her death sentence to be carried out, Mafi told reporters: "My mother doesn't visit me in prison. If you see her, tell her she promised to bring me cheese curls and chocolate. And she shouldn't forget to bring my red dress."[44]

If women convicted of having extramarital sex are not executed by hanging, they are executed by stoning. Hajieh Esmailvand, a seventeen-year-old minor, reflects that Iran is subject to outside international pressure. Esmailvand was sentenced to be stoned for having committed adultery with an unnamed man, subsequently identified only as "Ruhollah G," who at the time was also a seventeen-year-old minor. He was also convicted but sentenced to death by hanging. In November 2004 the Supreme Court of Iran upheld Esmailvand's death sentence and indicated that the execution could be carried out as early as December 21, 2004.

The case produced an urgent call from Amnesty International for letters and faxes to be sent to the Iranian Ministry of Justice in Tehran and the Iranian embassy in London, providing names, addresses, fax numbers, and e-mail addresses of specific officials to contact.[45] In a ten-day worldwide campaign, Iran was inundated with thousands of appeals from all over the world. The campaign received huge international publicity, including Internet discussions around the globe on Web sites and blogs devoted to Iran, talk-radio shows, and the international press reporting in many different languages.

On December 21, as rumors circulated worldwide that Esmailvand was going to be stoned that day, protest vigils were held in Stockholm, Gothenburg, and Cologne. Then on December 22, 2004, the Iranians buckled under the international pressure and announced that Esmailvand's stoning sentence had been suspended. The leader in Iran of the campaign to save Esmailvand from stoning, Mina Ahadi, was relieved: "We succeeded because a large number of people were determined that such a horrific violation of human rights would not be tolerated."[46] Nothing was said about suspending the sentence of Esmailvand's lover, nor was there any indication what would next happen to Esmailvand.

The Iranian Penal Code specifies in Article 102 that men who are to be stoned will be buried up to their waists and women up to their breasts for the purpose of execution. Article 104 specifies, that with reference to the crime of adultery, the stones used should "not be large enough to kill the person by one or two strikes, nor should they be so small that they could not be defined as stones."[47] Stones had to be "just right": large enough to cause significant harm and considerable pain, but not so large as to kill the person immediately.

The mullahs objected that anyone might think they were cruel. On January 11, 2005, judiciary spokesperson Jamal Karimi-Rad came forward to complain to the international press that "bringing up the issues of stoning and the execution of under-18s comes from outside the country and is aimed at distorting the image of the Islamic Republic." While denying that such punishments were continuing, Karimi-Rad insisted that such reports were "foreign propaganda."

The judiciary spokesperson did not deny that courts in Iran were issuing death sentences to individuals under eighteen, or that execution by stoning was still permissible. Instead, the spokesperson insisted that the Iranian Supreme Court was not approving such executions, stating "no such verdicts have been carried out." But stoning executions have been documented as having been carried out in Iran through 2002. At the moment the mullahs seem particularly sensitive to criticism from the EU countries, especially since

Iran is relying on the EU's support in negotiations with the IAEA to obtain nuclear fuel. Iran also expects major economic and trade concessions from the EU in return for the mullahs "promise" that they will stop enriching uranium to weapons grade.[48]

On January 6, 2005, Ayatollah Khamenei came out with a remarkable statement that revealed more than he probably intended to about how fundamentally threatened the mullahs are over sexuality. In their twisted view of Islam, Iran's supreme leader wanted to make sure the world knew what a devious plot it would be if Iran's enemies tried to destroy the country with miniskirts. He said:

> More than Iran's enemies need artillery, guns and so forth, they need to spread cultural values that lead to moral corruption. They have said this many times. I recently read in the news that one of them, a senior official in an important American political center, said: "Instead of bombs, send them miniskirts." He is right. If they arouse sexual desires in any given country, if they spread unrestrained mixing of men and women, if they lead youth to behavior to which they are naturally inclined by instincts, there will no longer be any need for artillery and guns against that nation.[49]

The mullahs are so threatened by women that they must keep them covered, segregated, and basically out of sight. Even more they are threatened by America, a country where women have equal rights with men. The mullahs' twisted, radical version of Islam may be at war with Israel, but even more, they are at war with the United States, the "Great Satan," a country where women are allowed to wear miniskirts and are not hanged or stoned for "acts incompatible with chastity."

Public Hangings, Public Mutilations

THE MULLAHS have perfected their own particular style of public hangings. Industrial cranes are used to lift victims into the air in a slow process that produces a grueling death and a grotesque display. For multiple hangings, multiple cranes are used, so a field can be filled with cranes from which bodies can be hanged, their feet tied together, their hands tied behind their backs.

The spectacles of public hangings have become commonplace in Iran. Consider the case of Ahmad Dowlatyari. He was condemned to death by hanging for murdering his crime partner in a disagreement over a stolen gold watch. Defiant, Ahmad kissed the rope before he was hanged: "I am not scared," he told those assembled at sunrise to watch him die. "My life is over now. I want to go with a smile." The description of his death was particularly graphic: "A tow truck's crane rose with a hydraulic hiss. The orange rope stiffened. Dowlatyari gasped once and was dead."[50]

There are many such stories of public hangings in Iran. On Thursday, January 6, 2005, thirty-two-year-old Bagher Soleimani was hanged in the northern Iranian town of Noshahr after he had served five years in prison. What was his crime? On February 4, 2004, he had killed a man during a fight over a coat. The Iranian Supreme Court rejected Soleimani's plea to escape the hangman.[51]

The mullahs also exact their version of Islamic law by performing public amputations when, in their view of justice, the crime calls for that punishment. In December 2004 the Islamic Supreme Tribunal approved a sentence to publicly amputate the hand of a man known only as "K.K." He was accused of stealing, and the fingers of his right hand were to be removed in public on Sunday, December 19, 2004, at 3:00 p.m. in the southwestern Iranian town of Izeh.[52]

The FIDH reported that in Iran in 2003 there were at least 108 executions by hanging, at least 4 executions by stoning, at least 197 persons who were flogged or sentenced to be flogged, and at least 11 amputations. Nor was the FIDH encouraged when the mullahs defended themselves by saying that the judiciary in 2003 had imposed a moratorium on death by stoning. The FIDH noted that even after this supposed "moratorium," four men were condemned to death by stoning in November 2003. Moreover, moratoriums were not permanent. A decree "can be reversed at any moment: it should be enshrined in a law adopted by the Parliament," the FIDH insisted.[53]

On October 20, 2003, a special U.N. reporter looking into arbitrary executions sent a communication to the Iranian Islamic Republic "regarding the case of four Iranian prisoners who were allegedly hanged in public in different locations in the city of Arak on 30 January 2003. One of them was reportedly executed in front of the university's main entrance, allegedly to create a climate of fear after recent demonstrations staged by Arak university students." In her report, the special reporter noted that paragraph 9 of the safeguards guaranteeing protection of the rights of those facing death penalties specifies that "where capital punishment occurs, it shall be carried out so as to inflict the minimum possible suffering."[54]

The mullahs, however, prefer cruel displays of hangings by hydraulic cranes, carefully staged to produce the maximum horror to the public who witness the events or whoever might happen to see the aftermath.

Mullahs Repress Baha'i Religion

BAHA'ISM IS a religion that believes God has been made known to man through various prophets, including Abraham, Moses, Jesus, and Mohammad. What the mullahs cannot stand is that Baha'is believe in the unity of all religions. Even worse, the Baha'is believe in the equality of men and women, even that women should be educated equally with men. There are some five million Baha'is in the world, with the largest communities in India and Iran. The religion dates to 1844, when Bahaullah, a Shi'ite Muslim living in Iran, had a divine revelation that communicated to him the spiritual unity of all human beings. With some three hundred thousand believers in Iran, Baha'ism is the country's largest minority religion.[55]

Put simply, the mullahs hate Baha'is. The Baha'i International Community believes that the policy of the Islamic Republic of Iran is to deprive all Baha'is of all rights. This paragraph from the FIDH Report on human rights in Iran is worth considering in its entirety:

> Baha'is in many different localities in Iran are still subject to arbitrary arrest, short-term detention, and persistent harassment, intimidation and discrimination. All attempts to obtain redress are systematically denied as officials continue to confiscate Baha'i homes, deny them their rightful earned pensions and inheritances, block their access to employment or impede their private business activities. The authorities also interfere with classes given to Baha'i youth in private houses and persist in banning the sacred institutions that perform, in the Baha'i Faith, most of the functions reserved to clergy in other religions.[56]

The mullahs detain, sometimes on life sentences, Baha'is simply for what they believe, not because they have committed any crime.

Mullahs Crack Down on the "Cyberdissidents"

ALWAYS ANXIOUS to quash any outlet for free expression, the mullahs have launched a repressive campaign to shut down Internet communication that in any way opposes the regime. In September 2004 the mullahs arbitrarily arrested twenty Internet journalists, webmasters, and bloggers who are opposed to the regime—"Cyberdissidents," as they are known. They were taken to a secret detention center where they were tortured to produce confessions. The Internet activists "have been beaten, humiliated and sometimes threatened with rape by their jailers. Many of them have been accused of moral crimes, that is, having sexual relations outside of marriage, a pretext often used in Iran to attack political dissidents."[57] Most confessed, and most were released on bail.

On December 10, 2004, Ali Mazroi, the father of one of the detainees wrote a public letter to President Khatami and charged that the judiciary was involved in the torture and detention of Internet journalists. Mazroi could not be simply dismissed; he is president of the Association of Iranian Journalists and a former member of parliament.

In retaliation, the chief prosecutor of Tehran, Judge Saeed Mortazavi, immediately filed libel charges against Mazroi. On December 11 Mortazavi ordered that three of the recently released dissidents be arrested again. The three, plus one journalist who was still in custody, were brought to Mortazavi's office and threatened with lengthy prison sentences if they did not denounce Marzoi's allegations. Once again, the four were brought back to interrogation where they went through the ordeal on three consecutive days for eight hours of questioning each day.

Then, on December 14, the four journalists were brought in front of a televised "press conference" where they denied that they had been subjected to solitary confinement, torture, or any other form of maltreatment during their detention. With their "statements" taped, Iran's government-controlled television station broadcast the four detainees' statement that they were treated as "gently as flowers."

The whole episode was closely monitored by Human Rights Watch. Joe Stork, the Washington-based director of Human Rights Watch's Middle East division, summed up the organization's assessment as follows: "If there are any credible charges against these journalists, the judiciary should hold fair trials instead of forcing them to appear on television to say their torturers treated them well."[58] According to Human Rights Watch, the journalists originally had been kept at a secret location within one hour of Tehran, where they were "held in solitary confinement in small cells for up to three months. During the entire length of their detention they were subjected to torture—including beatings with electrical cables—and interrogations that lasted up to 11 hours at a stretch."

The detainees had no legal representation or medical assistance. They were threatened that their family members would also be detained if they did not cooperate. Other reports indicated that during the interrogations the detainees had been beaten severely, then dragged outside, stripped naked, and doused with ice water; then they were dragged back into interrogation and forced to sit next to heaters and radiators as the questioning continued.[59]

The point of the regime in exacting confessions was to get an admission that reformist politicians and various prominent dissidents had worked with these Internet journalists to get information that would violate national security laws. Clearly, the mullahs feared the open communication that free Internet access allowed cyberjournalists and bloggers to express their grievances. President Muhammad Khatami made clear the regime's concern: "It's deplorable even if 10 percent of what the Web bloggers allege is true."[60] Khatami then called for an investigation into allegations that the cyber-dissidents had been tortured to admit that they had insulted Islam or sacrificed Iran's national security by making their insinuating but completely unsubstantiated charges.

At least the mullahs have learned that calling for an investigation is a good ploy when taking international heat for their repression of fundamental rights of expression.

The Mullahs' Greatest Accomplishments

FOR TWENTY-FIVE years the mullahs have ruled Iran. What is their legacy? An anonymous poster on an Internet blog listed the mullahs' greatest accomplishments. The list makes clear why the mullahs hate the Internet. Because expression over the Internet is so open and available, the mullahs have no choice but to repress it, just as they repress every human freedom they encounter.

The Mullahs' List of 50 Top Islamic Republic
Achievements in the 25 Years Since the Revolution

1. Execution, flogging, stoning, and amputation of limbs in public.
2. Mass killings of political prisoners.
3. Assassination of political dissidents outside of Iran.
4. Political serial killings in Iran.
5. Public hangings of sexual offenders, including minors, using hydraulic cranes.
6. Construction of many new prisons holding thousands of political prisoners.

7. Political oppression.
8. Promotion of international and domestic terrorism.
9. Violation of human rights in every category.
10. Lack of civil liberties.
11. Improvement and growth of Iran's cemeteries.
12. Killing and imprisonment of journalists.
13. Violation of women's rights.
14. Execution by stoning of women accused of sexual infidelity.
15. Punishment of women for being attractive to men.
16. Censorship and closure of all publications opposed to the regime.
17. Forcing Iranians to flee the country, resulting in five million refugees throughout the world and "brain drain."
18. Oppression of religious minorities.
19. Disallowing opposition political candidates to run for parliament.
20. Filtering Internet content to repress and control cyberdissent.
21. Jamming out-of-country satellite television and radio stations.
22. Stealing Iran's wealth and transferring the funds to overseas banks.
23. Destruction of Iran's economy.
24. Widespread poverty throughout Iran.
25. Severe inflation.
26. Devaluation of Iranian Rial.
27. Increase in unemployment.
28. Increase in the crime rate.
29. Promotion of corruption, prostitution, and drug addiction.
30. Housing crisis in Iran.
31. Malnutrition, retarded growth, and increased rate of psychological depression among Iranian youths.
32. Public health crisis in Iran.
33. Air and environmental pollution crisis in Iran.
34. Making Iran an international "embarrassment."
35. Occupation of the U.S. embassy in Tehran and holding hostages for 444 days.
36. Causing economic sanctions against Iran.
37. Producing a nuclear technology whose goal is to make atomic bombs.
38. Promoting regional conflicts in the Middle East.
39. Supporting terrorist groups who send suicide bombers to kill Israeli civilians.

40. Broadcasting to the world Suicide TV.
41. Destructions of fine arts, theater, cinema, and music in Iran.
42. Promoting a perverted form of Islamic Fundamentalism that has nothing to do with true religion.
43. Attacking university campuses to kill and crack down on students.
44. Violating the constitution of the "Islamic Republic."
45. Arbitrary arrests.
46. Interrogation under torture.
47. No legal representation for those accused of crimes.
48. Killing foreign journalists.
49. Hiring hooligans to beat and crack down on Iranian citizens.
50. Selling Iranian women as sex slaves in the United Arab Emirates.[61]

What allows a regime so unpopular to stay in power? The mullahs rule with an iron hand. Anyone who opposes them learns firsthand how a reign of terror works. As long as the mullahs are not bound by any code of civil liberties, they are free to ignore the rights of their citizens and use the typical terrorists' array of regime-control techniques to suppress any possibility of organized dissent while they achieve their number-one goal—making sure they stay in power at all costs.

There is not a single credible human rights organization in the world that has anything good to say about how the mullahs have conducted themselves at home. The conclusion of the all the world's human rights organizations is that the mullahs simply have no conscience when it comes to using force to repress their citizens so they can keep their own version of a fundamental Islamic theocracy going for the benefit of themselves.

PART 3

DISARMING THE BOMB

10

The Samson Option

Israel's Preemptive Strike

THE BIBLICAL STORY OF Samson and Delilah is familiar (Judges 16:4–30). Delilah deceives her husband, Samson. She betrays him to her people, the Philistines, who are the enemies of the Israelites. The Philistines put out Samson's eyes and rob him of the source of his strength by cutting his hair. Samson repents of his sin, his hair grows back, and he regains his strength. Not letting on that his strength has returned, Samson in turn deceives his captors. When the opportunity arises, he uses his renewed strength to bring down the two middle pillars of a great temple when the Philistines are assembled to sacrifice to their god. Samson kills a large number of the Philistines and in the process he kills himself.

Applied in the context of the Middle East, the Samson Option, has important ramifications.

Israel's Samson Option

ISRAEL MIGHT well launch a preemptive strike against Iran, even if the international military and diplomatic reprisals that follow might bring disastrous consequences upon Israel itself. Why? Because Israel might well calculate that Iran armed with nuclear weapons would be too unpredictable and dangerous to tolerate. At any moment and for any reason, Iran might simply launch a nuclear attack on Israel. Since Iran's irrationality cannot be ruled out, Israel could calculate there is no rational option except to attack Iran first.

Ironically, there is also a Samson Option calculated from Iran's perspective. (Nothing is ever easy or simple in the Middle East.) Allowing the mad mullahs in Iran to have a nuclear bomb might be the same as giving them a button with which they could blow up the world. The mullahs might just decide to push the End of the World button, acting as irrational terrorists unable to resist the temptation, or acting "rationally" in the calculation that they will soon be in heaven for their glorious deed. Even knowing that to launch a nuclear strike on Israel would result in a devastating nuclear retaliation being launched on them might not be enough deterrence for these radical clerics who have a history of embracing suicide as martyrdom. That the world would be destroyed because they pushed the button might perversely be an inducement to the mad clerics in charge of a radical terror-supporting theocracy.

Why Israel Strikes First

ISRAEL HAS sworn "Never again!" Reasoning that the Holocaust occurred in part because European Jews did not resist, the Israelis have determined that never again will Israel be passive in the face of its enemies. Since the late 1940s first strikes have characterized the Israeli's foreign policy. The highly effective Israeli first-strike air assault on June 5, 1967, destroyed the entire Egyptian air force on the ground at the start of the Six-Day War. But more parallel to the urgency surrounding the situation of Iran's having nuclear weapons is the June 1981 air attack that took out Iraq's Osirak nuclear reactor.

The "Never again!" resolve would tolerate annihilation only if it followed a massive Israeli military attempt to first annihilate the foe. Put another way, the possibility of annihilation would not stop Israel from attacking first if it felt its survival was on the line anyway.

The Samson Option psychology would be different for the Iranian mullahs even though the result might be the same. In its extreme form, the most radical Islamic terrorist accepts suicide to advance his cause. But the mad mullahs typically motivate others to commit suicide while they remain safe at home. Yet, presented with the opportunity to destroy Israel gloriously, even the mad mullahs might accept their own ticket to heaven as the price they had to pay to achieve their goal.

Thinking from a more rational perspective, an Iran armed with nuclear weapons could announce that it would launch a nuclear strike on Israel should Iran ever come under military attack by the United States, even if the United States were to launch a purely conventional strike on Iran. This would be Iran's version of the "tripwire" theory the United States used to justify maintaining a small conventional army in Europe in the 1950s. If the Soviets launched even a conventional attack against U.S. forces in West Germany, so the theory went, the United States would retaliate immediately with a massive nuclear strike. Similarly, Iran could announce that any conventional attack against it would result in a nuclear response by the mullahs.

Once Iran has a nuclear weapons capability, the mullahs suddenly have calculations and threats that were not available to them before. Armed with atomic weapons, for instance, Iran could make extremely aggressive foreign policy demands, threatening a nuclear attack on Israel if the demands are not met. The mullahs might command the withdrawal of all U.S. military forces from the Middle East, or else they would be "forced" to launch a nuclear strike on the U.S. bases in Iraq or Saudi Arabia or on Israel itself. Such nuclear brinksmanship instantly advances the situation to a whole new plateau of international danger.

Thought through from Israel's perspective, Iran must never be allowed to possess nuclear weapons. Iran has made its intentions abundantly clear. Any stoppage to enriching uranium will only be temporary. Iran has announced to the world that the mullahs will have atomic bombs. The only question is when.

Israel will watch for the moment of no return, the time when Iran has everything necessary on its own to make a deliverable nuclear weapon. Just after Israeli intelligence is convinced that Iran has reached that point, Israel will feel compelled to strike.

In June 2004 a report out of Tel Aviv confirmed that Israel already had rehearsed a military first strike on Iran. "Israel will on no account permit Iranian reactors—especially the one being built in Bushehr with Russian help—to go critical," an Israeli defense source told reporters. Prime Minister Ariel Sharon went on the record that Iran was the "biggest danger to the existence of Israel." Sharon also left no doubt as to his meaning: "Israel will not allow Iran to be equipped with a nuclear weapon."[1] Put in terms of the Samson Option,

Israel will feel compelled to strike first, before Iran has the ability to make its own first-strike decision.

Israel: A One-Bomb State

ISRAEL HAS only two major cities: Jerusalem and Tel Aviv. At the height of any business day, Tel Aviv has a population of between two million and three million people. Strategically, it is the business and finance center of Israel. Jerusalem is the religious center and the governmental capital of the nation.

If Iran were to launch a nuclear strike on Israel, the logical target would be Tel Aviv, because Jerusalem is also a holy site to Islam. The Dome of the Rock, built over the rock supposedly bearing the hoof print of Mohammed's horse as the Prophet ascended to heaven, is the third holiest city to Muslims. The golden dome of the mosque is a physically recognizable landmark on what the Jews call the Temple Mount, the raised land above Jerusalem that was the site of three Jewish temples (Solomon's, Zerubbabel's, and Herod's). Adjoining the Dome of the Rock is the Al-Aqsa Mosque, the largest mosque in Jerusalem. Part of the mosque's extended surrounding wall is the Western Wall, which is revered by Jews as a surviving foundation wall from the third temple. Destroying Jerusalem would be catastrophic to both Judaism and Islam.

A nuclear strike on Tel Aviv, however, would severely cripple the economic base of Israel. Depending upon the nature of the weapon and how the explosion occurred, hundreds of thousands would be killed in the first instant. Subsequent damage from fires and radiation would kill thousands more, either in the first hours after the attack or the days immediately after. Instantly the city would lose electricity, making it difficult for survivors of the blast to get a clear idea of what had happened. Panic and confusion would create additional problems as survivors tried to escape the city on the few roads leading to safety. In the confused aftermath, rescue services would also be in confusion as ambulances, fire, and police would be swamped with overwhelming needs to respond, inadequate resources, difficult communication, and problems finding open access routes.

The power outage that struck the northeastern United States from Ohio to New York City in August 2003 gives a mild idea of the confusion and problems that would result from a blackout, absent the horror, loss of life, fear, and devastation of a nuclear blast. Add in the physical elements of destruction and the psychological consequences of appreciating the loss and remaining threat, and the full impact of a nuclear explosion in any major urban area is almost unimaginable. An explosion similar to the Hiroshima blast or smaller would create horrible realities of death and destruction and ghoulish photographic images that would permanently scar human memory.

Nor would Israel readily recover from the consequences. The impact on the economy of Israel would throw the nation not only into an immediate emergency but most likely a loss of gainful subsequent activity that would challenge the severity of the worst economic depressions of the twentieth century.

Israel is a one-bomb state, meaning that a single nuclear weapon would dramatically change the nature of the country.[2] The country could not tolerate the human or economic disaster that would result from a single low-yield nuclear explosion. This is the nightmare image that Israeli nuclear scientists and government officials have calculated over and over again, ranging across various scenarios regarding type of weapon, nature of impact, and probabilities of secondary and tertiary crisis waves spreading through the metropolitan area, the nation, and the world. The "Never again!" resolve takes on new meaning when one bomb promises to bring the entire nation of Israel to its knees.

How Israel Strikes First

ONE SHOULD assume that Israeli and U.S. military planners have already worked out dozens of scenarios of possible military strikes against Iran. The permutations and combinations would be too extensive to enumerate here, even if the information were available to the public. In writing this book, I have had no access to classified information nor any briefings from administration officials regarding strategic military options in Iran.

At the end of the 2004 presidential campaign, the Bush administration announced it was utilizing $319 million in military aid to Israel to provide Israel with five thousand smart bombs. The sale included five hundred "bunker-buster" warheads, technically BLU-109s, two-thousand-pound warheads that can be used in combination with a GPS guidance system (GBU-31 or JDAMs). The JDAM (joint direct action munition) involves a special tail kit, enabling the bombs to be guided to the target by satellite. Bunker-buster bombs are capable of penetrating up to fifteen feet of fortified concrete. The weapons equipped with the GPS tail section can be delivered by F-15 and F-16 fighter jets the United States has sold to the Israeli Air Force. When the decision to sell Israel these advanced munitions was made, there was speculation in the worldwide press that the purpose was to prepare Israel for a strike against Iran's nuclear facilities.[3]

There are numerous complications to an Israeli strike on Iran's nuclear facilities. To begin with, with more than three hundred sites dedicated to nuclear technology, hitting most of the sites is a physical impossibility. Besides,
Iran has embedded many of the sites within populated urban areas, raising the
risk of collateral damage to civilians with the resultant adverse political consequences certain to result from the subsequent press coverage of the strikes.

Israel would undoubtedly concentrate on hitting five or six of the sites.
Clearly, the Soviet-built reactor at Bushehr is a logical target, as would be the
heavy water reactor facilities at Arak. One additional target might be the underground uranium enrichment facility at Natanz. While a strike limited to a
defined number of targets would not eradicate Iran's nuclear capabilities,
eliminating several key sites would represent a major setback.

Iran is farther from Israel than is Iraq, another factor making the strike on
Iran's nuclear facilities more difficult to pull off than was the 1981 attack on
the nuclear reactor at Osirak. Currently, U.S. troops in Iraq and Afghanistan
have Iran surrounded on the western and eastern borders. Still, Israel would
need to obtain or violate flyover rights involving several other countries, including possibly Iraq, Jordan, Lebanon, Saudi Arabia, and Syria. For political
reasons, these countries cannot cooperate with Israel in a strike on Iran; these
Islamic neighbors would undoubtedly deny flyover rights for an attack and
would object vociferously if their air rights were violated.

Because of the distances involved, Israel would have to refuel even their
long-distance F-15I and F-16I fighters en route or use U.S. airbases in Iraq for
refueling. One other alternative would be for Israel to launch the strike in part
or in whole from U.S. aircraft carriers in the Persian Gulf. This alternative
would shorten the distances involved and would eliminate flyover problems.
But for the United States to allow Israeli fighters to use U.S. aircraft carriers
to launch the raid would have enormous political consequences. Still, logisti-
cally, Israel could plan a three-pronged attack, two coming from carriers in the
Persian Gulf, one to the northwest near Bushehr, the other to the southeast,
perhaps as far east as the Gulf of Oman. The third prong could come over-
land, through Iraqi airspace.

An approach might be to launch the attack on a surprise basis, perhaps a
night assault, to minimize Iran's opportunity to activate air defense systems effectively. The entire strike could be planned to be over Iran for only a few
hours, with the combat activity coming to an end at the conclusion of the
three-pronged attack.

Dozens of other scenarios can be imagined. Given the history of Israeli first-strike operations, the best guess is that Israel would launch a surprise attack focused on a few targets with a reasonable chance of attack, planning that the entire operation would be concluded within a few short hours.

Israel might combine commando raids on the ground with the timing of select air attacks. Such land operations would increase the ability to inflict damage on targets that may be more difficult to destroy from the air, either because they are adequately protected from all but the most accurate air strikes, or because they are embedded in population areas where the collateral damage risk is high.

Israel has proven very successful in commando-type strikes targeted to kill leaders of Hamas, the mullah-supported terrorist group dedicated to the destruction of the Jewish state. There are probably 100,000 clerics of some significance in Iran. Of these, maybe 500 to 1,000 are reasonably important. To further specify the target universe, 100 to 200 of these clerics play political roles, of whom 10 to 20 are probably of national renown. Simply killing three to five of these clerics in the first hour would send fear throughout the Iranian world. Judging the reaction of radical Islamic extremists from experience in the Middle East, once a few key mullahs were assassinated, the rest could be expected to scurry to safety. A mullah may preach in the boldest statements of hate from the security of a mosque when he is surrounded by devoted followers. Yet the moment that cleric feels his life is threatened, he might just compete with the likes of Saddam Hussein for first position in a spider hole.

Israel has demonstrated with its assassination attacks on the Hamas leadership that it can damage the operational efficiency of the group by taking out the effective leadership two or three tiers down. Whichever mullah replaced one who has been assassinated would certainly think about the risk. From Osama bin Laden forward, we have yet to find a single radical Islamic extremist leader in the current war against terrorism who stood and fought. They are all brave when it comes to sending children in suicide attacks for Allah. Yet when it comes to threats to their own lives, they prefer to run and hide so they can rise again from the shadows and record one more surreptitious message of still more hate to their always admiring followers.

The goal of inflicting even partial damage by a limited first strike would be to set back Iran's timetable for obtaining nuclear weapons. While Iran may be on the verge of having those weapons, damage to some of the critical facilities could take months or even years to repair.

But the moment Israel makes a first-strike attack against Iran's nuclear fa-cilities, the political dynamics in the Middle East would change. Reaction from surrounding Islamic states would be severe. The United States, to the extent of its participation or acquiescence in the attack were clear, would re-ceive severe approbation from the world community that now supports a diplomatic solution with Iran over its pursuit of nuclear weapons.

If Israel struck before Iran had a deliverable nuclear weapon, retaliation by Iran would be limited to conventional means. Given the current limita-tions of Iran's military and air force, the retaliation would most likely be a conventional missile attack. The damage from such an attack, while severe, would be nowhere near as severe as the consequences of a nuclear attack.

Done in the most limited way imaginable, the first-strike by Israel would be the only strike planned. While it would be easier for the United States than Israel to send land forces into Iran, that type of action could be held as a contingency. Israel and the United States could plan to stand by after the first strike, to see how Iran would respond. After the 1981 Israeli strike on the Iraqi nuclear reactor at Osirak, Saddam Hussein did not launch a retaliatory strike against Israel. The United States and Israel might well suggest to Iran the wisdom of just such a stand-by response.

Iran might engage in suicidal military activity, but only if Iran calculated that its retaliation would inflict severe if not mortal damage on Israel. Iran probably would not engage in a suicidal military action if the likely calculation were that the ultimate result of the attack against Israel would inflict limited damage upon Israel while raising the possibility that accelerated military action by Israel (with or without the United States) would be suicidal only to Iran.

Undoubtedly the war scenarios game-played by military planners in the United States and Israel have calculated the difficulty of limiting any subse-quent war that would follow an Israeli first strike against Iran. The options available for retaliation by Iran or the involvement of other countries are too numerous and difficult for reliable probabilities to be assigned.

U.S. war planners would be very reluctant to green light an Israeli attack on Iran, except that the U.S. military shares with Israel the determination that Iran must never be allowed to possess nuclear weapons. The trigger point remains the moment Israel perceives that Iran has reached the point of no re-turn, when the mullahs will have nuclear weapons.

Clearly, going to war with Iran is a last resort. There are too many down-sides, not only in the world's adverse reaction to the United States as aggressors, but also in the damage that could well be done to dissident groups within Iran now pressing for regime change. Countries under attack typically experience a resurgence of nationalism that unites the population behind the current leadership, no matter how problematic that leadership has been, even to dissidents. As the 9/11 attack demonstrates in the United States, nothing unifies a diverse population faster than an attack by a foreign enemy.

An Israeli-led attack on Iran would most likely set back indefinitely the opposition movement within Iran. Still, this result is not 100 percent certain. The only certain calculation after an Israeli-led attack is that the world would change, both internationally and within Iran. An opposition movement within Iran might also find that in the aftermath of the attack the mullahs are sufficiently disoriented that their movement might be more openly brought to the streets without experiencing severe and violent reprisals.

Interestingly, some of Iran's neighbors might be relieved to see Iran deprived of its nuclear weapons capabilities. Saudi Arabia, for instance, may feel compelled to go through the expense and effort to develop its own nuclear weapons program if Iran develops a nuclear arsenal. Turkey may feel it has to reconsider its nuclear weapons options if Iran develops atomic bombs. For the Turks, NATO's credibility as a deterrent against an atomic Iran may well be called into question.[4] Once Iran gets nuclear weapons, the proliferation of nuclear weapons throughout the region seems inevitable.

One point is certain, in authorizing Israel to launch a first strike, the United States would have to be prepared to follow up with military action against Iran, depending upon how the mullahs react. The dimensions of the current war against terrorism being waged in the Middle East would transform to a new, higher level of intensity after an Israeli-led first strike against Iran, even if Iran does not immediately retaliate. The United States might well calculate that since it would get blamed for the attack anyway, U.S. forces might as well participate. Still, the decision to attack would be Israel's, not ours. The instant the mullahs have the capability to make nuclear weapons, the immediate threat is to Israel, not yet to the United States.

Rumors of an "October Surprise" Prior to the 2004 Election

AT THE end of the 2004 presidential election campaign, rumors circulated in Washington DC that President Bush, to bolster what were thought to be weak poll numbers, would pull an "October Surprise" and attack Iran prior to the November voting. The assumption was that a Bush-ordered attack on the

Iranian nuclear reactor at Bushehr and the underground uranium enrichment facility at Natanz, plus one or two other targets, would ensure a landslide victory as Americans rallied around his leadership.

To make the rumor more credible, those advancing the rumor noted that the aircraft carrier USS *John F. Kennedy* had been deployed to the Persian Gulf to coordinate the attack. Supposedly, Defense Secretary Donald Rumsfeld had discussed the role of the carrier in the planned attack on Iran when he visited the ship on October 9, 2004, and briefed the ship's commanders. Key U.S. allies in the region had reportedly been briefed on a dual-track military strategy aimed at conducting military operations simultaneously in Iraq and Iran. The goal of the U.S. attack on Iran was argued to be twofold: to take out Iran's key nuclear facilities while securing Iran's oil fields for use in the U.S. economy.[5]

But none of this happened. The United States did not attack Iran during or after the 2004 presidential election. Instead, the United States allowed the EU-3 and the IAEA to continue negotiating with Iran, all the while pressing that an agreement by Iran to stop enriching uranium had to be fully verifiable to be acceptable. The circulation of the October Surprise rumor could have been calculated to rile the president's opponents to increase their resolve to vote against him. Or the gambit may have been to announce the possibility of a strike beforehand, so as to blunt the political advantage any strike launched against Iran might have gained for the president.

Regardless of the motivation for circulating the rumor, the political swirl around Iran as the election cycle came to a conclusion served to heighten the importance of the question. The strong possibility that Iran was secretly developing nuclear weapons, following the North Korea track of using the negotiation process as a ruse to buy time, meant Iran was certain to be an issue at the top of the agenda for the party occupying the presidency on January 20, 2005. The controversy surrounding the alleged October Surprise signaled the certainty that however Iran would be handled by George Bush during his second term or by John Kerry in his first administration would draw fire from the political party out of power.

Should President Bush decide that war with Iran was inevitable, either through direct U.S. military action or by supporting an Israeli first strike, the political stakes were high. Done incorrectly, leftist Democrats could be counted upon to look into the possibility of holding impeachment hearings. Second administrations have been problematic for sitting presidents who cannot run for reelection a third time per the Twenty-second Amendment to the

Constitution. In 1974 Nixon in his second term resigned as the Watergate scandal lead to impeachment hearings, despite his having been reelected in a landslide in 1972. President Reagan was plagued by the Iran-Contra affair during his second term. President Clinton was impeached for lying under oath regarding the Monica Lewinsky sex scandal in his second term.

The arguments aligned against President Bush would be strong, especially if he does not build a credible case to the American people about going to war against Iran. Bush was under fire that no WMDs had been found in Iraq, despite the charges before the war that Saddam Hussein had stockpiles of WMDs that represented a threat to U.S. national security interests. How could President Bush be sure Iran was going to develop nuclear weapons? Democrats such as John Kerry could continue the arguments made during the campaign, namely that Iran would eventually succumb to international pressure if only the U.S. president would allow the IAEA to proceed in building an international coalition to pressure Iran to stop permanently enriching uranium.

Should President Bush decide that war with Iran was necessary, the first step would have to be to take the case to the U.N. Security Council, even though there is little reason to believe that the Security Council would be receptive to the argument. Russia, a permanent member to the Security Council, had spent approximately one billion dollars building the Bushehr reactor. China, another permanent U.N. Security Council member, had just signed a major oil and gas deal with Iran, a development that had analysts speculating that China would quickly become the world's largest importer of Tehran's oil and gas production. Chinese Foreign Minister Li Zhaoxing capped a year-long negotiation with Iran by paying a November 2004 visit to Tehran to meet with Iranian President Muhammad Khatami. During the visit, Li told the press that China was prepared to oppose any move by the United States to take the issue of Iran's nuclear program before the Security Council.[6]

Then the EU-3 of France, Germany, and Great Britain had been the prime movers in assisting the IAEA to negotiate yet another agreement with Iran, this time getting Iran to agree to stop enriching uranium, with the strategy that getting an agreement would keep the issue out of the Security Council. If the United States were to reject the agreement, perhaps because no reliable verification method was in place, the Security Council would certainly block further sanctions against Iran.

Still, for domestic political reasons, President Bush would have no alternative. Time would have to be spent taking the issue to the Security Council, or his leftist domestic opponents would be sure to hammer him with John Kerry's campaign accusation that he was inclined to take "cowboy" initiatives in his foreign policy implementation, lacking the skills to build the type of international coalition his father had fashioned for the first Gulf War.

All this played out against the developing oil-for-food crisis in the United Nations, a crisis that increasingly looked as if it might reach the office of the U.N. secretary-general, Kofi Annan.[7] This development was causing many in the U.S. public to question the honesty and the efficacy of the United Nations, an argument that might work this time in President Bush's favor should he have to take the Iran nuclear weapons issue before a nonreceptive Security Council. If the nations of the Security Council, possibly with the complicity of the secretary-general, could be bribed by Saddam Hussein's oil money, then their support for yet another rogue state in the Middle East might be equally suspect—or so the argument would go.

At any rate, the stakes are high, and President Bush can count on an uphill battle against the political left in the United States if he decides there is no alternative but war to stop Iran from developing nuclear weapons clandestinely. This was especially true if the president were to conclude that Iran had already reached the point of no return and could produce nuclear weapons on its own with no further assistance from outside foreign powers.

The Extreme Left and the Extreme Right Abandon Israel

As THE United States approached Election Day 2004, analyst Charles Krauthammer wrote a provocative editorial examining John Kerry's position on Israel. Krauthammer took seriously Kerry's mantra that he wanted the United States to more successfully enlist the support of the Europeans in the war in Iraq. Kerry had an unannounced strategy in mind, Krauthammer argued, to achieve this goal—once elected to the White House, Kerry would throw Israel to the dogs, giving the Europeans a key concession in their equation to solve the mess in the Middle East.

Krauthammer analyzed the words of Kerry's foreign policy adviser, Sandy Berger, the former Clinton national security adviser who was derided during the campaign when he was caught stuffing classified documents into his socks to steal them from the National Archives. Berger urged Kerry to steer the United States to "reengage" in ending the Israeli-Palestinian conflict, code words Krauthammer interpreted as a prescription to move the United States away from Israel. "Do not be fooled by the euphemism 'peace process,'"

Krauthammer warned. "We know what 'peace process' meant during the eight years Berger served in the Clinton White House—a White House to which Yasser Arafat was invited more often than any other leader on the planet. It meant believing Arafat's deceptions about peace while letting him get away with the most virulent incitement to and unrelenting support of terrorism. It meant constant pressure on Israel to make one territorial concession after another—in return for nothing. Worse than nothing: Arafat ultimately launched a vicious terror war that killed a thousand Israeli innocents."[8]

For decades the Islamic countries of the Middle East had been arguing that Israel was their key problem, that the Jews had stolen Palestine and deprived the Palestinians of their birthright. Give Palestine back to the Palestinians, so the argument went, and peace in the Middle East would be at hand. The one rub was that few countries outside the United States—not the Europeans nor the Russians, not the vast majority of the United Nations—cared if the Palestinians guaranteed the Israel's safety. "Why are they so upset with President Bush's Israeli policy?" Krauthammer asked. "After all, isn't Bush the first president ever to commit the United States to an independent Palestinian state? Bush's sin is that he also insists the Palestinians genuinely accept Israel and replace the corrupt, dictatorial terrorist leadership of Yasser Arafat."[9]

As proof of how isolated Israel had become in the United Nations, Krauthammer pointed to the 150-to-6 vote in which the General Assembly had declared Israel's security fence illegal. Nor did the Europeans, Russia, or the United Nations support Israel when the Israelis decided to defend themselves and attack the terrorists leading the Intifada (efforts that produced a remarkable 84 percent decrease in innocent Israeli casualties).

Kerry's supporters came to his defense, loudly arguing that he was pro-Israel. But their defense was somewhat undercut when Kerry's top foreign policy adviser, Richard Holbrooke, appeared on Fox Network's *O'Reilly Factor* and argued just what Krauthammer predicted the Kerry position would be. Holbrooke explained how Kerry would improve relations in the Middle East: "He [Kerry] has said already he would start intense talks with the allies . . . and he would reach out to the moderate Arab states. He'd put more pressure on Israel, Syria, and Saudi Arabia above all."[10] Pressuring Israel was a key part of the Kerry formula for bringing our supposed allies into closer working relationships with us in Iraq and Afghanistan.

David Horowitz, in writing his book *Unholy Alliance*, analyzed the support the extreme Left in the United States had given the Islamic terrorists who were opposing us internationally. In trying to explain the Left's underlying sympathy for the grievances expressed by Islamic radicals, Horowitz argued that the "leftist jihad" against America (which has its roots in the Left's support for communism during the 1950s and its opposition to the Vietnam War) had found common ground with the Islamic jihad that became evident in the 9/11 attacks. Again, Israel was caught in the middle, without the support of the American Left. Horowitz wrote: "In the Islamic war against the West, Israel is like the canary in the mine. It is targeted not only as a non-Islamic state, but also as the Middle East outpost of the chief infidel power, the United States."[11]

The "Goldwater Right" of the conservative movement has also moved closer to abandoning Israel. In an important book published during the campaign, *Where the Right Went Wrong*,[12] Pat Buchanan came out strongly in support of a position reminiscent of George Washington's famous Farewell Address, in which he argued that America should avoid foreign entanglements. Buchanan argued strongly that the Iraq War was ill conceived, that the U.S. military was overcommitted in a war that had been poorly planned. Buchanan from the Right was making almost the identical argument against the Iraq War that Kerry supporters were making from the Left.

Buchanan railed against neoconservatives, whom he saw as responsible both for our military policy in Iraq and for our encouragement of Sharon's hard-line policy in Israel. "Might is on Israel's side in this conflict," he wrote, "but time and demography are not. The Arab population of Israel, the West Bank, and Gaza is 4.5 million. Its birth rate is among the highest in the world. Outside of Palestine, Arab populations are exploding, Islam is growing more militant, and pro-American regimes are under strain, if not under siege."[13] Writing in December 2004, Buchanan spoke very clearly: "As for the neocons' insistence on 'regime change' in Iran, that is a deal-breaker, which is why Israel and the neocons have made it their non-negotiable demand. They don't want a deal. They want war."[14]

What it comes down to is clear. The crisis with Iran's getting nuclear weapons is only a life-or-death crisis to America if we remain committed to Israel's survival. In the extreme, if we are willing to see Israel sacrificed to the wave of Islamic radicalism surging in the Middle East, then our crisis would diminish in intensity. Iran is a considerable distance away from having a deliverable nuclear weapon that could hit the continental United States; certainly North Korea is much closer to that capability.

Even if we were to compromise Israel and reapply pressure for major Israeli concessions to the Palestinians, extreme liberals and extreme conservatives might argue that Iran could be held off, threatening to develop nuclear weapons, yes, but still coming under international control. Maybe Iran could be permitted to come within one turn of a screw from having a deliverable nuclear weapon, promising not to go the extra distance as long as Iran was given everything the mullahs wanted internationally, especially with regard to weakening the State of Israel.

If we accept that the hatred of Iran extends beyond Israel to include the United States, then David Horowitz has a point—as was argued at the time of the Holocaust, the Jews are once again the canaries in the mine of freedom.

Fundamentalist Christians and the Defense of Israel

TODAY ONE of the strongest sources of support for the State of Israel comes from fundamentalist, even evangelical, Christians. Hundreds of thousands, probably millions of Christians today view events unfolding in the Middle East in biblical terms. For Christians of this viewpoint, the survival of Israel takes on apocalyptic meaning. Viewed from the perspective of "the end days," the consequences of America abandoning Israel would be catastrophic.

A third influential book was published during the presidential campaign of 2004: *The American Prophecies*[15] by Michael Evans, founder of a group of Christians known as the Jerusalem Prayer Team. "I believe," Evans wrote, "there is a direct correlation between current events and prophecy. I am firmly convinced that President Jimmy Carter unlocked Pandora's box in the Middle East, and that President Bill Clinton stepped into the maelstrom."[16] Evans argues that Clinton abandoned Israel, not pursuing bin Laden's organization aggressively after the 1993 attack on the World Trade Center, and later that same year in forcing Israel to accept the Oslo Accords. Evans argues that God removed his protection from the United States because Clinton broke faith with Israel and that the 9/11 attacks were a direct consequence of Clinton's actions and God's punishment.

Most secularly trained Americans instinctively reject religious arguments of this nature as nothing more than superstition. Yet during the 2004 presidential campaign, I became aware of how deep the Christian conservative movement remains throughout the heartland of America. We touched a deep chord in America by arguing forcefully that the two and a half million Americans who went and fought in Vietnam did so honorably; that they had been horribly wronged when John Kerry in his 1971 testimony to the Fulbright Committee said that the U.S. military in Vietnam were war criminals, that war crimes were committed on a daily basis and were approved up and down the chain of command. This "silent majority," as Richard Nixon dubbed the millions of conservative Americans who populate the so-called Red States, included millions of fundamentalist Christians who have a deep, personal, almost religious commitment to the Jews who founded Israel and the freedom the State of Israel represents.

Remarkably, sorting out politics in the Middle East draws out ancient, biblical considerations. We should never forget that the Jews and Christians see their roots trace back to Abraham through his son Isaac; at the same time, Muslims see their roots trace back to Abraham through his son Ishmael. For secular Americans with a modern educational viewpoint as their intellectual frame of reference, these biblical considerations seem irrelevant at best, possibly even dangerous or just plain silly.

Yet for millions of Christians, Jews, and Muslims involved in these conflicts, the biblical frame of reference is ever-present as the context against which current events are played out. American politicians who forget the importance of religion in sorting out these political questions risk defeat—something the extreme liberal and highly secular wing of the Democratic Party is forced to sort out right now, especially in the face of John Kerry's unexpected loss in the presidential campaign of 2004. Kerry lost for many reasons, one of which was his inability to connect with fundamentalist Christians throughout America who take their religion seriously.

Ironically, a biblical connection ties together the ancient Persians and the Jews. As told in the book of Ezra (1:1–11), God brought in Cyrus of Persia to end the Babylonian captivity of the Jews and to provide them the necessary riches to return to Jerusalem to rebuild the temple. For Christians trained to appreciate the Jewish tradition as their own, this connection to the ancient Persians is revered, as it is for Jews. Looking beyond the mad mullahs who have hijacked both Islam as a legitimate religion and the thousands of years of proud Persian history, these roots of unity cut across the layers of religious intolerance and prejudice.

None of this is to argue that the problems of atomic Iran have to be viewed in biblical or religious terms to be understood. On the level of secular geopolitics, strong arguments are advanced that Israel must be supported as the only genuine democracy in the Middle East. The point here is that the perspective of fundamentalist Christians must be appreciated and entered into the political equation. In addition to the Jews living in America, there is a strong base of support for Israel among America's fundamentalist Christians, many of whom share the concerns of the Israelis themselves that a state like the current Islamic Republic of Iran represents the destruction of Israel and must never be allowed to possess nuclear weapons.

The Quagmire Argument

ANOTHER FAMILIAR attack from the Left, one recently also taken up by the extreme Right, is that America is in a quagmire in Iraq. The argument is meant to call to mind the Vietnam War and to suggest that the U.S. military is in a war over its head, that our enemies are so difficult to defeat that we are lost in a morass trying to stay alive and keep even with the challenges.

Underlying the argument is a suggestion charging that our military policy in the Middle East was formulated by a group of neoconservatives. The term is meant to bring to mind a group of individuals who have come to conservative principles rather recently, with a confidence in American military that might not be generally shared by traditional conservatives. A related charge is that while conservatives believe our moral and political values are right for us, neoconservatives want to expand our morals and values around the world.

President Bush's assertion that the urge for democracy lives in every human heart is viewed with skepticism by both extreme leftists and traditional conservatives. With a raised eyebrow, both the Far Left and the Far Right would question whether the historical traditions in any Islamic country in the Middle East give the people there any idea of what Americans mean by democracy. Our institutions do not apply to cultures this distant and distinct from ours, or so the critics argue.

Both the Far Left and the Far Right come together then on the conclusion that President Bush and the neoconservatives currently in charge of the Pentagon and the National Security Council are self-deluded at best, grandiose in their thinking, one-dimensional in the extension of their values to other cultures, probably silly in their understanding of world history and religions, but certainly naïve.[17]

A great divide separates those who view 9/11 as a watershed event in American history and those who do not. Those who see 9/11 as a defining moment tend to view the attack on the World Trade Center and the Pentagon as a major attack against America, an attack on our own soil, launched by radical

Islamic terrorists willing to commit suicide to kill us, all to advance their religious and political goals. Those who do not see 9/11 as a defining moment tend to wonder what the overreaction is all about. Seeing terrorism as a law-enforcement problem, these critics may want us to secure our borders, but they feel the danger is overstated, that a few extremists do not make a world war.

If we are involved in a world war against radical Islamic terrorists, as President Bush insists, then any measures we take to protect ourselves and to win are justified, regardless of cost or sacrifice. The Clinton administration proceeded for eight years on the law-enforcement hypothesis. That approach did not anticipate 9/11 or stop it from happening. We are at a threshold in history. As our forefathers warned, liberty requires constant vigilance. Within the lives of many of us, the United States has fought against a series of "isms"—Nazism, fascism, communism, to name three of the most important. Now we face another tyranny in the form of radical Islamic terrorism—Islamofascism, as some have named the threat.

Nothing would be more satisfying than to be able to make the threat disappear through clever diplomacy and multinational organizations. But since the 1930s that approach has been found wanting. Today the threat is not only Tel Aviv being destroyed by a nuclear weapon, the threat is also that a softball-sized lump of uranium-235 could be smuggled across our borders, much like drugs are commonly smuggled into the United States every day.

Can Israel tolerate the threat that Tel Aviv might be wiped off the face of the earth by a mad mullah who only has to push a button and launch a nuclear strike? Can we risk that an Iranian sleeper cell might be smuggled into our midst to detonate a suitcase nuke in New York or Washington DC or Los Angeles?

One person who cannot afford to make the wrong calculation here is the president of the United States. Should President Bush choose the negotiation-and-diplomacy route, and should Iran launch a nuclear attack either against Israel or the United States, the very critics today who are urging negotiation and diplomacy would be the first to accuse the president of being negligent in the conduct of his duty to protect the security of the American people and our key allies.

These are the questions Iran's nuclear program forces us to consider. Can any of us afford to be wrong?

11

The Movement for Freedom in Iran

TERRORISTS ARE LIKE BAD playwrights. They frequently have great openings, maybe even great first acts. The problem is that terrorists generally have poorly thought-out second acts and almost always terrible endings. Our goal in stopping terrorists is to rewrite their play with our ending, making sure we engineer the second act to get to a conclusion that makes sense.

So, for example, the 9/11 terrorists had a great opening. The drama began with their hijacking four airplanes simultaneously, taking over the cockpits, and flying them as suicide bombers into some of America's most important landmarks—the World Trade Center in New York City, a symbol of American business and economic strength, and the Pentagon, a symbol of America's military power. Then what was supposed to happen? Americans were supposed to feel afraid. Yes, that happened. Next, Americans were supposed to capitulate to the terrorists' demands, abandon Israel, and pull out of the Middle East. None of that happened.

The ending Americans are in the process of writing is that we are hunting down the radical extremist Islamic terrorists and eliminating them before they have a chance to pervert any further our freedoms and the freedoms of others around the world. The second act is very difficult. We have had to attack and destroy the Taliban in Afghanistan. We have attacked Saddam Hussein and removed him from power. We have accepted the capitulation of Muammar Qaddafi and moved to remove all weapons of mass destruction in Libya.

For a quarter of a century since the Islamic revolution in Iran that put the mullahs in power, there has been an expectation among freedom-loving people that Iran would experience a revolution from within. This has not yet happened. Still, we must continue to search through the many options available until we find something that works.

So how do we write the ending with the mad mullahs in Iran? The play should end with an opposition movement that rises from within Iran and successfully removes the mullahs from power. Peaceful regime change from within is the best possible ending.

A Congressional Resolution Supporting Regime Change

THE MULLAHS will press hard for the international community to unite behind them, arguing that for the United States to support regime change in Iran would be a criminal act.

Within our own domestic politics, the Far Left of the Democratic Party is certain to scream and object to anything other than supporting the Europeans who want to work with the mullahs. Since the Watergate era, the Far Left of the Democratic Party has consistently objected to the United States interfering in the domestic politics of another nation, no matter how anti-democratic the regime may be, no matter how much harm the regime in question may want to cause the United States. In any action concerning the mullahs, the far left wing of the Democratic Party will come out on the side of the mullahs, not those who want to oppose them.[1]

Even the Far Right of the Republican Party, the paleo-conservatives as we have referred to them before, will object to our meddling in Iran. The mullahs may be anti-freedom and anti-democratic, the paleo-conservatives would agree. Yet since the mullahs do not represent a clear and present danger to vital U.S. national security interests, we should leave them alone.[2] The argument of the Far Right is fundamentally different than the argument from the Far Left. The Far Right argues not that radical Islamic extremists are right in their hatred of America but that there are severe limits to our ability to defeat them using military power as our primary weapon.

Study after study affirms that the mullahs are extremely unpopular in Iran. But the difficulty any Iranian opposition has in gaining any momentum is that the mullahs are so ruthless. At the first sign a resistance movement is gaining ground, the mullahs employ the terror tactics of arbitrary arrests, confinement without legal representation, torture, and murder. By removing the opposition leaders, the mullahs cripple the movements. By causing fear among the followers, the mullahs destroy any organized opposition. When a rogue regime effectively controls the internal mechanisms of social control, including the police and the courts, dissidents are soon isolated and eliminated. When confronted by the world, the mullahs simply lie, deny that they are repressing anyone's freedoms, or even more creatively, they blame the dissidents themselves for the trouble.

The United States must reach out and provide moral and intellectual support for the opposition groups fighting for freedom in Iran. This initiative can start with the U.S. Congress. A resolution passed by the Senate and the House of Representatives should affirm a number of specific steps:

- That the State Department will be authorized to award competitively substantial funds to Iranian American radio and television broadcasting organizations willing to carry the message of freedom to the Iranian people. Additional funds should be awarded competitively to individuals and groups operating freedom-supporting Internet sites and blogs dedicated to communicating with the Iranian people. As much as one hundred million dollars should be committed to this effort immediately.

- The official policy of the U.S. government, including all policy statements issued by diplomatic representatives of the government around the globe, should reflect and support the theme of regime change to remove the mullahs from power and should express America's support for opposition groups championing the cause of freedom within Iran.

- We should make every effort through the State Department and the Immigration and Naturalization Service to assist any and all political refugees who manage to escape Iran so they can fly to freedom and asylum in America. Procedures to validate Iranian refugees and to assist them financially should be expedited and given top priority.

- Funds should be made available to support groups in Iran who are dedicated to freedom. We should look to support opposition groups who show a commitment to human rights, equality of women, and freedom of religion, as well as to those fighting to champion the cause of free speech and association, and the rights of equal economic opportunity. Another one hundred million dollars should be committed to this effort immediately.

- Congress should call on the president and the executive branch to pursue any international diplomatic efforts to oppose the mullahs' rogue regime and to support opposition groups within Iran. This should include, but not be limited to, introducing resolutions at the United Nations and making efforts with as many nongovernmental agencies as possible to support these goals. The entry of Iran into the World Trade Organization should be blocked by the administration as long as the mullahs remain in power.

- Congress should call upon the president and the Department of Justice to investigate and prosecute all U.S. corporations and individuals who attempt to circumvent the economic and diplomatic sanctions currently in place against the mullahs, being particularly sensitive to corporations operating through foreign subsidiaries and individuals acting through appointed international agents seeking to achieve indirectly what is forbidden by law. The resolution should support existing U.S. sanctions on Iran as well as the Iran-Libya Sanctions Act, tightening enforcement provisions of the original legislation and expanding on the president's discretion to impose additional sanctions and/or other penalties to punish the mullahs for misdeeds.

A resolution passed by both houses of Congress firmly stating these principles and actions should give strong moral, economic, and political support to those freedom fighters within Iran seeking to gain ground. Important resolutions along these lines are currently under consideration by Senators Rick Santorum (R-PA), Sam Brownback (R-KS), and Norm Coleman (R-MN). In the House of Representatives, strong support for such a movement has been expressed by Representatives Ileana Ros-Lehtinen (R-FL) and Steve King (R-IA). Many more can be expected to come forward as sponsors.

The Model of the Ukraine

THE UNITED STATES expended sixty-five million dollars in 2002–4 to support opposition groups in Ukraine, with the goal of electing Viktor Yushchenko president. The money was spent through organizations such as the U.S. Agency for International Development (USAID), the Carnegie Foundation, and the National Democratic Institute. The funds were used to promote democracy, not to support Viktor Yushchenko's candidacy directly.[3]

Still, the expenditure of public funds to cause regime change came under intense partisan attack. Democratic congressmen, such as Representative Edolphus Towns (D-NY), called for an investigation of the matter, charging that U.S. taxpayer funds were allocated to support organizations with a known preference for candidate Yushchenko, and that these organizations were key elements in mobilizing Ukraine's "Orange Revolution."[4]

Towns sent a letter to Andrew Natsios, the administrator for USAID, charging: "Information in the public domain indicates that a significant portion of the reportedly $65 million spent during the past two years, for such programs in the Ukraine, may have been given to organizations with a known partisan agenda in support of one of the presidential candidates. Such a bias would be inconsistent with public claims by the administration that the United States is impartial in the Ukraine election, and this would constitute a negative image of the United States for unwarranted interference in that country's domestic affairs."[5]

The Bush administration noted that the State Department spends about one billion dollars annually to support pro-democracy activities worldwide. Ken Wollack, president of the National Democratic Institute, insisted: "All the effort that has been made on the part of organizations like ours and on behalf of the U.S. government was to support the process, not the outcome."[6]

The National Democratic Institute is composed of a group of Democratic Party foreign policy experts; former Secretary of State Madeleine Albright chairs the board of directors. The institute spends approximately forty-eight million dollars per year for democracy-building programs around the globe. In response to criticism, the National Democratic Institute pointed out that representatives of all parties and all blocs in Ukraine attended its seminars to learn fundamental democracy skills, including writing party platforms, organizing voter support bases, and developing internal party structures. The institute was a main supporter of the Committee of Voters of Ukraine, a group constituted to be a watchdog to make sure the presidential vote was conducted fairly.[7]

Applied to the situation in Iran, those opposed to any U.S. meddling in the internal politics of another state will certainly object to any strong congressional resolution that authorizes the government to spend funds to promote democracy in Iran. The problem is that, without resources, a resolution lacks the ability to achieve results other than through moral persuasion. If we are to communicate to opposition groups within Iran that we support their efforts to establish democracy through peaceful processes, making financial resources to their efforts is important.

What is our partisan purpose? Our goal in Iran should be to replace the current anti-democratic government of the mullahs with a new government dedicated to freedom. Our ultimate goal should be to support a process of democracy, not simply one candidate over another. What the Ukraine model shows us is that we can reasonably hope change in the direction of freedom can be stimulated from within, without any need for military intervention.

Why Can't We Just Work with the Mullahs?

IN JULY 2004 the Council on Foreign Relations issued a report entitled "Iran: Time for a New Approach." The report was the product of an independent task force whose cochairs were Zbigniew Brzezinski, national security adviser to President Carter during the 1979 hostage crisis with Iran, and Robert Gates, who stayed on after Carter to serve as deputy director of the CIA under President Reagan during the dark days of the Iran-Contra affair. Neither gentleman was evidently deterred by prior policy failures.

The report criticized the "old direction" resulting from sanctions as a "lack of sustained engagement" with the government of Iran; the recommendation for a "new direction" was to open up "dialogue" with Iran, "selectively engaging Iran on issues where U.S. and Iranian interests converge, and building upon incremental progress to tackle the broader range of concerns that divide the two governments." The report also cautioned against talking about regime change, preferring instead to focus the rhetoric and policies on "promoting political evolution that encourages Iran to develop stronger democratic institutions at home and enhanced diplomatic and economic relations abroad."[8]

The language of engagement may have sounded more determined than merely saying "use more diplomacy," but the result was the same—more appeasement. The mullahs reading the Council on Foreign Relations report could be assured that any government following the recommendations of this report would be setting out to work with them, not remove them from control. That message was certain to be reassuring to the mullahs while at the same time being devastating to the opposition groups trying to change the government from within. The idea that we might convince the mullahs to give up the despotic control they enjoy as a result of their position at the head of the theocracy is wishful thinking.

Then, in July 2004, a group reconstituting the old Committee on the Present Danger (CPD) came out with some more recommendations along the appeasement line. The first Committee on the Present Danger had been a 1950s group of conservatives organized to resist Communism in the Soviet Union. The group began from an important premise. As explained by Frank J. Gaffney Jr., head of the Center for Policy Security in Washington DC: "The CPD brilliantly waged a 'war of ideas' against an earlier, hostile ideology with global ambitions—Soviet Communism. Now it must help defeat today's ideological threat: Islamofascism."[9] The group included other prominent conservatives, including former U.N. Ambassador Jeanne Kirkpatrick and former CIA Director James Woolsey. The group also included prominent liberals, with Senator Joseph Lieberman (D-CT), Al Gore's vice presidential running mate in 2000, serving as co-chairman.

The CPD searched for ways the U.S. government could communicate with the people of Iran to achieve democracy. Action steps included reopening our embassy in Tehran, to be headed by a "counselor" whose job would be to "generate support from our allies, speak frequently with the Iranian people via radio/tv/internet and meet directly with Iranians wherever possible."[10]

While the CPD took a strong stance that the regime must never be allowed to possess nuclear weapons, many of the practical recommendations seemed unrealistic. For instance, the counselor at our reopened embassy in Tehran would try to establish programs of visiting scholars or would enlist young Iranians to go abroad for seminars with counterparts in democracies around the world. The whole idea was for the U.S. government to reestablish a presence in Iran through which we could encourage international dialogue, meetings, and people exchanges that would teach principles of freedom and techniques of democracy to the Iranian people.

Like the Council on Foreign Relations, the CPD entitled its position paper "Iran—a New Approach." Like the Council on Foreign Relations, the CPD was implicitly admitting that the current policy of sanctions was failing. What then was needed? Both groups came up with virtually the same answer—dialogue, otherwise phrased as "engagement." How this differed simply from the old failed alternative of diplomacy was not made clear. Still the groping was for a way to talk to the Iranians and get them to see reason. We are reminded of the quip usually made about Lyndon Johnson's idea in the 1960s that civil rights activists and segregationists could make progress if only they would "come, let us reason together."

Yet unlike the Council on Foreign Relations, the CPD believed Iran needed a regime change. Its major contention was that the strategy to impose sanctions had cut off any possibility of America reaching the Iranian people to communicate directly with them to stimulate regime change from within.

The problem with the CPD approach was that Iranians closed our embassy during the revolution because they did not like what the United States and our democracy stood for. The mullahs have not invited us to reopen the embassy. If we were to agree with them, the mullahs would probably be interested in talking with us. But if we expect them to start agreeing with us, we are just wasting our time. The mullahs have not agreed with us for twenty-five years, and the reason is probably not that they don't understand what we are saying. Nor do the mullahs want us communicating with the Iranian people. For twenty-five years the mullahs have done everything imaginable to imprison or kill dissident journalists, and now they are attacking free speech on the Internet.

For the marble to go through the hole at the bottom of the bowl takes a while. Then finally, when it does, we have to realize that the mullahs understand us just fine, which is probably why they continue to call us the Great Satan. The mullahs do not want Americans talking with anyone.

Pat Buchanan Reacts

WHEN THE CPD came forward with its recommendations, Pat Buchanan went ballistic. He ridiculed the "feel good" nature of the CPD's recommendations, claiming that the declaration of the group "is pure mush. It reads like the final communiqué, negotiated in some all-night session of deputies, of a contentious meeting of the G-8."[11]

Buchanan's major criticism of the CPD was not its wanting to reestablish the U.S. embassy in Tehran so we could open up a dialogue with the Iranian people. Buchanan objected to the underlying position taken by the CPD, namely, that there was something so wrong with the mullahs that we couldn't work with them. Buchanan's position was that the United States has worked with many corrupt regimes, why not one more? He wrote: "But terrorism is a tactic, a weapon used in wars of liberation by the IRA, the Irgun, the Stern Gang, the Mau Mau, the Algerian FLN, the Viet Cong, the ANC and a dozen other movements. Not only have we made accommodations with the regimes that came out of these movements, we are giving most of them foreign aid. And some of the ex-terrorists, like Menachem Begin and Nelson Mandela, have gotten Nobel Peace Prizes."[12]

Like the Council on Foreign Relations, Buchanan wanted us to work with the mullahs. Strangely, the Far Right was coming to the same conclusion as the Far Left, but for a different reason. The Council on Foreign Relations thought we should work with the mullahs because a policy of "creative engagement" might change them fundamentally so the mullahs would begin to think more like freedom-loving democrats. Buchanan didn't particularly care what the mullahs thought, and he doesn't seem to expect them to convert to our position on issues of human rights. But what Buchanan is saying is that the United States has worked with international bad guys before, what's the problem with working with yet one more group of bad guys? Buchanan's realism is almost so hard-nosed it becomes cynical. Consider this extract:

> One imagines most signers of the CPD declaration would consider Arafat a terrorist. But not only does Yasser share a Nobel Prize with Yitzhak Rabin and Shimon Peres, he was handed Hebron by Benjamin Netanyahu and offered 95 percent of the West Bank and co-tenancy of Jerusalem by Ehud Barak. Can it be that four Israeli prime ministers have engaged in accommodation with terrorists?
>
> Was FDR wrong to accommodate Stalin to defeat Hitler? Was Nixon wrong to go to Beijing and accommodate Mao Tse-tung in the Shanghai Communiqué? Were not Stalin and Mao two of the greatest terrorists of the twentieth century?
>
> Bush's father made an accommodation with Hafez al Assad, who had slaughtered thousands of Muslims in Hama, for help in ousting Saddam from Kuwait. Was he wrong to do so? In ousting the Taliban, George W. Bush enlisted a Northern Alliance of warlords whose hands were soaked in blood. Was he wrong to do so?

Buchanan has a point. From the perspective of Machiavellian "real politics," there may be times to accommodate terrorists. The point is that we tried that approach for eight years under the Clinton administration. Bill Clinton's approach, however, was to see terrorism as a law-enforcement problem. He hesitated to retaliate against terrorists because we had insufficient legal proof or we lacked the jurisdiction to indict them. Clinton worried about collateral damage to civilian populations if our military strikes were not sufficiently surgical to wound or kill only the terrorist "criminals" we were after.

The result of Clinton's approach was that the terrorists concluded we were weak, they were emboldened, and they grew in strength. Their increased determination to attack us was evident as the first 1993 attack on the World Trade Center during the Clinton administration was seen by the terrorists as a minor setback, or an experiment that showed them what really needed to be done if the buildings were to be taken down.

Accommodation will not work with the mullahs. The mullahs have figured out that the game of diplomacy and negotiation only gives them time to build nuclear weapons while they gain strength in collecting the investment dollars of the Europeans and other newfound allies, such as the Indians and Chinese. We will never deter the mullahs from their ultimate goals, which remain to destroy Israel and America while spreading their perversion of Islamic extremism worldwide, using terrorism as much as necessary and practical. The mullahs are religious extremists, and their fundamental beliefs are not subject to negotiation or modification, no matter how persuasive our arguments for freedom are or how effectively we open channels to communicate those ideas.

The Damocles Proclamation

THE NEXT suggestion can be termed a ploy just to get their attention. The idea comes from a story told by Cicero, the great Roman orator, of Dionysius, a Greek king of Syracuse who ruled in Sicily from 432 to 367 BC.

As the story goes, Damocles, an admirer of the king, wished he could enjoy the king's wealth and power for a day. The king granted his wish, and Damocles was very pleased with his fate, until he noticed a sword hanging over his head, suspended by a mere horsehair. If the horsehair should break, the sword would fall and kill him instantly. When Damocles complained, the king explained that there was always a sword hanging above the life of a king because he could at any instant lose his kingdom and his head by a single wrong move.

Conservative thinker Jack Wheeler applied the concept of the Sword of Damocles to the situation of deterring al-Qaeda from further 9/11-type attacks on the United States.[13] If we modify the suggestion somewhat, we come up with a Damoclean Sword threat to use against the Islamic Republic of Iran. Here's how it would go: If Iran were to launch a nuclear weapon on Israel, the United States would immediately retaliate by unleashing a massive nuclear strike on Mecca. This is a version of the mutually assured destruction scenario, in that the loss of Israel would be as devastating to the Jews as the loss of Mecca would be to the Muslims.

There are several obvious problems with the idea. First, the destruction of Mecca would mean that the United States was at war with Islam itself, but our true enemy is much narrower—the terror-supporting radical Islamists who have hijacked both the religion and the government of Iran. Second, the mullahs have preached suicide, and the loss of Mecca would be horrible. Still, the mullahs might calculate that the State of Israel would still be destroyed, and there would remain hundreds of millions of Muslims whose zeal to defeat America would now be truly unstoppable. And the mullahs might be crazy enough to calculate that destroying Mecca and Medina might not be too bad after all; as a result, their Shi'ite holy sites would become even more important.

The reason to consider the idea is that a Damoclean Sword proclamation issued against the mullahs might reframe their thinking and have a positive effect, provided the threat was formed correctly and was credible. Historically, similar threats have formed the core of international compacts such as NATO, where we swore that a military attack against any NATO member country would automatically trigger a military response from all the members.

The president could make clear that if we had proof that the mullahs were constructing a nuclear weapon clandestinely in contravention of their agreements with the IAEA, then the United States would consider that an act of war necessitating a military attack on Iran. This would at least define a zero-tolerance approach to what reasonably appears to be the current Iranian effort to achieve secretly what they have agreed publicly they would not do. After the president made such a proclamation, no person or nation should be able to see the situation the same again. There would be no doubt that continued cheating by the Iranian government would mean war.

The only problem here is that the mullahs are clever. The nuclear negotiators for the Iranian government has already suggested to the EU-3 and the IAEA that it would be entirely reasonable for the Iranian government to develop everything necessary to have a nuclear weapon. The mullahs would just stay a few steps away from putting one together. They would refrain from making nuclear weapons until an international threat to their national security left them no choice but to defend themselves by assembling in final form one or more deliverable nuclear devices.

Should the president decide to issue a Damoclean Proclamation, the speech would have to make clear that continuing nuclear weapons development to all but the last stage would be considered tantamount to building nuclear weapons and making them operational. Delivering such a speech would communicate seriousness to those opposition groups inside Iran that are looking for a clear message from the United States.

The Mullahs Make a Fashion Statement

THE MULLAHS are famous for their proclamations regarding how women should dress. The state-run television station has even dedicated part of its main news program to a series of segments dedicated to the question "What is fashion?" The programs feature warnings based on the Tehran chief of police's admonition that women were not to dress like "models," that a general clampdown was in order to round up women seen wearing flimsy headscarves, three-quarter-length trousers, and shape-revealing coats.[14]

What does not draw as much journalistic comment are the fashions the mullahs have created for themselves. The black or white turban and the long, draped gray robes are standard wardrobe items for regulation mullahs. So are the stylishly trimmed beards and the unobtrusive simple-rim eyeglasses. The well-dressed mullah pays attention to how the cloth on the robe drapes, how different layers of the robe hang, how robe inside pockets are designed to hold prayer books. Fashion statements can be made on whether collars are round or high, whether sleeves are tight or loose, whether trousers are worn under robes or not. Yet regardless of the variations that define higher style, a definite "mullah look" has evolved.

So, too, the government representatives venturing forth for international meetings are developing a style. Expensive, well-tailored suits are required. Iranian diplomats are designing what appears to be a signature variation—shirts are tailored with a tieless short collar cut to be pinned together with a gold pin fastener. This variation is being seen as a distinct Iranian fashion statement that is recognizably different from the traditional suits and ties common for decades in diplomatic meetings.

These are not trivial points. All terrorist groups in the Middle East make fashion statements—Hezbollah with its yellow banners, Osama bin Laden with his untrimmed beard and a turban-robe combination more suitable for a mountain terrain than an urban setting.

There is precedent here. Where did Adolf Hitler as chancellor get his military uniform? He may have considered himself the head of the military, but he held a civilian position. The short mustache suggests a direct copy from one of his favorite movie actors, Charlie Chaplin.

Then we have the early photographs taken by his personal photographer, Heinrich Hoffman, who followed Hitler everywhere. In Heinrich's photographs, Hitler poses in sometimes ridiculous gestures, highlighted by exaggerated facial expressions, all staged before the camera so he could perfect his dramatic speaking style, a style audiences were supposed to assume had been completely natural. Hoffman was later ordered by Hitler to destroy these early photographs, but he disobeyed the order.[15] In retrospect, the entire Nazi production was carefully staged and choreographed.

If the mullahs are to be defeated, their imagery must be broken. Photographs of the regime's brutal repression of its own citizens must be shown to the world. Images of women and their second-class status, their loss of rights, even their abusive clothing must be presented so the world can see.

What impact will this have? The mullahs are desperate to have themselves considered a legitimate government that deserves to be taken seriously. Show the brutal images, and the world will question the mullahs about their true purposes, no matter how well their fashionable clothes are stylishly tailored. Play for the world the mullah-produced hate television, with subtitles so the full extent of their anti-Jewish hatred can be appreciated.

To survive, the mullahs depend upon a closed society. Open the society so the world can see. Every tyranny depends on secrets and shadows to survive. The mullahs are no exception. Hatred hates the light of day.

The Case of Ahmed Batebi

AHMED BATEBI is one of many Iranian students the mullahs arbitrarily arrested during the student demonstrations of July 1999 in Tehran. The students were protesting the closure of the newspaper *Salaam*, which translates as "peace."

Batebi became famous internationally when his photograph was picked up by the world press. The image is striking. Batebi, bearded with a headband around his forehead, was photographed holding up a bloody T-shirt, his hands stretched above his head, an Iranian flag filling the background, an anguished look upon his face. The photograph communicated the intensity of the student protest movement, desiring against all odds to bring freedom to Iran by getting rid of the mullah's harsh and repressive rule. The image was made more poignant by Batebi's subsequent arrest and imprisonment.

Batebi was sentenced to death on charges relating to national security, a sentence determined by a secret revolutionary court trial where he had no legal representation. Not even a transcript of the trial is known to exist. His sentence was later commuted on appeal to a fifteen-year prison sentence, later reduced to ten years, all suffered because of his brave act of protest. Even today, his lawyer is pressing for his release, uncertain that Batebi is even still alive.[16]

A February 4, 2003, letter written by Batebi and other imprisoned students was given wide distribution. The statement is important and dramatic:

> We want to show our respect for the Universal Declaration of Human Rights, Universal Peace, Non-violence, Environmental Protection, Permanent Progress, and all the other noble covenants sanctioned by mankind. We hope to alleviate despotism and totalitarianism, setting the vote of the people as the gauge for governance. We aspire to redeem the rights of our sisters which have been ignored for so long, and establish an all encompassing equality between men and women. We want to promote the Persian creed of "good deeds," "good speech," and "good thoughts." We have borne the burden of endless tortures. We have actually witnessed executions of our friends.[17]

Every successful social and political movement needs someone to come forward to represent the cause. Ahmed Batebi's haunting image as presented in the now-famous photograph of his protest act, his long imprisonment and suffering, the eloquence of his statement from prison—all these qualify Batebi to be a candidate to represent the cause of Iranian freedom internationally.

A worldwide movement to learn the exact situation of Batebi's imprisonment and, if he is alive, to press for his release could well set in motion an international movement the mullahs could not ignore.

The Importance of the U.S. Military

THOSE WHO have opposed the war in Iraq have argued that the nation's military forces are stretched to the limit, that we will need to reinstitute a draft if we need to fight yet another war in the Middle East or in some other part of the world. Critics on the Left forget that it was President Clinton who dramatically reduced the size of the American military. Between 1992 and 2000, the eight years Bill Clinton was in office, national defense was cut by more than half a million personnel and fifty billion in inflation-adjusted dollars. The army lost four active divisions and two reserve divisions. Air force personnel decreased by 30 percent. The total number of navy ships decreased from around 393 ships in the fleet in 1992 to 316 today. Even the marines dropped twenty-two thousand personnel.[18] President Clinton did not believe we were at war. He saw radical Islamic terrorists as a problem within the purview of the FBI. When the question came to rogue states, Clinton thought Madeleine Albright and the State Department were in business to speak with them, to see if diplomacy might position them more favorably vis-à-vis the vital security interests of the United States.

Americans have had to fight many tough wars. In Iraq less than 2,000 soldiers have died. In Vietnam, the number was 58,000 honored dead, their names inscribed on The Wall memorial in Washington. During the Civil War, some 624,511 Americans died on the battlefield. President Franklin Roosevelt won a world war fought across both the Atlantic and the Pacific oceans, yet he was crippled from polio and could not even walk across a room without using crutches.

The men and women serving today in the armed forces of the United States are some of the bravest and most skilled military personnel to honor this nation with their unselfish service. The American armed forces are patriots who have volunteered for duty. Billions of dollars spent to make sure these men and women are properly rewarded for their service is money well spent. If we need more troops, we should improve the incentives, and more brave Americans will come forward to increase the ranks. There is no need for conscripts when the nation has the economic resources to reward those who come forward of their own will.

Then, too, businesses around the country should organize to adopt those serving so that our armed forces know they will have meaningful and relevant career opportunities awaiting them when they leave the service. We owe the brave veterans of all our wars more than a parade on Veterans Day.

We can expect the war we are fighting today, the war against radical Islamic terrorists, to be a long and difficult war. Yet the costs of not fighting the war include very possibly more dramatic attacks on U.S. soil and possibly even the loss of our cherished freedoms. When called forth properly, America has never lacked the men and women to fight for freedom.

The Need to Call the United Nations' Bluff

THE UNITED NATIONS has never been able to stop a single nation in the world from developing nuclear weapons once that nation has announced its desire to do so. Libya gave up its program to develop weapons of mass destruction only after the United States eliminated the Taliban from Afghanistan and removed Saddam Hussein from power in Iraq.

On January 13, 2005, Israel broke its silence on the nuclear freeze deal brokered with the mullahs by the EU-3 and the IAEA. Israel's Foreign Minister Silvan Shalom told a Jerusalem news conference that the Europeans "have achieved an agreement now with Iran. We do not like it very much but still it is much better than it was before. We believe that it should be moved, should be transferred to the Security Council, in order to stop the Iranians from what they are doing."[19]

Israel has a point. Iran's agreement with the IAEA will be meaningful only if Iran allows open and complete inspection of the country's nuclear facilities. Even then, the opportunity for subterfuge is considerable, especially in a country as large as Iran. IAEA inspectors will have to be free to investigate claims made even by international groups opposed to the Iranian regime.

There is one more important point here. The United Nations has a horrible record of protecting tyrants and allowing them to steal huge amounts of money. The allegations in the U.N. oil-for-food scandal with Saddam Hussein even suggests that U.N. officials may be willing to be bought, given the billions of dollars flowing around loosely or under the influence of creative accounting.

Still, taking the matter to the Security Council may be a prerequisite to a responsible approach to the problem for both the United States and Israel. If military action is required as a last resort, both the United States and Israel will have to make the case that the United Nations was given ample opportunity to act to prevent Iran from developing nuclear weapons, even clandestinely.

Besides, taking the question to the Security Council puts the question of Iranian nuclear weapons on a larger world stage. What is said here is certain to be followed by opposition groups within Iran. If the United States and Israel were to use the forum of the Security Council effectively, then how they make the case could well give support and encouragement to the dissidents seeking to organize for peaceful regime change effected from within.

A War of Ideas

FRANK GAFFNEY was right. We need a "war of ideas" to defeat the mullahs. How best will this happen?

The mullahs are fighting the Internet right now in Iran because they realize it has the power to communicate and change ideas. Bloggers in the United States caused a huge shake-up at a communications giant like CBS News over the Dan Rather scandal with forged documents set up to defeat President Bush in the 2004 presidential campaign. This gave encouragement to bloggers around the globe. Producing peaceful regime change in Iran is not too large a concept to be taken on by the "pajamahudeen" of recent blogger fame.

Internet Web sites can reach across borders, even more easily than television or radio signals. Two excellent pro-freedom blogs on Iran come to mind as candidates to lead the charge. One is maintained by Aryo Pirouznia on behalf of the Student Movement Coordination Committee for Democracy in Iran (www.daneshjoo.org). The other is maintained by Gary Metz, known on the Internet as "Dr. Zin," and is titled Regime Change Iran (www.regimechangeiran.com). Other innovative Web sites are in development. In addition to sharing information and providing a forum for robust discussion, the bloggers can open international petitions for peaceful regime change in Iran. Drawing thousands, possibly even hundreds of thousands of signatures, an Internet-based regime-change petition could easily draw the attention of activists worldwide. The word would circulate in the mainstream media once the petition gained enough momentum, inevitably reaching the mullahs in Tehran.

We should not neglect broadcasting both radio and television into Iran. The Internet should supplement these efforts, providing an alternative channel of communications with its own unique characteristics and advantages for reaching and impacting people.

All the content—whether delivered by radio, television, or the Internet—should be active, interesting, and interactive. Dull programming and uninteresting content will get nowhere. Lively discussions and open forums, challenging ideas and ready access to news as it develops—these can be sufficiently compelling to command attention.

The mullahs will be hard pressed to stop altogether a persistent barrage of interesting information supporting concepts of freedom delivered by an assortment of creative media. If we are going to remove the mullahs from power, we must grow the seed of freedom in Iran by winning the war of ideas.

A War of Economics

ISHAQ SHAHRYAR presented his credentials as Afghanistan's ambassador to the United States to President George W. Bush on June 19, 2002, at a ceremony in the White House. Ambassador Shahryr was the first recognized Afghan ambassador to the United States since 1978.

The event was recognized by the administration as a great victory for freedom. Ambassador Shahryar has had a distinguished career as a scientist known for inventing low-cost solar cells. He was instrumental in the development of ultraviolet sensitive solar cells for NASA's Jupiter Project. In 1993 he was awarded U.S. patent rights for a 20 percent efficient silicon solar cell. He has been quoted as saying: "My role is to help Afghanistan enter the twenty-first century. It's my mission to take my business skills and help revolutionize the Afghan economy." Shahryar is taking steps to accomplish that mission.[20]

On October 9, 2004, Afghanistan held the country's first-ever free elections to select a president. The event was historic.

Moving beyond the threshold of freedom, we must realize that the expectations of the Afghan people have been raised. If nothing materially changes after a free election has been held, many will begin to wonder what difference freedom makes.

This is the problem Ambassador Shahryar has begun to address. The idea is to involve and organize private capital to invest in Afghanistan. With the assistance of Wall Street, Shahryar is developing a program to assist corporations who want to set up not only markets but also business operations within Afghanistan. The opportunities are huge. The entire infrastructure of the country has been destroyed by decades of war. Every basic need from housing to education, from roads to airports, from consumer goods to entertainment, needs to be delivered to a waiting public.

If we wait for government to take the initiative, we will wait a long time. Bureaucratic and legislative process are rarely quick to respond. If we want to demonstrate to the Afghan people the benefits of freedom, we must activate our most creative minds and our most productive corporations to get involved. The goal is to build Afghan business, not simply to transplant American companies there. The desire is to build jobs for the Afghan workforce, not to rely on public subsidies.

If Ambassador Shahryar makes progress with this effort in Afghanistan, the results are certain to be seen throughout the Middle East and beyond. Nothing will impact the imaginations of others, including those in both Iraq and Iran, as to see a demonstration of progress put in place when governments and private enterprise cooperate.

If in Afghanistan an economic model of success can be set in a Middle Eastern country that has already been liberated from the tyranny of radical Islamic extremists, then those planning for similar peaceful and constructive change in Iraq and Iran may well take hope and follow the lead.

Conclusion

For the past twenty-five years the mullahs controlling Iran have been a threat to the citizens of Iran and to peace in the region. The Iranian theocracy has appropriately been labeled by the Bush administration as part of the "Axis of Evil," along with Saddam Hussein's Iraq and North Korea under Kim Jong Il.

Now, as the mullahs advance to obtain nuclear weapons, the threat they represent is ever wider and more serious. One nuclear weapon could destroy Israel as we know it. The mullahs are well aware how close they are to fulfilling their dream of "Death to Israel," a dream that is not just mad rhetoric but a core belief of their insane religious extremism.

The minute the mullahs reach the point where they can make a nuclear weapon without further assistance from any outside power, the political calculation of the world changes. Many of us have lived our entire adult lives under the threat of a nuclear war. Yet, somehow, most of us have never imagined a nuclear war could actually happen. The mullahs will change that calculation. If we allow these mad terror-supporting clerics to get their hands on atomic bombs, we may be only a countdown away from the ultimate terror of experiencing a nuclear war in our lifetime. The mullahs getting their hands on atomic bombs may be how apocalyptic scenarios begin.

George Soros Joins Forces with the AIC to Support the Mullahs

On January 13, 2005, the pro-mullah American Iranian Council (AIC) joined forces with George Soros's Open Society Institute to host Javad Zarif, Iran's ambassador to the United Nations, to give a talk entitled "The View from Tehran."

Soros did not waste any time after supporting John Kerry's losing 2004 presidential bid with millions of his own money. Even before George Bush could be inaugurated the second time, Soros was rolling out the carpet for the mullah's top man in New York. Soros invited Zarif to his New York base to explain why Kerry had been right to insist that the United States needed to grant Iran full economic and diplomatic recognition, as well as nuclear fuel, all the while trusting that the mullahs would keep their word and not make bombs.

In announcing the event, Iranian government spokesperson Abdollah Ramenzanzadeh told reporters that Tehran "had not yet decided on a third party" to mediate "negotiations" with the United States. What negotiations? Investigative reporter Kenneth Timmerman, writing in the *New York Post,* commented: "There are no ongoing negotiations between the United States and Iran. However, whenever the regime has felt under pressure from a vigorous U.S. policy, it has dangled the prospect of such negotiations in an attempt to discredit and to weaken the American side."[1]

Once again the mullahs were being clever. The staged event gave the appearance of putting pressure on the Bush administration to go along with the EU-3 and the IAEA and accept Iran's word that it would stop enriching uranium. Now President Bush would appear to be unreasonable if he did not assign some third party to mediate these nonexisting negotiations. Moreover, the American Left would have even more ammunition to make the case that the president was on yet another preemptive warpath against a presumed Islamic enemy who had no intention of possessing weapons of mass destruction.

The Iranian foreign ministry went further, suggesting that Secretary of State Colin Powell has determined that a "future Iraqi government dominated by the Shi'a and influenced by Iran will not be a threat to the United States or its interests" and "that Washington and Tehran have reached an understanding on how Iraq needs to be stabilized."[2]

Once again the pro-mullah public relations effort in the United States was hard at work, trying to pin on outgoing Colin Powell, known to be one of the administration's more liberal foreign policy officials and generally in favor of negotiations, the presumptive conclusion that Iran could be constructive in Iraq. This was not something the Bush administration itself would readily concede, not when the reports coming from the U.S. military in Iraq were presenting evidence that the mullahs were sending terrorists across the border into Iraq to harass American troops and create as much instability as possible prior to the scheduled elections on January 30, 2005.

Timmerman was accustomed to the mullahs' shenanigans: "What Tehran wants is abundantly clear. Iran's ruling clerics want to continue mucking around in Iraq and to complete their nuclear weapons development, without the United States intervening."[3]

The key story here was not that the mullahs and their cohorts in America were dissembling—that was old news. What this event signaled was that George Soros and the American Far Left were ready to continue spending millions of dollars to support America's enemies, including radical Islamic extremists from a terror-supporting rogue state like Iran.

"Soros is once again showing his true colors," Timmerman wrote. "He is anti-American, anti-freedom and pro-tyranny, for America and for America's friends overseas."[4]

Hassan Nemazee, as was seen earlier, one of John Kerry's top fund-raisers in his 2004 presidential campaign, was a board member of the AIC. Nemazee has funded a long list of Democratic party candidates, including Bill and Hillary Clinton, Ted Kennedy, and Joe Biden. At every event where Democratic candidates have been present, the AIC has been certain to press its agenda to restore economic and diplomatic ties between Iran and the United States.

Aryo Pirouznia, the Iranian freedom fighter whom Nemazee sued for defamation when Aryo called him an agent of the mullahs, was extremely upset by this Soros-sponsored get-together between the AIC and the Open Society Institute in New York.

> It seems once again the very same individuals and groups of interest, who tried to sell the false idea of any possibility of reforming an ideologically rogue and tyrannical regime, have mobilized in order to influence the second Bush administration. These are the very same circles that pushed for Mr. Kerry's presidency and now they're intending to avoid the formation of a strong U.S. policy, which might back the Iranian people morally and financially in their struggle to overthrow the illegitimate and shaky Iranian regime.[5]

There was no doubt in Aryo's mind that the mullahs needed America's economic and diplomatic support to prop up their regime. What Aryo wanted was freedom in his country, something he knew in his heart could only be achieved if the mullahs were thrown out of power.

More than ever the Bush administration should avoid engaging the Mullahcracy and must increase its political and economic pressures on the totality of the Islamic regime and its partners in order to favor the opposition groups in Iran pushing for a popular take-over of power. Only an elected Iranian secular and democratic state, issued from a real and genuine referendum, can answer the aspirations of the Iranian people and fulfill the world's legitimate concerns about freedom, fanaticism, Islamism, terror, and the dangers of nuclear weapons.[6]

Timmerman was equally strong in his conclusion: "Soros' prescription for America's future was bad for America. His prescription for the future of America's relations with Iran is bad for the world. Strengthening Tehran's mullahs means a nuclear-armed Iran."[7]

Jack Kennedy's Calculation No Longer Applies

ON JUNE 10, 1963, President John F. Kennedy gave a commencement address at American University in Washington DC. In that speech, he made a statement about the nuclear standoff between the United States and the Soviet Union that changed the nature of the arms race then raging between the two countries. Speaking of the Soviets, Kennedy chose to focus on what ultimately brought us together: "For, in the final analysis, our most basic common link is that we all inhabit this small planet. We all breathe the same air. We all cherish our children's future. And we are all mortal."

Here is the great difference. The mullahs do not share our love of life. For the mullahs, the prize is in the anticipated life after death, an afterlife where the rewards of martyrdom are promised to be sublime. The legacy mullahs have left the world is their invention of the suicide bomber, a young man or woman who can be convinced to strap on a belt of explosives so he or she can sneak into the midst of unsuspecting civilians, all too often innocent Jews, and blow themselves up. The mullahs preach the glorification of self-destruction as a pinnacle experience of the short lives of those they indoctrinate to do their lethal bidding. Killing one's self so as to kill the enemy in the process is the distinguishing thought the mullahs propagate.

The EU-3 and the IAEA see no problem in giving mad religious fanatics like these access to nuclear fuel. That is the greatest madness of all.

The Soviets fought bravely in many wars, yet there was no streak of suicidal heroism fundamental to Soviet Communism. The Soviets wanted to beat the United States, yet they wanted to live to enjoy the victory.

As we have pointed out before, if the mad mullahs had a world annihilation button that they could press to end the world, the probability is that they would push the button. How can people who think like this be deterred by the fear of mutual assured destruction, which stopped both the United States and the USSR from launching a first strike against the other? The mullahs might simply launch a nuclear weapon because of the chaos that would result, even if it meant their subsequent self-destruction.

On December 14, 2001, at Friday prayers in Tehran, Ayatollah Ali Akbar Hashemi-Rafsanjani in his "Jerusalem Day" speech told those assembled that "one atomic bomb would wipe Israel out without a trace." But the Islamic world, he added, would only be damaged, not destroyed, by Israeli nuclear retaliation.[8] How many suicidal deaths in the Islamic world were acceptable to Ayatollah Rafsanjani? One million? One hundred million? A billion? If the hated Jews could be wiped clear from the Holy Land, the ayatollah may well have accepted whatever Islamic casualties it took.

The nuclear weapons strategic thinking since the end of World War II has been predicated on a presumption that those nations who possessed nuclear weapons would not calculate in a suicidal manner. The mad mullahs in Iran, with their radical version of their Islamic faith, have changed that calculation. The mullahs preach suicide.

Warren Buffett Expects Nuclear War

IN 2002 Warren Buffett, one of the wealthiest people in the world, gave a frightening prediction to the shareholders of his Berkshire Hathaway holding company: "We're going to have something in the way of a major nuclear event in this country. It will happen. Whether it will happen in 10 years or 10 minutes, or 50 years . . . it's a virtual certainty."[9]

Buffett has built his career on the insight needed to be a major investor across many different industries, including insurance. If he perceives the risk of nuclear war, we probably all should give considerable thought to the warning.

For more than half a century the world has lived with the threat of nuclear war, but only rarely has the world felt that nuclear war could actually happen. Nuclear war seemed a real possibility for a few days during the 1962 Cuban Missile Crisis. Various subsequent crises in Berlin again raised the specter of nuclear war. Many do not yet realize how real the possibility of nuclear war will be the minute the Islamic Republic of Iran gets its first deliverable nuclear weapon. And that day is imminent.

The Logic of Asymmetric Warfare

THE CONSTRUCTION of the World Trade Center took seven years, from the time construction began on One World Trade Center in 1966 until Two World Trade Center was finished in 1973.

American Airlines Flight 11 out of Boston began the attack by striking the North Tower of the WTC at 8:45 a.m. on September 11, 2001. The north tower, the first hit but the second to collapse, went down at 10:28 a.m. So the total elapsed time from the first impact to the collapse of both towers was one hour and forty-three minutes.

This is a key principle of effective terrorism. Destruction is much easier and more dramatic than creation. Building something takes time; blowing up something can be done relatively quickly. There is a corollary principle. Complex systems fail for relatively simple faults. The Space Shuttle *Challenger* blew up because a relatively inexpensive part, an O-ring seal malfunctioned between the booster sections of the rocket.

Without electricity, our advanced civilization comes to a halt—televisions no longer work, elevators may stop at midfloor, computers cannot function, the Internet cannot be accessed, our cell phones run out of batteries and cannot be recharged, lights go off, and the world turns to darkness. We live in a complex world that is yet dependent on the availability of many components we take for granted. Eliminate running water and every major city enters a sanitation crisis within forty-eight to seventy-two hours.

If terrorists were truly politically or militarily strong, they would simply go to war, as would a nation-state of some considerable significance. Because terrorists are weak, they seek to exploit weaknesses in their enemies with dramatic violence that will cause massive chaos or produce psychological havoc out of proportion to the terrorists' own lack of strength.

To prevent terrorism from being successful requires a massive expenditure of the nation-state under attack. We in the United States of America have already expended billions of dollars and sacrificed previously enjoyed freedoms to combat radical Islamic terrorism. To prove the point, just consider the relative ease of boarding an airplane prior to the 9/11 attack and realize how much has been spent since 9/11 to reinforce airline security. Today we are inconvenienced as passengers and intruded upon as citizens because the entire system of air travel has been transformed to a new level of cost and difficulty. Yet the only alternative is to allow our complex systems to be victim to random, calculated violence to the point where no one feels safe, whether they have ever planned to take an airplane trip or not.

Nuclear terrorism raises the stakes. If the world permits a rogue terror-supporting state like the theocracy currently ruling Iran to have nuclear technology and fuel, we will be starting a short clock ticking down to the time where we will most certainly experience nuclear war of one form or another.

Terrorists communicate their purposes in advance, and they attack their enemies systematically. We should not underestimate the ability of the mullahs to win, given the religious zeal with which they pursue their perceived holy mission. The promise of a reward in heaven permits suicidal calculations that take the potential for terrorism and violence to a new plateau of seriousness.

If we fail to take seriously the threat represented by Atomic Iran right now, we may well doom ourselves to experience a nuclear war in our lifetime.

A World Without Israel?

FOR THOUSANDS of years the Jews have been hated by enemies who wanted desperately to remove them from Israel. Egyptians. Philistines. Assyrians. Babylonians. Two of these forcibly removed the Jews from the Holy Land. The Jews returned, but the ancient kingdoms of Assyria and Babylon are long gone.

The history of Jewish persecution is long. We cannot begin to enumerate the list of powerful people and nations that have decided their purpose in life in large part depended upon hating Jews. The most notable example in modern times is, of course, Hitler and Nazi Germany. The Holocaust resulted, and six million Jews were killed. The concentration camps known as Auschwitz and Birkenau produced haunting images of barbed wire and gas chambers, which only Jew-haters choose to ignore or even deny altogether.

Hating Jews is a collective historical sickness of the human race. Whether we will emerge from it unscathed today is an open question. What hangs in the balance is the possibility within our lifetime of the nuclear annihilation of the human race as we know it, should we not be able as a species to overcome this perverse tendency to hate Jews.

Right now the radical Islamic extremists are attempting to convince the world that we can have peace only if we will eliminate Israel. Those Muslims who have tried to make peace, such as Anwar Sadat of Egypt, run the risk of being assassinated by radical extremists within their own midst. This may have been a reason Yasser Arafat turned down Bill Clinton's remarkable offers at Camp David. Clinton desperately wanted to be remembered as the president who made peace in the Middle East, and he was willing to press Israel for major concessions so that personal goal could be accomplished. Clinton failed.

That a world without Israel would be peaceful is yet another deceitful ploy being advanced by the radical Islamic extremists.[10] Our recent history proves that tyrants set on world domination cannot be appeased. What other radical Islamic terrorists learned when the United States and Israel pulled out of Lebanon was that Hezbollah was right, their suicidal terror tactics worked. Rather than being appeased, the most insane among the radical Islamic terrorists were encouraged to press even harder.

The same will happen if the mad mullahs have their dream come true. A world without Israel would be a huge victory to these extremist clerics who want the world to conform to their theocracy. The real enemy, the Great Satan, has always been the United States of America. Our music, our economic lifestyle, our treatment of women, our openness in discussing topics such as sex—all these and many more themes are an affront to the radical Islamic sensibility. Mad clerics in extremist mosques in Tehran and around the world would see the elimination of Israel as a victory.

"Just give us Jerusalem," might be the way the argument starts, or even more deceitfully, "Just let us share Jerusalem, that will be good enough for now." We make a mistake if we think that the elimination of Israel will ever leave the imagination of the extreme Islamic mind.

What are we to do? Unfortunately, we must respond with force. Hitler occupied the Sudetenland in part because most Americans and many others in the world had never even heard of the Sudetenland at the time. "Give him the Sudetenland," was a seemingly reasonable response, "then he'll leave us alone." Hitler did not leave anyone alone, not even his temporary friends, the Soviets.

This is the problem with hate. We begin by thinking it is only hatred of Israel. Then we realize it is also hatred of us. Finally we are forced to acknowledge that the hatred was always about everyone and everything, except for the hater themselves and those few ideas the hater wished to impose on the world as their self-imprint.

Mad ideas are exactly that—mad, totally insane. No one in the history of the world has ever dominated the world, and most likely no one ever will. The idea is a bad one to begin with. World domination is hard; it requires constant repression, as was proved by Stalin and many others before him. The only sane idea in the world is freedom. As precious and as delicate as freedom is, the concept is the strongest ever devised by the human species. The logical corollary of freedom is religious tolerance. Without religious tolerance, freedom will not long live.

Those of goodwill have always hesitated to use war to defend freedom. We may be forced to do so again, but even then, we will not do so with any sense of pleasure or enjoyment. We are engaged in a world war against the radicals who hijacked Islam, but we do not need to be at war with Islam itself. Whether we will win or lose this war remains to be seen. Yet the consequences of not fighting the war are unimaginable. Many of the ideas presented in these pages were not presented to be sensational. No, they were presented because they must be contemplated. We have no choice but to take steps right here and now to see these horrific images never come to pass.

Consider these notes of a Jewish inmate, found in a concentration camp at the end of World War II:

> It is already dark in the yard. An electric lamp shines in the distance, casting a faint light. The only strong illumination comes from a big floodlight mounted above the gate, visible from far away. We stumble along the soggy, clayey ground, full of fear and exhaustion. We are approaching our new graves, as we call our new homes. Before we even got to the new place, before we drew in a breath of air, some of us had our heads clubbed. Blood was already flowing from split heads or injured faces. This was the first welcome for newcomers. All of us are bewildered, looking around the place where we are brought. Now they inform us that this is a sample of camp life. Iron discipline reigns here. We are in the death camp. It is a lifeless island. A man does not come here to live but to die, sooner or later. There is no room for life here. It is the residence of death. Our brains are dulled, thoughts are numbed, this new life is impossible to grasp. Everyone is wondering where his family is. Where were they taken and how will they manage in the new conditions? Who knows how their terrified children will behave when they see how their mothers are mistreated? Who knows how these thugs will treat the sick, the weakened mothers, and the sisters they love? Who knows what human grave received their fathers and brothers, or what they are going through? They all stand helpless, full of anxiety, in despair, lonely, wretched, broken.[11]
>
> Handwritten notes of Zalman Gradowski found at Auschwitz

That the mullahs would exact extinction upon the Jews if they had the opportunity to do so should never be doubted. "May it never happen again," the prayer that is central to every Holocaust museum around the world, is the responsibility all people of goodwill are forced to take up once again.

If this world is to remain civilized, we must encourage everyone to once and for all lay down the hatred of Jews. Ultimately, the only people destroyed are the Jew-haters themselves. Today, in a world where the Jew-haters have nuclear weapons, the price we all have to pay for tolerating their hatred is horribly unimaginable.

The Last, Best Hope of Mankind

STANDING ON the battlefield at Gettysburg in 1863, Abraham Lincoln reflected on America's importance, a nation brought forth in liberty and dedicated to the proposition that all are created equal. Lincoln saw that the Civil War was a great test whether America, or any nation brought forth on those principles, could long endure. Lincoln was well aware how powerful are the forces of hate that seek to dominate humans in one form of slavery or another.

We are still today engaged in that test. The mullahs currently ruling Iran want to impose on us all their particular vision of radical Islam. We will only be free, so the mullahs proclaim, when we believe what they preach and do as they instruct. To be truly free, one must follow their version of Islam, or so the mullahs proclaim. America is founded on a different principle, the principle of freedom of religion, where no one may rightfully dictate to anyone else whether or how to believe in God.

Tyranny in the name of God is still tyranny. All the repressions and violence that come with the mullahs come because they are insecure at their core. Those who truly trust in the rightness of their beliefs will allow others to come to the same conclusion of their own free will.

America would have preferred to pass on participating in the war against terrorism. Yet, once again, Americans are fighting and dying in lands most Americans have never visited, in places with names most of us cannot correctly pronounce. We went to war against the radical Islamic terrorists because we were attacked and, even then, as a last resort.

Were the mullahs truly to lay down their ambitions to advance their extreme religious views through violence, including nuclear violence, we could easily make peace with them without contemplating difficult processes such as regime change. We are not at war with Islam itself, just the perverted version of Islam that these mad mullahs have hijacked to fly the airplane of their personal ambitions. We are at war because we have no choice.

In his second inaugural address, President Lincoln noted that the Civil War began because one side, the South, would *make* war rather than let the Union survive, while the other side, the North, would *accept* war rather than let the nation perish.

We are much in that same difficulty today. The mullahs have determined to make war on the world rather than allow others to be free. We accept war rather than see our freedoms perish from the face of the earth.

This, then, is the great challenge we face today. Will we and our children remain free? If that is to be, then we have hard tests before us that we must face resolutely and with great courage.

Radical Islamic extremists must never be allowed to possess nuclear weapons. May the better angels of our nature once again prevail.

Notes

Index

Notes

Foreword

1. John E. O'Neill and Jerome R. Corsi, *Unfit for Command: Swift Boat Veterans Speak Out Against John Kerry* (Washington DC: Regnery, 2004).
2. Jerome R. Corsi, "Terrorism as a Desperate Game: Fear, Bargaining, and Communication in the Terrorist Event," *Journal of Conflict Resolution* 25, no. 1 (March 1981): 47–85.

Introduction

1. Michael Ledeen, "Europe's Ritual Dance. The Western Counterpart of Iran's Deception," *National Review Online*, November 29, 2004.
2. Commission on Presidential Debates, Debate Transcript: The First Bush-Kerry Presidential Debate, University of Miami, Coral Gables, Florida, September 30, 2004. The complete transcript can be found at http://www.debates.org/pages/trans2004a.html.
3. Ibid.
4. The President's State of the Union Address, the United States Capitol, Washington DC, September 29, 2002. Archived at WhiteHouse.gov. http://www.whitehouse.gov/news/releases/2002/01/20020129–11.html.
5. National Commission on Terrorist Attacks upon the United States, *The 9/11 Commission Report: Final Report of the National Commission on Terrorist Attacks upon the United States* (New York: Norton, 2004). The heading on page 240 reads "Assistance from Hezbollah and Iran to al-Qaeda."
6. "Kerry Says He Will Repair Damage if He Wins Election," *Tehran Times*, February 8, 2004. The article is online at http://www.jihadwatch.org/dhimmiwatch/archives/000856.php.
7. Kenneth R. Timmerman, "Kerry Will Abandon War on Terror," *InsightMag.com*, March 1, 2004, http://www.insightmag.com/news/2004/03/16/PoliticsKerry.Will.Abandon.War.On.Terrorism-621288.shtml. Timmerman noted, "By claming that the Kerry campaign had sent the message directly to an Iranian news agency in Tehran, the paper indicated that the e-mail was a demonstration of Kerry's support for a murderous regime that even today tops the State Department's list of international terrorism."

8. "Khamenei: 'Have 2 bombs ready to go in January or you are not Muslims,'" reported in the October 5, 2004, issue of Geostrategy-Direct.com. See also "Iranian leader wants nukes in 4 months," on WorldNetDaily.com, October 2, 2004.

Chapter 1: Iran's Quest for Nuclear Weapons

1. Bill Gertz, *Trechery: How America's Friends and Foes Are Secretly Arming Our Enemies* (New York: Crown Forum, 2004), 92.
2. Attachment A, Unclassified Report to Congress on the Acquisition of Technology Relating to Weapons of Mass Destruction and Advanced Conventional Munitions, 1 July–31 December 2003. See http://www.cia.gov/cia/reports/721_reports/july_dec2003.htm. Referred to hereafter as the 721 Report.
3. Robin Wright and Keith B. Richburg, "Powell Says Iran Is Pursuing Bomb," *Washington Post*, November 18, 2004.
4. Ibid.
5. Dafna Linzer, "Nuclear Disclosures on Iran Unverified: U.S. Officials Checking Evidence Cited by Powell," *Washington Post*, November 19, 2004.
6. Steven R. Weisman, "Bush Confronts New Challenge on Issue of Iran: Ominous Disclosures on a Nuclear Program," *New York Times*, November 19, 2004.
7. Liza Porteus, "State, Powell Defend Comments About Iran's Nuke Program," Fox News, November 21, 2004. See http://www.foxnews.com/story/0,2933,139076,00.html.
8. Eli Lake, "Bush Skeptical of Atom Accord with Iranians: Verification Is Key, President Asserts," *New York Sun*, November 23, 2004.
9. Quoted in Elaine Sciolino, "Exiles Add to Claims on Iran Nuclear Arms," *New York Times*, November 18, 2004. See also "Iran Bought Blueprints of Nuclear Bomb, Opposition Group Says," *NewsMax.com*, November 17, 2004 (http://www.newsmax.com/archives/articles/2004/11/17/102110.shtml.
10. Dafna Linzer, "U.N. Finds No Nuclear Bomb Program in Iran: Agency Report and Tehran's Deal with Europe Undercut Tougher U.S. Stance," *Washington Post*, November 18, 2004. Note the political message conveyed in the subtitle to the article, emphasizing that the statement by the IAEA "undercuts" the "tougher U.S. stance," or to paraphrase the undertone more directly, "the warmongering hawks in the Rumsfeld Department of Defense."
11. Ibid.
12. A series of Internet articles announced Iran's surprise request for a "research" loophole to allow some centrifuges to remain operational. See "Iran Wants to Amend Nuke Freeze, EU Says No," *Reuters.com*, November 24, 2004; "Iran's last minute backtrack on nuclear 'deal,'" *Telegraph.Co.Uk*, November 24, 2004; "Iran asking IAEA to exempt some centrifuges from nuclear suspension deal," *TurkishPress.com*, November 24, 2004.

13. Elaine Sciolino, "Board Accepts Nuclear Vow by Iranians: A Tepid Resolution Angers U.S. Envoy," *New York Times*, November 30, 2004.

14. Ibid.

15. Ibid.

16. Ibid. for ElBaradei's statement. For Hassan Rohani's remarks, see Caroline Glick, "H-hour Has Arrived," *Jerusalem Post*, November 18, 2004.

17. Caroline Glick, "Feith to 'Post': US Action Against Iran Can't Be Ruled Out," *Jerusalem Post*, December 12, 2004.

18. Arieh O'Sullivan, "Ya'alon: West Must Be Prepared to Strike Iran," *Jerusalem Post*, December 13, 2004.

19. Elaine Sciolino, "Iran and Europeans Open a New Round of Negotiations," *New York Times*, December 14, 2004.

20. A similar analysis can be found in the insightful article by Stuart E. Eizenstat, "Iran: A Test for the European Approach," *International Herald Tribune*, December 14, 2004. See also William Danvers, "Outside View: Between Iran and a Hard Spot," *Washington Times*, December 14, 2004.

21. See GlobalSecurity.org. This Internet site contains an extensive discussion of Iran's nuclear facilities, including a site-by-site description (Iran > Facilities > Nuclear).

22. David Albright and Corey Hinderstein, "Countdown to Showdown," *Bulletin of the Atomic Scientists*, November–December 2004.

23. "UN Offers to Guarantee Fuel for Iran—Diplomats," *TehranTimes.com*, October 30, 2004, reprinting a Reuters report from Vienna.

24. "Bushehr" at GlobalSecurity.org (Home > WMD > World > Iran > Facilities > Nuclear > Bushehr). See http://www.globalsecurity.org/wmd/world/iran/bushehr .htm.

25. Maria Golovnina, "Russian Announces Completed Nuke Plant," *Washington Times*, October 15, 2004.

26. GlobalSecurity.org, see note 23 above.

27. The report is available at the Web site of the Federation of American Scientists, www.fas.org (FAS > Nuke > Guide > Iran > Facility). See http://www.fas.org/ nuke/guide/iran/facility/esfahan.htm.

28. Information provided by the National Council of Resistance of Iran, U.S. Representative Office, "Information on Two Top Secret Nuclear Sites of the Iranian Regime (Natanz and Arak)," December 2002. See IranWatch.org, http://www .iranwatch.org/privateviews/NCRI/perspex-ncri-natanzarak-202.htm.

29. David Albright and Corey Hinderstein, "The Iranian Gas Centrifuge Uranium Enrichment Plant at Natanz: Drawing from Commercial Satellite Images," The Institute for Science and International Security (ISIS), March 14, 2003; http://www.isis-online.org/publications/iran/natanz03_02.html.

30. NCRI report, http://www.fas.org/nuke/guide/iran/facility/esfahan.htm.
31. Richard Boucher, U.S. Department of State, Washington DC, May 9, 2003. The question was taken from the May 8, 2003, daily press briefing, "Iranian Nuclear Facilities: Arak and Natanz," http://www.state.gov/r/pa/prs/ps/2003/20439.htm.
32. Ibid.
33. James R. Bolton, "Preventing Iran from Acquiring Nuclear Weapons," Hudson Institute, Washington DC, August 17, 2004. See http://www.state.gov/t/us/rm/ 35281.htm.
34. Ibid.
35. Anthony H. Cordesman and Arleigh A. Burke, "Iran's Developing Military Ca- pabilities," Main Report,Washington DC Center for Strategic and International Studies, Center for Strategic and International Studies, December 14, 2004, working draft. The discussion of the Shahab-3 missile is drawn from pages 25–27.
36. Ibid.
37. Gertz, *Treachery*, 110.
38. National Council for Resistance in Iran, press release, December 3, 2004.
39. Bill Gertz, "U.S. Told of Iranian Effort to Create Nuclear Warhead," *Washington Times*, December 3, 2004.
40. "Abdul Qadeer Khan 'Apologizes' for Transferring Nuclear Secrets Abroad," http://www.fas.org/nuke/guide/pakistan/nuke/aqkhan020404.html.
41. Peter Slevin, "U.N. Nuclear Chief Warns of Global Black Market," *Washington Post*, February 6, 2004.
42. 721 Report.
43. Douglas Jehl, "C.I.A. Says Pakistanis Gave Iran Nuclear Aid," *New York Times*, November 24, 2004.
44. Louis Charbonneau, " Exiles Say Iran Obtained Bomb Design, Uranium," Reuters Wire, November 17, 2004.
45. Khatami's statements are posted at the Web site of the Middle East Media Research Institute (www.memri.org). See Special Dispatch Series, no. 723, May 28, 2004, http://www.memri.org/bin/articles.cgi?Page=archives&Area=sd&ID=SP72304.
46. David G. Hubbard, *Winning Back the Sky: A Tactical Analysis of Terrorism* (San Francisco: Saybrook, 1986).

Chapter 2: Kerry-Edwards '04 Endorse the Mullahs

1. Glen Kessler and Robin Wright, "Edwards Says Kerry Plans to Confront Iran on Weapons," *Washington Post*, August 30, 2004.
2. Ibid.
3. Ibid.
4. David M. Halbfinger, "Kerry Denounces 'Inept' Bush Foreign Policy," *New York Times*, December 4, 2003.

5. Ibid.
6. "Jewish Involvement in 9/11," The Middle East Media Research Institute (MEMRI), *Special Dispatch Series*, no. 735, June 29, 2004.
7. "Iranian TV Series Based on the Protocols of the Elders of Zion and the Jewish Control of Hollywood," The Middle East Media Research Institute (MEMRI), *Special Dispatch Series*, no. 705, April 30, 2004.
8. Arieh O'Sullivan, "Target: The Jewish State—Threatening Israel Remains a Way of Life for Iranian Clerics," *Jerusalem Post*, December 10, 2004.
9. See http://www.johnkerry.com/pressroom/releases/pr_2004_0319b.html.
10. The Web site for Pirouznia's group, the Student Movement Coordination Committee for Democracy in Iran is www.daneshjoo.org. A description of the organization can be found at http://www.daneshjoo.org/article/publish/article_2566.shtml.
11. Graham Button and Kerry A. Dolan, "America's Man in Buenos Aires?" *Forbes*, May 3, 1999. See http://www.forbes.com/global/1999/0503/0209066a.html.
12. Ibid.
13. Kenneth R. Timmerman, "Dirty Moolah," *American Spectator* (October 2004), reports the sentence is from Nemazee's June 1, 2002, speech to the AIC in San Francisco. The sentence does not appear in the archived speech at http://www.american-iranian.org/Pages/Speeches/hasannamazi.htm. All quotes from the Kerry speech are drawn from the text at the AIC Web site at the same URL.
14. Kenneth R. Timmerman, "Kerry's Iran Scandal," *Washington Times*, October 15, 2004.
15. Ibid.
16. Timmerman, "Dirty Moolah."
17. Ibid.
18. Ibid.
19. Paul Hughes, "Iran's Clerics Lean Toward Kerry to Ease Pressure," Reuters, October 27, 2004.
20. Ibid.
21. Ibid.

Chapter 3: Pro-Mullah Democrats, Pro-Mullah Lobbies

1. This policy is discussed in Kenneth M. Pollack, *The Persian Puzzle: The Conflict Between Iran and America* (New York: Random House, 2004). Pollack served from 1995 to 1996 and from 1999 to 2000 as the director for Gulf affairs on the National Security Council during the Clinton administration. He introduces the policy of "dual containment" in detail on page 259.
2. Madeleine K. Albright, to the American Iranian Council, Washington DC, March 17, 2000. The text of her speech can be found at http://www.american-iranian.org/beta/publications.php?Perspective=1&PerspectiveID=46.

3. Pollack, *Persian Puzzle*, 338.

4. This fund-raiser was reported in Kenneth R. Timmerman, "Biden Buddies Up to Pro-Iran Lobby," *InternetMag.com*, March 4, 2002, http://www.insightmag.com /main.cfm/include/detail/storyid/195020.html.

5. Ibid.

6. Carl Weiser and Patrick Jackson, "Iranian-American Fund-raiser Sparks Political Spat in Del," *News Journal*, March 28, 2002.

7. Editorial, "Iran and Its Apologists," *Washington Times*, March 29,2002.

8. Joseph Biden on NBC's *Today Show*, May 27, 2003. The quotation is taken from the transcript on Biden's Web site: http://biden.senate.gov/pressapp/record .cfm?id=204474.

9. "Senior US Senator Joseph Biden Meets Iranian FM Kamal Kharrazi in Davos," Payvand News Release, January 24, 2004, http://www.payvand.com/news/ 04/jan/1173.html); "Kamal Kharrazi Meets US Senator Joseph Biden at Davos," Iran Press Release, Paris, January 25, 2004, http://www.iran-press-service.com/ articles_2004/Jan_04/iran_usrelations_25104.htm; "Senior US Senator Slammed Washington's Anti-Iran Policies," Islamic Republic News Agency (IRNA), Tehran, January 23, 2004, see http://www.globalsecurity.org/wmd/library/news/ iran/2004/iran-040124-irna01.htm.

10. Reza Aslan, "A Cult Is Trying to Hijack Our Iran Policy," *Los Angeles Times*, December 10, 2004.

11. For a discussion of the history of the NCRI and the Mujahedeen Khalq, see Elizabeth Rubin, "The Cult of Rajavi," *New York Times*, July 13, 2003.

12. Drawn from Sam Dealey, "'A Very, Very Bad Bunch': An Iranian Group and Its Surprising American Friends," *National Review*, March 25, 2002, http://www .nationalreview.com/25mar02/dealey032502.shtml.

13. Ibid.

14. An important analysis of the Alavi Foundation and its origins is presented by Kenneth R. Timmerman, "Clinton Betrayed Anti-terror Pledge: Administration's Secret Iran Policy Superseded Law, President's Promises," WorldNetDaily .com on September 29, 2002, http://www.worldnetdaily.com/news/article .asp?ARTICLE_ID=20216.

15. Known in Iran as Bonyad: The Mostazafan & Janbazan Foundation. See http:// www.iran-bonyad.org/.

16. Timmerman, "Clinton Betrayed Anti-terror Pledge."

17. The Alavi Foundation's Web site is www.alavifoundation.org.

18. Cited in John Mintz, "U.S. Keeps Close Tabs on Muslim Cleric: Officials Suspect Activist Has Close Ties with Iranian Regime," *Washington Post*, January 1, 2003.

19. Art Moore, "U.S. Muslim Event Hails Khomeini: Mainstream Figures Speak at 'Tribute to the Great Islamic Visionary,'" WorldNetDaily.com, December 15,

2004, http://www.worldnetdaily.com/news/article.asp?ARTICLE_ID=41939.
See also Todd Bensman and Robert Riggs, "The Investigators," in a television
news article titled, "Texas Muslims Host Ayatollah Komeini Tribute: Internet
Fuels Controversy over Conference Attended by 'Mainstream' Muslims," December 17, 2004, http://www.cbs11tv.com/localnews/local_story_352163501
.html.

20. Tom Perrotta, "Police Papers Stir Islamic Group's Ire," December 22, 2004,
http://www6.1aw.com/lawcom/displayid.cfm?statename=NY&docnum=172729
&table=news&flag=full.

21. Timmerman, "Clinton Betrayed Anti-terror Pledge."

22. Madeleine Albright, Robin Cook of Britain, Herbert Vedrine of France, Lam-
berto Dini of Italy, Lloyd Axworthy of Canada, Niels Helveg Petersen of Denmark, Ana Palacio of Spain, and Jozias van Aarsten of the Netherlands, "How to
Approach Iran," *Washington Post*, December 13, 2004.

23. Ion Mihai Pacepa, "Kerry's Soviet Rhetoric: The Vietnam-era Antiwar Move-
ment Got Its Spin from the Kremlin," *NationalReview.com*, February 26, 2004.
See John E. O'Neill and Jerome R. Corsi, *Unfit for Command: Swift Boat Veterans
Speak Out Against John Kerry* (Washington DC: Regnery, 2004), chapters 6 and 7.

24. Louis Charbonneau and Mark Trevelyan, "EU, Iran Clash over Terms of Nuclear
Freeze," *Reuters*, November 25, 2004.

25. John Loftus, National Intelligence Conference and Exposition, Arlington, Virginia, February 8–10, 2005, reported on RegimeChangeIran.blogspot.com,
http://regimechangeiran.blogspot.com/2004/11/why-iran-must-to-shut-down-its
-last-20.html.

26. George Jahn, "Iran Using Loophole in Nuclear Agreement," Associated Press
News Release, December 21, 2004.

27. Ibid.

28. Amir Taheri, "Eye of the Storm: Iraq Gets an Arab 'Helping Hand,'" *Jerusalem
Post*, July 8, 2004. See Also, "Iranian Leader Wants Nuke in 4 Months," World
NetDaily.com on October 2, 2004.

29. "Photos Indicate Improvements to Iranian Shahab-3," *Ha'artz*, August 30, 2004.

30. Information in this paragraph is drawn from "Iran Conducts Battlefield Test of
Shihab-3 Missile, Spends $1.5 Billion on WMD Warhead," GeoStrategy-Direct
.Com, December 28, 2004, http://www.geostrategy-direct.com/geostrategy
-direct/secure/2004/12_28/2.asp.

31. "Iran, EU to Resume $20b Trade Ties Soon," *Persian Journal*, December 29, 2004,
http://www.iranian.ws/iran_news/publish/article_5171.shtml.

32. "Iran to Purchase Russian Passenger Planes," IranMania.com, January 1, 2005,
http://www.iranmania.com/News/ArticleView/Default.asp?ArchiveNews=Yes&
NewsCode=27348&NewsKind=BusinessEconomy.

33. "Direct Flights Between Brussels and Tehran soon," IranMania.com, January 1, 2005, http://www.iranmania.com/News/ArticleView/Default.asp?NewsCode= 28290&NewsKind=Current%20Affairs.

34. Ayelet Savyon, "The Iran-E.U. Agreement on Iran's Nuclear Activity," www.memri.org, December 21, 2004, no. 200, http://memri.org/bin/articles .cgi?Page=archives&Area=ia&ID=IA20004.

35. Atieh Bahar Consulting, "Oil & Gas, Market Overview, Oil Reserves," http:// www.atiehbahar.com/Resources/Oil&Gas.htm.

36. U.S. Energy Information Administration, "Iran: Country Analysis," http://www. eia.doe.gov/emeu/cabs/iran.html.

37. Mehrdad Valibeigi, "More Unintended Consequences: US Sanctions and Iran," *Daily Star,* February 3, 2004, http://www.dailystar.com.lb/article.asp?edition_id= 10&categ_id=15&article_id=154.

38. Michael Rothschild, "Iran Lures BNP, HSBC for Loans, U.S. Banks Barred," Bloomberg.com, December 23, 2004, http://www.bloomberg.com/apps/news?pid =10000102&sid=apxPmkzkceWc&refer=uk#.

Chapter 4: The Nemazee Double Take

1. Hassan Nemazee's deposition was taken on October 18, 2004, in New York City at the Courtland Marriott, 866 Third Avenue, New York, NY. This account is drawn from the stenographer's official transcript: "In the District Court, Dallas County, Texas, 68th Judicial District. Hassan Nemazee, Plaintiff, Against Aryo B. Pirouznia and Student Movement Coordinating Committee for Democracy in Iran ('SMCCDI'), Index No. 04–7359-M." Hereafter referred to as "Nemazee Deposition." The deposition began at 9:07 a.m. and concluded at 10:15 a.m. A videotape was made of the deposition and is archived on WorldNetDaily.com at http:// www.worldnetdaily.com/news/article.asp?ARTICLE_ID=41084. Copies of the deposition can be purchased on WorldNetDaily.com.

2. In the deposition, Nemazee took exception to the published version of the speech he gave at the AIC's meeting in San Francisco on June 1, 2002, which John Kerry attended. Nemazee claimed that the sentence of the speech supporting the reestablishment of normal diplomatic relations with Iran was only in a draft of the speech. Even though Nemazee acknowledged that the draft including the suspect sentence was published on the AIC Web site, he insisted that he omitted the sentence when he gave the speech. He said the speech without that sentence could be found on his computer. Nemazee had no explanation why the AIC published an incorrect version of the speech, nor why he did not contact the AIC to correct the error. The discussion of the AIC speech begins at page 29 of the deposition.

Chapter 5: Democrats Attack America's Intelligence Operations

1. "Democrats Mull Politicizing Iraq War Intelligence," *Fox News*, November 2, 2003, http://www.foxnews.com/story/0,2933,102206,00.html. The memo is published in "Raw Data: Dem Memo on Iraq Intel," *Fox News*, November 6, 2003, http://www.foxnews.com/printer_friendly_story/0,3566,102258,00.html.
2. James G. Lakely, "Memo Infuriates Senators," *Washington Times*, November 6, 2003.
3. Pat Roberts, "A Panel Above Politics," *Washington Post*, November 13, 2003.
4. Lakely, "Memo Infuriates Senators."
5. Robert Novak, "Democrats Ruin the Intelligence Committee," TownHall.com, November 18, 2003, URL: http://www.frontpagemag.com/Articles/ReadArticle .asp?ID=10856.
6. "Senate Intel Report Mirrors Dems' Anti-Bush Memo," NewsMax.com, July 12, 2004, http://www.cshink.com/dems_anti-bush_memo.htm.
7. Ibid.
8. "Democrats Again Say Iraq Intel Misused," *Associated Press*, October 21, 2004.
9. "Responding to President Bush's challenge to clarify his position, Sen. John F. Kerry said Monday that he still would have voted to authorize the war in Iraq even if he had known then that U.S. and allied forces would not find weapons of mass destruction"; Jim VandeHei, "In Hindsight, Kerry Says He'd Sill Vote for War," *Washington Post*, August 10, 2004.
10. James Mann. *Rise of the Vulcans: The History of Bush's War Cabinet* (New York: Viking Penguin, 2004), 90–94.
11. "Neocon 101: Some Basic Questions Answered," *Christian Science Monitor*, 2004, http://www.csmonitor.com/specials/neocon/neocon101.html. The brief biographies of these neocons are drawn from this source.
12. Ernest F. Hollins, "Bush's Failed Mideast Policy Is Creating More Terrorism," *Charleston Post and Courier*, May 6, 2004. See also http://hollings.senate.gov/ ~hollings/opinion/2004506A17.html.
13. Lauren Markoe, "Hollings Defends His Statements on Israel: Column Alleging Bush Invaded Iraq to Please Jews Draws Accusations of Anti-Semitism," The State.com, May 19, 2004, http://www.thestate.com/mld/thestate/8699824.htm.
14. "Gen. Zinni: 'They've Screwed Up,'" May 21, 2004, http://www.cbsnews .com/stories/2004/05/21/60minutes/main618896.shtml. See also Ellis Shuman, "Former Mideast Envoy Zinni: U.S. Went to War in Iraq to Help Israel," Israel Insider, May 24, 2004, http://web.israelinsider.com/bin/en.jsp?enPage=Article Page&enDisplay=view&enDispWhat=object&enDispWho=Article%5E13672 &enZone=AntiSemi&enVersion=0&.
15. Shuman, "Zinni."

16. Seymour M. Hersh, "Selective Intelligence: Donald Rumsfeld Has His Own Special Sources—Are They Reliable?" *The New Yorker*, May 12, 2003. In response to this article, Bryan G. Whitman, deputy assistant secretary of defense for media, wrote to David Remnick of *The New Yorker*. Whitman objected to the inaccuracies and expressed disappointment that Hersh ignored written answers the Department of Defense had submitted in response to questions posed by Hersh before writing the article. An attachment noted twenty specific inaccuracies and/or distortions the Department of Defense cited in the article.

17. John D. Rockefeller IV to to Douglas Feith, October 1, 2003.

18. Carl Levin to Douglas Feith, November 25, 2003.

19. Marc Cooper, "Soldier for the Truth: Exposing Bush's Talking-points War," LA Weekly, February 20–26, 2004, http://www.laweekly.com/ink/04/13/news-cooper.php.

20. Ibid. A long list of Kwiatkowski's articles can be found at libertarian Lew Rocklwell's Web site (www.lewrockkwell.com) at (http://www.lewrockwell.com/kwiatkowski/kwiatkowski-arch.html).

21. The words of the senator are quoted directly, despite their faulty grammatical structure. The ellipsis is in the original source. Rowland Scarborough, "Pentagon Challenges Rockefeller on Feith Hit," *Washington Post*, July 14, 2004.

22. Powell A. Moore to John D. Rockefeller IV, July 9, 2004.

23. Three CBS News reports are relevant: "Spy Arrest Said Possible Soon," CBS News.com, August 28, 2004, http://www.cbsnews.com/stories/2004/08/29/national/main639286.shtml?CMP=ILC-SearchStories; "FBI in Contact with Suspected Spy," August 30, 2004, http://www.cbsnews.com/stories/2004/08/30/national/main639409.shtml?CMP=ILC-SearchStories; "2 Officials Briefed in Spy Probe," August 30, 2004, http://www.cbsnews.com/stories/2004/08/30/national/main639542.shtml?CMP=ILC-SearchStories.

24. This paragraph is drawn from the CBS News report "FBI in Contact with Suspected Spy."

25. Edwin Black, "Feeding Frenzy," *Jerusalem Report*, October 4, 2004.

26. NBC News, *Meet the Press*, September 5, 2004, http://www.msnbc.msn.com/id/5921259/.

27. Juan Cole, "Spy Scandal's Roots Are Deep," ProgressiveTrail.org, December 25, 2004, http://www.progressivetrail.org/articles/040902Cole.shtml. Cole's Web site is www.juancole.com.

28. Letter and accompanying notes from Michael Ledeen to Jerome R. Corsi, December 20, 2004.

29. Ibid. The information in the subsequent paragraphs about the two Ledeen meetings in Rome are taken from the notes that accompanied Ledeen's December 20, 2004 letter.

30. Ibid.
31. Joshua Micah Marshall, Laura Rozen, and Paul Glastris, "Iran-Contra II? Fresh Scrutiny on a Rogue Pentagon Operation," *Washington Monthly*, September 2004, http://www.washingtonmonthly.com/features/2004/0410.marshallrozen.html.
32. Ledeen to Corsi.
33. Curt Weldon to I. Lewis Libby Jr., November 26, 2003. The bullet points in the text are quoted directly from this letter.
34. Eli Lake, "Congressman Warns of Iranian Attack on U.S., *New York Sun*, December 14, 2004.
35. The Church Committee was officially known as the Senate Select Committee to Study Governmental Operations with Respect to Intelligence Activities, named after its chairman, Frank Church (D-ID). The Church Committee produced fourteen volumes of reports in 1975 and 1976, dealing with a wide range of U.S. intelligence-gathering operations.
36. Editorial, "Jamie Gorelick's Wall," *Washington Times*, April 14, 2004, http://washingtontimes.com/op-ed/20040415-094758-5267r.htm.
37. Seymour Hersh, "Selective Intelligence."The issue of Leo Strauss is also raised by James Mann, *Rise of the Vulcans*, 25–29.
38. Jerome R. Corsi, "Prior Restraint, Prior Punishment, and Political Dissent: A Moral and Legal Evaluation" (doctoral thesis, Harvard University, June 1972).

Chapter 6: Iran Exports Terror

1. The phrase "terror masters" and the comparison to America's Mafiosi are borrowed from Michael Ledeen, whose writings on radical Islamic terrorism are insightful, demanding serious consideration even from his critics. See Michael A. Ledeen, *The War Against the Terror Masters: Why It Happened, Where We Are Now, How'll We'll Win* (New York: St. Martin's, 2003).
2. The discussion presented in the following paragraphs of this section is drawn primarily from Magnus Ranstorp, *Hizb'Allah in Lebanon* (New York, St. Martin's, 1997); Amal Saad-Ghorayeb, *Hizbu'llah: Politics and Religion* (London: Pluto Press, 2002); *Hezbollah: Information Bulletin*, the Center for Special Studies (CSS), www.intelligence.org.il.; and Aaron Mannes, *Profiles in Terror: The Guide to Middle East Terrorist Organizations* (New York: Rowman & Littlefield, 2004).
3. Louis Freeh, former director of the FBI, made clear that Hezbollah was responsible for the attack on the Khobar Towers, see "Remember Khobar Towers: Nineteen American Heroes Still Await American Justice," *Wall Street Journal*, May 20, 2003, http://www.opinionjournal.com/editorial/feature.html?id=110003518.
4. Mannes, *Profiles in Terror*, 152–55.
5. Ibid., 154.
6. Ibid., 167.

7. The CSS Intelligence and Terrorism Information Center, *Hezbollah: Information Bulletin*. A discussion of the SIDE report can be found at http://www.intelligence .org.il/eng/bu/hizbullah/pb/app5.htm.

8. Imad Mughniyah is listed on the FBI's list of the most wanted terrorists at www.FBI.gov, http://www.fbi.gov/mostwant/terrorists/termugniyah.htm.

9. CSIS, *Hezbollah: Information Bulletin*.

10. Ibid.

11. Ibid. See also Gary Gambill, "Hezbollah's Strategic Rocket Arsenal," *Middle East Intelligence Bulletin* 4, no. 11 (November–December 2002), http://www.meib .org/articles/0211_12.htm.

12. Stephen Brown, "Canada—Terrorist Haven," FrontPageMagazine.com, December 9, 2002, http://www.frontpagemag.com/articles/ReadArticle.asp?ID=5007.

13. Associated Press, "Michigan Man Charged with Aiding Hezbollah." Reported on CNN.com, January 15, 2004, http://www.cnn.com/2004/LAW/01/15/hezbollah .charges.ap/.

14. Gary C. Gambill, "Dossier: Hassan Nasrallah, Secretary-General of Hezbollah," *Middle East Intelligence Bulletin* 6, nos. 2–3 (February–March 2004), http://www .meib.org/articles/0402_ld.htm.

15. Ibid.

16. Ibid.

17. Ibid.

18. Ibid. For the photograph of Nasrallah and Annan in Beruit in June 2000, see http://www.meib.org/articles/0402_ld.htm.

19. An excellent reference on Hamas is Khaled Hroub, *Hamas: Political Thought and Practice* (Washington DC: Institute for Palestine Studies, 2002).

20. Hamas (Islamic Resistance Movement) on GlobalSecurity.org, http://www.global security.org/military/world/para/hamas.htm.

21. See Mannes, *Profiles in Terror,*117. Much of the following is drawn from pages 117–21.

22. Drawn from: Zohar Palti, "Israel's Security Fence: Effective in Reducing Suicide Attacks from the Northern West Bank," *Peacewatch* 464, July 7, 2004, http://www.washingtoninstitute.org/watch/peacewatch/peacewatch2004/464.htm.

23. Yassin's assassination and funeral were extensively covered by the world press. See "Hamas Chief Killed in Air Strike," *BBC News World Edition*, March 22, 2004. For an Internet version, see, "Hamas Threatens U.S. After Israel Kills Terrorist Leader," NewsMax.com, March 22, 2004, http://www.newsma.com/ archives/articles/2004/3/22/102250.shtml.

24. Aaron Mannes, "Dangerous Liasons: Hamas After the Assassination of Yassin," *Middle East Intelligence Bulletin* 6, no. 4 (April 2004), http://www.meib.org/articles/ 0404_pa11.htm.

25. Craig Nelson, "Israel Kills New Chief of Hamas: Enraged Palestinians Vow Revenge for Missile Attack," *Arizona Daily Star,* April 18, 2004.

26. "UK Condemns Hamas Leader Killing," BBC News, April 18, 2004, http://news.bbc.co.uk/1/hi/uk_politics/3636179.stm.

27. "Israel Kills Hamas Operative in Syria," FoxNews.com, September 26, 2004, http://www.foxnews.com/story/0,2933,133564,00.html.

28. "Canada Looking at UN Agency over Palestinian Connection," CBC News, October 4, 2004. The satellite photo in question can be seen in the article on the Internet at http://www.cbc.ca/story/world/national/2004/10/03/unwra041003.html.

29. The ambulance incident is noted in Matthew Levitt, "Terror on the UN Payroll," *Peacewatch,* October 13, 2004, http://www.washingtoninstitute.org/watch/peacewatch/peacewatch2004/475.htm.

30. John Mintz, "Muslim Charity, Officials Indicted," *Washington Post,* July 28, 2004.

31. Associated Press, "Three Accused of Financing Hamas Plans: U.S. Accounts Allegedly Used to Support Terrorism," August 20, 2004, http://www.msnbc.msn.com/id/5770736.

32. Two background articles on the Council on American-Islamic Relations and the Holy Land Foundation are Joe Kaufman, "The CAIR-terror Connection," FrontPageMagazine.com, April 29, 2004, http://www.frontpagemag.com/Articles/ReadArticle.asp?ID=13175; Andrew C. McCarthy, "To Be Charitable, They're Terrorists," *National Review OnLine,* July 29, 2004, http://www.nationalreview.com/mccarthy/mccarthy200407290000.asp.

33. Ibid.

34. Eli Lake, "Hamas Agents Lurking in U.S., FBI Warns." *New York Sun,* April 29, 2004.

35. Avi Jorisch, "Terrorist Television," *National Review Online,* December 22, 2004, http://www.nationalreview.com/comment/jorisch200412220812.asp. The estimate of ten million to fifteen million daily viewers worldwide comes from this source. Avi Jorisch's work on *Al-Manar* television has been path-finding in its insight and importance. See Jorish, *Beacon of Hatred: Inside Hezbollah's Al-Manar Television* (Washington DC: Washington Institute for Near East Policy, 2004).

36. Jeffrey Goldberg, "In the Party of God: Are Terrorists in Lebanon Preparing for a Larger War?" *The New Yorker,* October 10–14, 21, 2002, http://www.newyorker.com/fact/content/?021014fa_fact4.

37. "MEMRI TV Project: Mothers of Hizbullah Martyrs: We Are Very Happy and Want to Sacrifice Our Children," Memri.org, Special Dispatch Series, November 25, 2004. http://www.memri.org/bin/articles.cgi?Page=archives&Area=sd&ID=SP81904.

38. Avi Jorish and Salameh Nematt, "Inside Hizballah's Al-Manar Television: A Special Policy Forum Report," *Policywatch*, October 18, 2004, http://www.washingtoninstitute.org/watch/policywatch/policywatch2004/917.htm.

39. "Hezbollah TV: French Ban Is 'Politically Motivated,'" Aljazeera.com, December 14, 2004, http://www.aljazeera.com/me.asp?service_ID=6152.

40. Ibid.

41. The official Web site of the Israel Defense Force (IDF) carries a full report of the incident: "A Briefing Following the Seizure of Karin A, A Palestinian Weapons Ship," http://www1.idf.il/dover/site/mainpage.asp?sl=EN&id=7&docid=22065. EN. For An article with photographs of the *Karine-A* and the weapons unloaded, together with a weapons inventory, see "IDF Seizes PA Weapons Ship," *Jewish Virtual Library*, January 4, 2002, http://www.jewishvirtuallibrary.org/jsource/Peace/paship.html.

42. "Captain: Weapons Were Intended for Palestinians," Jerusalem AP report, January 7, 2002, http://www.usatoday.com/news/world/2002/01/07/smuggling.htm.

43. Kenneth Jacobson, "ADL Analysis: Arafat Knew About Weapons Shipment," http://www.adl.org/israel/karine_a.asp.

44. Michael Ledeen, *War Against the Terror Masters*, 48.

45. "Iraq Accuses Iran and Syria of Backing Terror," NewsMax.com, December 15, 2004, http://www.newsmax.com/archives/articles/2004/12/15/83733.shtml.

46. Associated Press, "Iraq's Defense Minister Describes Iran as 'Number One Enemy,'" December 15, 2004. http://news.bostonherald.com/international/view.bg?articleid=59010&format=text.

47. "Iraq Defense Minister Says Iran Mainly to Blame for Iraq Unrest," Iran Press News, January 5, 2005, http://www.iranpressnews.com/english/source/002479.html.

48. "Iraq's DM: Over a Million Shi'ites Entered Iraq from Iran," *IranFocus.com*, January 6, 2005, http://www.iranfocus.com/modules/news/print.php?storyid=1167.

49. "King Abdullah Defends Statement on Shi'ite 'Crescent,'" Iran Press News, January 6, 2005, http://www.iranpressnews.com/english/source/002501.html.

50. Reuel Marc Gerecht, "Will Iran Win the Iraq War?" *Wall Street Journal*, December 14, 2004, http://www.aei.org/news/newsID.21706,filter.all/news_detail.asp.

51. "Iran's Role in the Recent Uprising in Iraq," Middle East Media Research Institute, Special Dispatch Series, April 9, 2009, http://www.memri.org/bin/articles.cgi?Page=archives&Area=sd&ID=SP69204.

52. Ibid.

53. Gary C. Gambill, "Iran, Sadr, and the Shi'ite Uprising in Iraq," Middle East Intelligence Bulletin 6, no. 4 (April 2004), http://www.meib.org/articles/0404_iraq1.htm.

54. Michael Ledeen, "The Fattest Terrorist: Sadr Denounced," National Review Online, May 25, 2004, http://www.nationalreview.com/ledeen/ledeen200405251028.asp.

Chapter 7: Sleeper Cells and Nuclear Bombs

1. Jerry Seper, "Terrorist Cells Too Close for Comfort," *Washington Times*, December 10, 2003, http://www.washingtontimes.com/national/20031209–114319–3699r.htm.
2. Eli Lake, "Hamas Agents Lurking in the U.S., FBI Warns," *New York Sun*, April 29, 2004, http://daily.nysun.com/Repository/getFiles.asp?Style=OliveXLib:Article ToMail&Type=text/html&Path=NYS/2004/04/29&ID=Ar00100.
3. Jerry Seper, "Islamic Extremists Invade U.S., Join Sleeper Cells," *Washington Times*, February 9, 2004, http://www.washingtontimes.com/national/20040209–115406–6221r.htm.
4. Jerry Seper, "'Sleeper Cells' of al-Qaeda Active in U.S. Despite War," *Washington Times*, February 10, 2004, http://www.washingtontimes.com/national/20040210–105654–8823r.htm.
5. Scott Wheeler, "Alleged Terror Threat Operates in DC Suburb," *CNSNews.com*, July 12, 2004, http://www.cnsnews.com/ViewSpecialReports.asp?Page='Special-Reports'archive'200407'SPE20040712a.html.
6. Mary Beth Sheridan, "Oxon Hill Development Has Ties to Terror," *Washington Post*, April 19, 2004, http://www.washingtonpost.com/ac2/wp-dyn/A22576–2004 Apr18?language=printer.
7. Michael Jacobson, "The Patriot Act and Middle Eastern Terrorists," *Policywatch*, November 1, 2004, http://www.washingtoninstitute.org/watch/policywatch/poli cywatch2004/912.htm.
8. For an important and insightful analysis of how the United States might profit by utilizing racial profiling in the war on terror, see Michelle Malkin, *In Defense of Internment*, Washington DC: Regnery, 2004).
9. Andrew Welsh-Huggins, "Cheney: Terrorists May Bomb U.S. Cities," October 19, 2004, http://apnews.myway.com/article/20041019/D85QOUF80.html.
10. CBS, "The Perfect Terrorist Weapon, *60Minutes*, broadcast September 7, 1977.
11. An excellent discussion of the suitcase nuclear bomb issue is found in Graham Allison, *Nuclear Terrorism: The Ultimate Preventable Catastrophe* (New York: Holt, 2004), 43–46.
12. "'Suitcase Nukes': A Reassessment," Monterey Institute of International Studies, September 23, 2002, http://www.cns.miis.edu/pubs/week/020923.htm. A photograph of Congressman Burton showing the suitcase bomb to the congressional committee can be found at this URL.

13. Carey Sublette, "Alexander Lebed and Suitcase Nukes," NuclearWeapons Archive.org, May 18, 2002, http://www.nuclearweaponarchive.org/News/Lebed bomb.html. This site also shows a photograph of Burton demonstrating the mock suitcase bomb to the congressional committee.

14. "Suitcase Nukes': A Reassessment"; "'Suitcase Nukes': Permanently Lost Luggage," Monterey Institute of International Studies, February 13, 2004, http://www.cns.miis.edu/pubs/week/040213.htm.

15. Ibid.

16. Research Abstracts translation of a foreign-language newspaper report printed on February 11, 2004, reported on NTI.com, http://www.nti.org/db/nistraff/2004/20040300.htm.

17. "Journalist Says al-Qaeda Has Black Market Nuclear Bombs," March 22, 2004, at http://www.smh.com.au/cgi-bin/common/popupPrintArticle.pl?path=/articles/2004/03/22/1079823250899.html. An author who believes the Chechen mafia sold suitcase nukes to al-Qaeda for thirty million dollars plus heroin with a street value of seven hundred million dollars is Paul Williams. See Williams, *Osama's Revenge: The Next 9/11* (New York: Prometheus Books, 2004), 37–49.

18. Scott Wheeler, "Alleged Terror Threat Operates in DC Suburb."

19. John Mintz and Susan Schmidt, "'Dirty Bomb' Was Major New Year's Worry," *Washington Post*, January 7, 2004, http://www.washingtonpost.com/ac2/wp-dyn?pagename=article&contentId=A60519–2004Jan6&notFound=true. Also reported in Charles D. Fergusen and William C. Potter, *The Four Faces of Nuclear Terrorism* (Monterey, CA: Center for Nonproliferation Studies, 2004), 261. Hereafter referred to as *Four Faces of Nuclear Terrorism*.

20. *Four Faces of Nuclear Terrorism*, 264. This work was enormously helpful. I have drawn heavily from the work's excellent analysis. The book can be purchased or downloaded online at http://cns.miis.edu/pubs/week/040618.htm.

21. "The Mechanics of a 'Dirty Bomb,'" CBSnews.com, http://www.cbsnews.com/stories/2002/04/23/attack/main507031.shtml.

22. *Four Faces of Nuclear Terrorism*, 265.

23. Ibid., especially chapter 4, entitled Making the Bomb.

24. Thomas B. Cochran and Christopher E. Paine, "The Amount of Plutonium and Highly-Enriched Uranium Needed for Pure Fission Nuclear Weapons," National Resources Defense Council, April 13, 1995. The National Resources Defense Council Web site is www.nrdc.org. A simple chart describing various kinds of fissile fuel needed for making nuclear weapons can be found on the USA Today Web site under the all-too-appropriate concept of "make-a-nuke" (http://www.usatoday.com/news/2003–02–27-make-a-nuke.htm).

25. "The Demand for Black Market Fissile Material," *Controlling Nuclear Warheads & Materials*, Nuclear Threat Iniative (hereafter refferred to as NTI), www.nti.org,

http://www.nti.org/e_research/cnwm/threat/demand.asp. The NTI Web site is an excellent resource for information about nuclear terrorism. I have drawn heavily from this source for this material.

26. Ibid. A good selection of photographs showing al-Qaeda documents captured in Afghanistan that show nuclear devices and research can be found at CNN.com, http://www.isis-online.org/publications/terrorism/images.html. These documents make clear that al-Qaeda's investigation into nuclear-weapons capability was extensive. A sketch of an al-Qaeda drawing for a crude nuclear device can be seen on the NTI Web site, http://www.nti.org/e_research/cnwm/threat/demand.asp.

27. "The ABC News Nuclear Smuggling Experiment: The Sequel—The Continuing Saga of NRDC's Uranium Slug and the Potential Consequences." The report is published at http://www.nrdc.org/nuclear/furanium.asp.

28. From http://www.usatoday.com/news/2003–02–27-make-a-nuke.htm.

29. Quoted in "The Uranium Threat," http://www.nci.org/new/nci-ura.htm. The NCI Web site (www.nci.org) is another excellent source of articles and discussions relevant to nuclear terrorism.

30. The quote and the discussion in the entire paragraph is drawn from *The Four Faces of Nuclear Terrorism*, 112.

31. Dafna Linzer, "Nuclear Capabilities May Elude Terrorists, Experts Say," *Washington Post*, December 29, 2004, http://www.washingtonpost.com/wp-dyn/articles/A32285–2004Dec28.html.

32. Ibid.

33. Ibid.

34. Ibid.

35. Ibid.

36. National Commission on Terrorist Attacks upon the United States, *The 9/11 Commission Report: Final Report of the National Commission on Terrorist Attacks upon the United States* (New York: Norton, 2004). The discussion of the 9/11 plot is drawn entirely from this source.

37. Ibid., 145.

38. Ibid.

39. This analysis is drawn from http://www.atomicarchive.com/Example/Example1.shtml, which has an analysis of a 150-kiloton nuclear bomb detonated at the base of the Empire State Building. The site was constructed with a solid understanding of the physics involved. The data here corresponds with similar damage and casualty data presented in the professional scientific literature.

Chapter 8: Oil Extortion

1. Data on world energy can be found at the U.S. Energy Information Administration Web site (www.eai.doe.gov). Much of the information presented here is

drawn from these profiles. For Iran, see http://www.eia.doe.gov/emeu/cabs/iran .html. For Saudi Arabia, see http://www.eia.doe.gov/emeu/cabs/saudi.html.

2. Ibid. *Bonyads* are typically Islamic charitable foundations. When the Shah was deposed, the mullahs established *bonyads*, supposedly to distribute the imperial wealth to the people of Iran. The largest *bonyad*, and probably best known, is the *Bonyad-e Mostazafan* ("The Foundation of the Dispossessed"), which took control of the Shah's Pahlavi Foundation and its many companies ranging over from mining and agriculture to factories and manufacturing. The *Bonyad-e Mostazafan* (http://www.iran-bonyad.org/) is a multibillion dollar enterprise with a reputation for crushing labor unions and funding Iran's surrogate state-supported international terrorist organization Hezbollah. See Michael Rubin, "Roots and Results of Revolution," a book review published in the *Middle East Quarterly*, June 22, 2004, http://www.aei.org/news/newsID.21217/news_detail .asp.

3. Agence France Press (AFP), "China Signs $70 Billion Oil and LNG Agreement with Iran," October 30, 2004, http://www.dailystar.com.lb/article.asp?edition_id= 10&categ_id=3&article_id=9713.

4. Sudha Ramachandran, "The Glue that Bonds India, Iran," *Asia Times*, January 12, 2005, http://www.atimes.com/atimes/South_Asia/GA12Df05.html.

5. Michael Blackman, "Abundant Oil Makes Kazakhstan a Country to Watch," *The Age*, December 1, 2004, http://www.theage.com.au/news/Business/Abundant-oil-makes-Kazakhstan-a-country-to-watch/2004/11/30/1101577481456.html?from= storylhs&oneclick=true#.

6. Ibid.

7. Thomas Gold, *The Deep Hot Biosphere* (New York: Copernicus Books, 2001).

8. Paul Roberts, *The End of Oil: On the Edge of a Perilous New World* (New York: Houghton Mifflin, 2004), 59.

9. Michael T. Klare, *Blood and Oil: The Dangers and Consequences of America's Growing Dependency on Imported Petroleum* (New York: Holt, 2004).

10. "The Price of Oil—In Context," CBC News Online, September 27, 2004, http:// www.cbc.ca/news/background/oil/.

11. William C. Thompson Jr., "One Year Later: The Fiscal Impact of 9/11 on New York City," September 4, 2002, http://comptroller.nyc.gov/bureaus/bud/reports/ impact-9–11-year-later.pdf.

12. See Adam Geller, "A Year After Attacks, Economic Impact Lingers," September 8, 2002, http://www.suntimes.com/special_sections/sept11/economy/economic impact.html.

13. Anthony H. Cordesman and Arleigh A. Burke, "Iran's Developing Military Capabilities," Main Report, Washington DC Center for Strategic and International Studies, Center for Strategic and International Studies, December 14, 2004,

working draft, http://www.csis.org/burke/mb/041208_IranDevMilCap.pdf. Referred to hereafter as CSIS Report.

14. Ibid., 4.

15. Ibid., 2.

16. U.S. Energy Information Administration, Department of Energy, "Persian Gulf Oil and Gas Exports Fact Sheet," http://www.eia.doe.gov/emeu/cabs/pgulf.html. The term "Tcf" refers to trillion cubic feet, a volume measurement of natural gas; 1 Tcf is enough to fuel all the gas-heated homes in Canada for approximately two years. The term bbl/d refers to barrels per day.

17. Ibid.

18. CSIS Report, 40.

19. Ibid. For Internet reports concerning Iran's purchase of Sunburn cruise missiles, see "A Weapons Analysis of the Iran-Russia-US Strategic Triangle," TBRnews .org, http://www.thetruthseeker.co.uk/print.asp?ID=2439. See also, Mark Gaffney, "Iran a Bridge Too Far?" on the Information Clearinghouse Web site, http://www .informationclearinghouse.info/article7147.htm. Neither of the Internet reports have been verified for authenticity.

20. A good twenty-years later perspective on the sinking of the HMS *Sheffield* is offered in "The Sinking of the Shiny Sheff," http://ayup.co.uk/shuttup/shuttup 2–0.html.

21. For a discussion of the attack on the USS *Stark* and how the attack fit into the Tanker War, see "Iran-Iraq War (1980–1988), The Tanker War, 1984–1987," http://countrystudies.us/iraq/105.htm.

Chapter 9: Repression in Iran

1. Michael Rubin, "Tyranny @ 25," National Review Online, April 1, 2004, at http://www.nationalreview.com/rubin/rubin200404010848.asp.

2. Fédération international des ligues des droits de l'Homme (FIDH), Ligue Iranienne de Défense des Droits de l'Homme. (International Federation of Human Rights Leagues; Iranian League for the Defense of Human Rights), "Appraisal of the EU Human Rights Dialogues: Assessment of the Human Rights Situation in Iran" (referred to hereafter as FIDH Report), http://www.fidh.org/article.php3?id _article=1678.

3. "Q&A: Iran Election Crisis," BBC News World Edition Online, February 1, 2004, http://news.bbc.co.uk/2/hi/middle_east/3389017.stm.

4. Ibid.

5. FIDH Report, 5.

6. "In Depth: Zahra Kazemi—Iran's Changing Story," CBC News Online, July 28, 2004, http://www.cbc.ca/news/background/kazemi/. See also, "Kazemi's Death an

'Accident': Iranian Judges," CBC News Online, July 29, 2004, http://www.cbc
.ca/story/world/national/2004/07/28/kazemi_judiciary040728.html.

7. FIDH Report, 10. An Article 90 Commission is a parliamentary body mandated
    by the Iranian Constitution that allows a citizen to submit a complaint in writ-
    ing, demanding that the assembly conduct an investigation and give a satisfac-
    tory reply.

8. Human Rights Watch, "Like the Dead in Their Coffins: Torture, Detention, and
    the Crushing of Dissent in Iran," June 7, 2003, http://hrw.org/reports/2004/
    iran0604/. Referred to hereafter as Human Rights Watch Report.

9. "Iranian Court Slaps Opponents with Terms," May 11, 2003, IranMania.com,
    http://64.233.161.104/search?q=cache:NScLAtMtPC0J:www.iranmania.com/
    News/ArticleView/Default.asp%3FNewsCode%3D15514%26NewsKind%3D
    Current%2520Affairs+reza+alidjani&hl=en.

10. Human Rights Watch, "Iran: Journalists Receive Death Threats After Testifying:
    Presidential Commission Heard Their Testimony of Torture During Detention,"
    http://www.hrw.org/english/docs/2005/01/06/iran9948.htm.

11. FIDH Report, 6.

12. Human Rights Watch Report, 15. A good description of the *Basiji* and the *Ansar-e
    Hizbollah* can be found in Kenneth M. Pollack, *The Persian Puzzle: The Conflict
    Between Iran and America* (New York: Random House, 2004),150–52.

13. Human Rights Watch Report, 12.

14. Ibid., 13–14.

15. Ibid., 13. Comment drawn from a Human Rights Watch interview with a former
    Iranian prisoner in London, December 2003.

16. Ibid., 17.

17. Ibid., 19.

18. Ibid, 24.

19. Ibid., 28.

20. *Tazir* is discretionary punishment, such as a sentence that could be suspended by
    a judge.

21. A *toman* is a term for old Iranian currency; a *toman* is equivalent to ten rials. A
    helpful site for Iranian currency is IranTour.org, http://www.irantour.org/currency
    .html.

22. Human Rights Watch Report, 51.

23. Ibid., 52.

24. National Coalition of Pro-Democracy Advocates, "The Situation of Human
    Rights in Iran," NCPDA.com, http://www.ncpda.com/humanrights.html.

25. "Women in the Middle East," no. 26 (July 2004), at the Web site of the Institute
    for the Secularisation of Islamic Society, at http://www.secularislam.org/women/
    bulletin26.htm. Hereafter referred to as ISIS Bulletin. An identical quote is found

at Donna M. Hughes, "Iran's Sex Slaves Suffer Hideously Under Mullahs," June 8, 2004, http://www.activistchat.com/phpBB2/viewtopic.php?t=2678.

26. Babak Seradjeh, "Gender Separation in Iran," posted on the Web site of Free Thoughts on Iran, October 25, 2003, http://www.freethoughts.org/archives/000212.php.

27. Homa Darabi Foundation, "Establishment of the Islamic Republic in Iran & Present Situation for Women," Homa.org, http://www.homa.org/Details.asp?ContentID=2137352848&TOCID=2083225444. Referred to hereafter as Homa Darabi Report.

28. Golnaz Esfandiari, "Violence Against Women—In Iran, Abuse Is Part of the Culture," http://www.parstimes.com/women/violence_culture.html. The Web site notes that the article is posted with the permission of Radio Free Europe/Radio Liberty, November 25, 2003.

29. Ibid.

30. Ibid.

31. Morteza Aminmansour, "Slavery of Children and Women in Persian Gulf Countries," June 20, 2004, *Persian Journal*, http://www.iranian.ws/iran_news/publish/article_2675.shtml.

32. Ibid.

33. ISIS Bulletin.

34. Hughes, "Iran's Sex Slaves."

35. Ibid.

36. Ibid.

37. Sohrab Morovati, "Iran-Society-Youth: Young Iranian Runaways Hit Dead End of Prostitution and Drug Abuse," Agence France Press, June 1, 2002, http://www.aegis.com/news/afp/2002/AF020601.html.

38. Homa Darabi Report.

39. Essential reading on the question of why the American Left is drawn to embrace radical Islamic extremism is David Horowitz, *Unholy Alliance: Radical Islam and the American Left* (Washington DC: Regnery, 2004).

40. Posted on the blog RogerLSimon.com, "August 25, 2004: The Public Hanging of a Sixteen Year Old Girl in Iran," http://www.rogerlsimon.com/mt-archives/2004/08/the_public_hang.php.

41. "Iran: 16-Year-Old Girl Hanged in Street for 'Acts Incompatible with Chastity," Amnesty International, August 24, 2004, http://www.amnesty.org.uk/deliver/document/15557.html.

42. "Under Iran's 'divinely ordained justice,' girls as young as nine are charged with 'moral crimes.' The best that they can hope for is to die by hanging," News Telegraph, December 19, 2004, http://www.telegraph.co.uk/news/main.jhtml?xml=/news/2004/12/19/wiran19.xml&sSheet=/news/2004/12/19/ixworld.html.

43. "Iran: Girl with Mental Age of Eight Given Death Sentence After Mother Forced Her into Prostitution from Early Age," Amnesty International, http://www.amnesty.org.uk/news/press/15803.shtml.

44. "Iran Confirms Death Verdict Against Woman," IranPressNews.com, December 22, 2004, http://www.iranpressnews.com/english/source/002230.html.

45. "Fear of Imminent Execution: Hajieh Esmailvand (f), An Unnamed Man (Aged 17 When Accused," Amnesty International, http://www.amnesty.org.uk/action/irandp1.shtml.

46. "Iran's Islamic Republic Caves in to International Pressure: Stoning of Hajieh Esmailvand Suspended," Organization for Women's Liberation, International Committee Against Stoning, http://www.wpiran.org/farsi1/archive/kampain/hajieh/2912_suspended.html. See also www.stopstoningnow.com.

47. Ibid., with reference to the Amnesty International article in note 45.

48. "We don't execute under 18's," Iranian news release, January 11, 2005, http://www.news24.com/News24/World/News/0,,2–10–1462_1645739,00.html.

49. "Iranian Leader Khamenei: Iran's Enemies Want to Destroy It with Miniskirts," Middle East Media Research Institute, TV Monitor Project, Clip No. 468, January 6, 2005, http://www.memritv.org/Transcript.asp?P1=468.

50. Quotations taken from Brian Murphy, "Public Hanging on the Rise in the Islamic Republic," Iran-Press-Service.com, http://www.iran-press-service.com/articles_2002/May_2002/iran_executions_21502.htm.

51. "32-Year-Old Man Hanged in Public in Northern Iran." January 6, 2005, http://www.iranfocus.com/modules/news/print.php?storyid=1169.

52. Iran Press News, "Sentenced to Public Amputation," December 17, 2004, http://www.iranpressnews.com/english/source/002084.html.

53. FIDH Report, 12.

54. Report submitted by the U.N. special reporter on extrajudicial, summary or arbitrary executions, Asma Jahangir, to the Commission on Human Rights of the U.N. Economic and Social Council, Doc. UN E/CN.4/2004/7, December 22, 2003, paragraph 50. Cited in FIDH Report, 13.

55. See Leela Jacinto, "School Under Threat of Death: Despite Grave Danger, Iran's Baha'is Study at Underground University," ABC News, 2005, http://www.abcnews.go.com/International/print?id=79489.

56. FIDH Report, 16.

57. "Reporters Without Borders Condemns Mistreatment of Cyberjournalists and Webloggers," Reporters Without Borders, RFS.org, January 6, 2005, http://www.rsf.org/article.php3?id_article=12246.

58. "Iran: Judiciary Uses Coercion to Cover Up Torture: On National TV, Journalists Forced to Deny They Were Tortured," December 20, 2004, Human Rights Watch, HRW.org, http://www.hrw.org/english/docs/2004/12/17/iran9913.htm.

59. "Obtaining Forced Confessions and Vicious Treatment of Political Prisoners in the Islamic Regime," Iran Press News, January 4, 2005, http://www.iranpress news.com/english/source/002464.html.

60. "Journalists Claims of Torture to Be Probed," *Salt Lake Tribune*, January 10, 2005, http://www.sltrib.com/nationworld/ci_2520828.

61. Anonymous comments posted by "Guest" at the following URL reference: http://www.pbase.com/zanoni/irans_street_art. The list in the text is based on this posting with some editing and addition of new material.

Chapter 10: The Samson Option

1. The information in this paragraph, including both quotes, is drawn from: Uzi Mahnaimi in Tel Aviv, with Peter Conradi, *The Muslim News*, reporting an article in the *Sunday Times*, June 18, 2004, http://www.muslimnews.co.uk/news/news .php?article=7761.

2. This point is made by Anthony Cordesman, a senior researcher at the Center for Strategic and International Studies in Washington DC. Cordesman is quoted in "Iran's Military Called No Match for U.S. But Its Missiles Pose Threat to Israel," GeoStrategy-Direct.com, January 4, 2005, http://www.geostrategy-direct.com/ geostrategy-direct/secure/2005/1_04/1.asp. See also Anthony H. Cordesman and Arleigh A. Burke, "Iran's Developing Military Capabilities," Main Report, Washington DC Center for Strategic and International Studies, Center for Strategic and International Studies, December 14, 2004, working draft.

3. One example of the news coverage of the bunker-buster bomb shipment to Israel was Aluf Benn, "U.S. to Sell Israel 5,000 Smart Bombs," Ha'aretz, September 21, 2001. This article was reprinted on www.fromoccupiedpallestine.org, http://www .fromoccupiedpallestine.org/node.php?id=1421. For a similar analysis, see "Israel Ready to Move Against Iran's Nuclear Facilities After Transfer of Advanced Munitions," www.geostrategy-direct.com, October 19, 2004, http://www.geostrategy-direct.com/geostrategy-direct/secure/2004/10_19/1.asp?

4. Mustafa Kibaroglu, "Iran's Nuclear Program May Trigger the Young Turks to Think Nuclear," Carnegie Endowment for International Peace, http://www. carnegieendowment.org/npp/publications/index.cfm?fa=view&id=16284.

5. An example of the Iran attack "October Surprise" rumors is discussed in Wayne Madsen, "A Bush Pre-election Strike on Iran 'Imminent,'" October 20, 2004, www.lebanonwire.com, http://www.lebanonwire.com/0410/04102002LW.asp.

6. Antoaneta Bezlova, "China-Iran Tango Threatens US Leverage," Asia Times On Line (www.atimes.com), http://www.atimes.com/atimes/Middle_East/FK30Ak01 .html.

7. After the presidential election, beginning in late November 2004, newspapers such as the *New York Post* were running multipage spreads dedicated to exposing

the U.N. oil-for-food scandal. See *New York Post*, December 13, 2004, which dedicated pages 4 and 5 to the scandal.

8. Charles Krauthammer, "Sacrificing Israel," *Washington Post*, October 22, 2004.

9. Ibid.

10. William Kristol, "Kerry Will 'Put More Pressure on Israel' According to His Own Foreign Policy Advisor," Weekly Standard, October 25, 2004, http://www .weeklystandard.com/Content/Public/Articles/000/000/004/832kszfc.asp.

11. David Horowitz, *Unholy Alliance: Radical Islam and the American Left* (Washington DC: Regnery, 2004).

12. Patrick J. Buchanan, *Where the Right Went Wrong: How Neoconservatives Subverted the Reagan Revolution and Hijacked the Bush Presidency* (New York: St. Martin's, 2004).

13. Ibid., 242.

14. Pat Buchanan, "Time to Engage Iran?" *Times Republican*, December 20, 2004, http://www.timesrepublican.com/columns/story/127202004_colcol.asp.

15. Michael D. Evans, *The American Prophecies: Ancient Scriptures Reveal Our Nation's Future* (New York: Warner Faith, 2004).

16. Ibid., 11.

17. For a key statement of the attack on neoconservatives as guilty of military hubris, lofty foreign policy visions, and insufficient appreciation of how limited U.S. military power is, see James Mann, *Rise of the Vulcans: The History of Bush's War Cabinet* (New York: Viking, 2004).

Chapter 11: The Movement for Freedom in Iraq

1. An essential book in understanding how the Far Left in America has united with radical Islamic extremists is David Horowitz, *Unholy Alliance: Radical Islam and the American Left* (Washington DC: Regnery, 2004). Consider, for example, Horowitz's analysis on how the American Left and radical Islamic extremists have joined to form "one jihad" on the theme of anti-Americanism with which the Far Left and the radical Islamic extremists both agree: "They [Western radicals] had already embraced the Palestinian movement in the 1960s, when Arafat, backed by the Soviet bloc, created modern terrorism. They did so because Soviet Communism and Palestinian terrorism presented themselves as enemies of the American Satan. With the help of the Castro dictatorship, which the American Left embraced for similar reasons, Arafat established the first terrorist training camps and launched the first international campaign of airline hijackings and hostage-takings. The attack of 9/11—whose weapon of choice was hijacked airlines loaded with hostages and whose targets were Wall Street and the Pentagon, the very symbols of American empire—was thus the juncture at which the two jihads finally met" (page 145).

2. An essential book to understand the important arguments made by the Far Right in America today is Patrick J. Buchanan, *Where the Right Went Wrong: How Neoconservatives Subverted the Reagan Revolution and Hijacked the Bush Presidency* (New York: St. Martin's, 2004). Buchanan makes a strong argument that fundamentalist Islamic extremists will not be beaten by force, instead they must be combated on the battlefield of ideas: "But Islamic fundamentalism is not an imminent or grave threat to America. Nor are U.S. combat divisions designed to defeat a fighting faith. If Islam is rising and its sons are prepared to die to enlarge the Dar al Islam and use terror to drive us out of their world, can we defeat it? No other Western empire did. If a clash of civilizations is coming, the West is unchallenged in wealth and weaponry. Yet, wealth did not prevent the collapse of Europe's empires, nor did awesome weaponry prevent the collapse of the Soviet Union. Rome was mighty, Christianity weak. Christianity endured and prevailed. Rome fell. America's enemy then is not a state we can crush with sanctions or an enemy we can defeat with force of arms. The enemy is a cause, a movement, an idea" (page 87).

3. Editorial, "U.S. Money and the Orange Revolution," *Kyiv Post*, January 14, 2005, http://www.kyivpost.com/opinion/editorial/22068/.

4. Press Release, "Senior Democrat on House Oversight Panel Demands Accounting for U.S. Government Funds Funneled to Back Yuschenko-Led 'Orange Revolution,' in Ukraine, Despite Official White House Denials," December 16, 2004, http://biz.yahoo.com/prnews/041216/dcth046_1.html?printer=1.

5. Ibid.

6. Anna Badkhen, "U.S. Poured Millions into Ukraine but State Department Denies Trying to Influence Vote," *San Francisco Chronicle*, December 19, 2004, http://sfgate.com/cgi-bin/article.cgi?f=%2Fc%2Fa%2F2004%2F12%2F19%2FMNG6LAE79M1.DTL.

7. Matt Kelley, "U.S. Money Has Helped Opposition in Ukraine," *San Diego Union-Tribune*, December 11, 2004, http://www.signonsandiego.com/uniontrib/20041211/news_1n11usaid.html. The Web site of the National Democratic Institute for International Affairs can be found at http://www.ndi.org/employment/currentemploy.asp.

8. Zbigniew Brzezinski and Robert M. Coles, "Iran: Time for a New Approach," the Council on Foreign Relations, Washington DC, 2003, 8–9. The report can be downloaded at http://www.cfr.org/pdf/Iran_TF.pdf.

9. Laura Rozen, "The Resurrection," AlterNet.com, August 25, 2004, http://www.alternet.org/story/19647.

10. "A Committee on the Present Danger Policy Paper: Iran—A New Approach," http://www.fightingterror.org/newsroom/CPD_Iran_policy_paper.pdf.

11. Patrick Buchanan, "The Committee on the Present Confusion," July 26, 2004. Buchanan's column is syndicated by Creative Syndicate, Inc. Interestingly, the

column is published regularly by the extreme Left group that runs AntiWar.com. This column, for instance, is archived at http://www.antiwar.com/pat/?articleid =3188. The Far Right paleo-conservatives have evidently now come full circle to where they have joined the extreme political left in an anti-war sentiment they both share, although for different reasons.

12. Ibid.

13. Jack Wheeler, "George Bush and the Sword of Damocles: Why There Hasn't Been Another 9-11," January 5, 2004, www.tothepointnews.com. A report on Wheeler's thinking is also available, see "Has U.S. Threatened to Vaporize Mecca? Intelligence Expert Says Nuke Option Is Reason bin Laden Has Been Quiet," WorldNetDaily.com, January 7, 2005, http://www.worldnetdaily.com /news/article.asp?ARTICLE_ID=42272.

14. "Iran Mullah-Run Parliament Proposes National Costumes," Iran News, August 21, 2004, *Persian Journal,* http://www.iranian.ws/iran_news/publish/article_3408 .shtml.

15. For an insightful discussion of Hitler as "the great pretender" and to view a selection of these early Hoffman photographs, see Colin Jacobson, ed., *Underexposed: Pictures Can Lie and Liars Use Pictures* (London: Vision On Publishing, 2002), 22–23.

16. See "URGENT ACTION—Iran: Possible "Disappearance"—Fear for Safety— Ahmed Batebi," Amnesty International, November 13, 2003, http://web .amnesty.org/library/index/engmde130362003. See also, Radio Free Europe, "Imprisoned Student's Case Comes Up for Review," Iran Press News, December 28, 2004, http://www.iranpressnews.com/english/source/002346.html.

17. Ibid. Quoted in the Amnesty International "Urgent Action" web posting, cited above.

18. Jack Spencer, "The Facts About Military Readiness," Executive Summary #1394, September 15, 2000, Heritage Foundation, http://www.heritage.org/Research/ MissileDefense/BG1394es.cfm.

19. Dan Williams, "Israel Breaks Silence on EU-Brokered Iran Nuke Freeze," Reuters, January 13, 2005; see also http://www.alertnet.org/thenews/newsdesk/ L13573530.htm.

20. The discussion in the text of Shahryar is based on conversations with the author in December 2004.

Conclusion

1. Kenneth R. Timmerman, "Shilling for the Mullahs," *New York Post,* January 11, 2005. Timmerman has consistently written important reports on the pro-mullah lobby in the United States and their efforts to recruit a long list of Democratic politicians, including John Kerry, to their side.

2. Ibid.
3. Ibid.
4. Ibid.
5. Aryo Pirouznia to Jerome R. Corsi (e-mail), January 12, 2005.
6. Ibid.
7. Timmerman, "Shilling for the Mullahs."
8. Reported in Robert S. Wistrich, "Muslim Anti-Semitism: A Clear and Present Danger," American Jewish Committee, http://www.ajc.org/InTheMedia/ Publications.asp?did=503&pid=1203. See especially footnote 145. Also reported by the Iran Press Service from Tehran on December 14, 2001, "Rafsanjani Says Muslims Should Use Nuclear Weapon Against Israel," at http://www.iran-press-service.com/articles_2001/dec_2001/rafsanjani_nuke_threats_141201.htm.
9. Reported in Joseph Farah's Between the Lines column, "The Global Strategic Threat," WorldNetDaily.com, July 23, 2002, http://www.worldnetdaily.com/ news/article.asp?ARTICLE_ID=28363.
10. A courageous book making an important statement on the need for Israel to survive is Alan Dershowitz, *The Case for Israel* (New York: Wiley, 2003).
11. Teresa Swiebocki and Henryk Swiebocki, eds., *Auschwitz: Voices from the Ground* (Krakow: PMO, 1992), 18.

Index